Credit Derivatives & Synthetic Structures

A Guide to Instruments and Applications

Second Edition

JANET M. TAVAKOLI

John Wiley & Sons, Inc.
New York • Chichester • Weinheim • Brisbane • Singapore • Toronto

Founded in 1807, John Wiley & Sons is the oldest independent publishing company in the United States. With offices in North America, Europe, Australia, and Asia, Wiley is globally committed to developing and marketing print and electronic products and services for our customers' professional and personal knowledge and understanding.

The Wiley Finance series contains books written specifically for finance and investment professionals as well as sophisticated individual investors and their financial advisers. Book topics range from portfolio management to e-commerce, risk management, financial engineering, valuation, and financial instrument analysis, as well as much more.

For a list of available titles, please visit our website at www.WileyFinance.com.

This book is printed on acid-free paper. ∞

Published by John Wiley & Sons, Inc.
Published simultaneously in Canada.

ISBN 0-471-41266-X

Printed in the United States of America.

10 9 8 7 6 5 4 3 2

acknowledgments

The concept of portfolio risk came alive for me in the spring of 1981 in Merton Miller's corporate finance class at the University of Chicago's 190 E. Delaware building. Just before class I would comb chemical dust out of my hair and brush white powdered phosphate residue off my jeans, the result of my day job as a chemical engineer. Then I prepared for the entertaining enthusiasm of my instructor who made risk and reward the subject of imaginative financial fun. Gimmicks and games were a key part of every class discussion in the good old days when the accrued income on zero-coupon bonds was taxed as capital gains at maturity. But times change. The IRS went on to tax implied accrued income as ordinary income on an annual basis. Merton Miller went on to win a Nobel prize in economics. I thanked Merton Miller for inspiring my enthusiasm for the new gimmicks and games, which inevitably evolve in the financial markets. I regret I won't have another opportunity. Merton Miller passed on June 3, 2000. He was a shining light in the world of finance.

Lauren Golden gave me help and advice with illustrations. Mox Tan encouraged me to write this book, when I preferred to go sailing. Steve Wade of Union Bank of Switzerland and Hei Wai Chan of JP Morgan helped me formulate my views and influenced my thinking through many discussions over several months. Stephen Partridge-Hicks of Gordian Knot inspired a clearheaded approach to the credit markets and taught me to carry a compass into the byzantine labyrinth of credit structures: "That sounds good, but I'll have to have my lawyers study the documents."

I would also like to thank others who offered their encouragement and perspective: Dan Stahle and Tom Boemio at the Federal Reserve, Mu Gu at Bank of America, Randy Allison Kaufman at Bank Boston, Vivian Bronk at the Bank of England, Philip Borg and Kave Taleghana at Bankers Trust, Carl Schuman at Westdeutsche Landesbank Girozentrale in New York, Isaac Efrat at Moody's Investors Service, Paul Varotsis at Chase in London, Kevin McGivern at Sumitomo Capital, Oliver d'Oelsnitz at DG Bank, Ethan Berman at CreditMetrics, Franklin Lee at Merrill Lynch, Ron Dembo at Algorithmics, Nancie Poulus Watson, and Patricia Sevening.

Adrian Hyde of Chase helped me correct typos and other errors for the first edition. Bin Hong of BankOne gave me technical advice on credit exposures. Sandy Sloane of Bank of America, Chris Culp of the Chicago Group, and Rupert Walsh and Chris Surr of Credittrade helped with various insights.

Special thanks to the excellent publishing and editing staff at John Wiley & Sons, especially Claudio Campuzano.

J. M. T.

contents

Introduction   1

CHAPTER 1
Credit Derivatives Market Overview   5

Estimated Market Size   5
Evolution of the Market   7
Techniques of Credit Risk Measurement   12

CHAPTER 2
Total Rate of Return Swaps—Synthetic Financing   19

Motivation of the Receiver of the Total Rate of Return   24
Motivation of the Payer   27
Regulatory Capital and Bank Motivation   28
Creating Synthetic Assets   35
Mismatched Maturities   35
Tranched Asset Swap versus TRORS   36
Funding Arbitrage and Joint Probability of Default   38
Balance Sheet Management   41
Advanced Balance Sheet Management   42
Relative Performance TRORS   44
Hedge Funds and Loan TRORS   44
Loan TRORS Mechanics   47
Hedge Funds and Leverage   55
Hedge Funds and Leveraged Exposure to Spreads   57
Relative Value and Balance Sheet Management   59
Credit Exposure and the Conditional Probability of Default   62
Maturity Mismatches: Loans and Synthetic CLOs   71

CHAPTER 3
Credit Default Swaps and Options   73

Traditional Credit Default Swap   77
Importance of the Default Protection Seller   82
Defining the Event   88
Default Language for Nonsovereign Debt   91
Redefining the Credit Default Event as a Credit Event   96
Basis Risk: Imperfect Correlation between the
    Reference Asset and Risk   99
Variations in Sovereign Default Language   101
Materiality, Price Adjustments, and Substitution:
    More Potential Sources of Basis Risk   103
Basis Risk and Substitution   106
Termination Payments   108
Pricing and Applications   122

CHAPTER 4
Exotic Structures   141

Asset Swap Switches   142
Knock-in Options, Credit Spread Options, and Forwards   145
Balance Sheet Swaps and Exposure Management   149
Callable Step-Ups   155
Synthetic Lending Facilities   159
Geared Default Options   160
Basis Risk: Delivery, Hedge Costs, and Calculations   165
Basket Credit Default Swaps   171
Pricing Basket Credit Default Swaps   175
Regulatory Viewpoints   181
Knock-in Basket Options   184
Reduced Loss Credit Default Options   184
Pro Rata Default Structures   186

CHAPTER 5
Sovereign Risk and Emerging Markets   189

The Guesstimaters' Market   191
Tax Arbitrage   196

Credit Plays—The Home Currency Advantage   198
The Currency Question in Sovereign Default Protection   201

CHAPTER 6
Credit-Linked Notes   **223**

Reasons for the Existence of Credit-Linked Notes   223
Credit Default–Linked Notes   224
Credit-Sensitive Notes   233
Index-Linked Notes   233

CHAPTER 7
Synthetic Collateralized Loan Obligations   **237**

General Comments on Securitization   237
Unwind Triggers   240
Synthetic CLOs   241
Rating Criteria   245
Black Box Structures   246
Secured Loan Trusts: Synthetic CLOs and TRORS   247
Equity Piece Buyers   249
Cash Flow Overview   250
Risks to the Bank Sponsor   251
The Bank Sponsor and Counterparty Risk   251
Structural Considerations   253
Synthetic Securitizations for Highly Rated Banks   254
BISTROs   256
The Super Senior Tranche   259
Securitizing First Loss Risk with Principal Protected Notes   259
Credit Arbitrage Funds   261

CHAPTER 8
Selected Documentation, Regulatory, Booking, and Legal Issues   **265**

Hidden Costs in Default Language   267
Guarantees, Insurance, and Credit Derivatives   272
Booking Issues   273
Regulatory Capital   274
Booking in Nonbank Entities   281
Selected Cross-Border Issues   281

CHAPTER 9
Future of the Global Market   **283**

Basis Risk: Delivery Options and Credit Events   285
Bank Best Practices   288
Internet Trading   294
An Inevitable Shake-Up   296
Trend to a Commodity Market   298

Selected Bibliography   **299**

Index   **302**

introduction

Credit derivatives are revolutionizing the financial industry and will for ever change the way banks do business. Although many securities firms are currently active providers in this market, global banks with large balance sheets and low funding costs will eventually dominate the market. Investors and end users include the interbank market, corporations, insurance companies, hedge funds, mutual funds, and securities firms. Most investors and end users are just beginning to scratch the surface of understanding how these products can be applied to credit line management, portfolio management, arbitrage opportunities, and creation of synthetic assets.

This book presents current applications of the various types of credit derivative products currently available in the market. New structures constantly emerge, and printed material cannot keep up with the variations on the original theme. Nonetheless, the basic groundwork for understanding the existing and future structures in this market are presented here.

The philosophy of this book is that the timing of cash flows, the magnitude of cash flows, and the certainty of cash flows determine value. Relative value is further determined by regulatory, accounting, tax, and risk profile constraints. The reader must firmly hold on to these concepts in any discussion of financial products. It is easy to lose sight of cash flows when the mind walks through a maze of jargon, equations, and diagrams. I can't spend jargon. I can't spend equations. I can't spend diagrams. But I can spend cash. If I'm constrained by regulations, tax, or accounting, then these constraints have a real value to me, and I'll factor them into my thinking along with figuring out the cash.

Whether I'm evaluating a credit derivative, an interest rate option, an interest rate swap, or my private investment portfolio, I ask the same basic questions: How much cash will I get? When will I get the cash? How certain am I that I will get the cash? Are there any government regulations that make me better off? Is there an accounting method that makes me appear better off? Can I use less capital to improve my rate of return? Is there a tax regulation I can use to my economic advantage? How much of the cash do I get to keep?

This book is both accessible to the lay reader and challenging to the experienced market professional as it delves into the principles and processes of the credit derivatives market using only the fundamental rules of investment theory. The book does not deal with models and pricing theory; there are dozens of books on models crowding technical bookshelves. This book does deal with the framework—the method of questioning one must employ before applying a model. This book also points out the limitations of trying to apply mathematical models to define unknowable unknowns. Using current market models to price credit derivatives is a bit like trying to apply Euclidean geometry to describe the shapes found in nature. The formulas and curves look neat, regular, and well defined. Unfortunately, nature just doesn't look that way. It looks more like a Mandelbrot set, a fractal. We can't force our observations of nature into those neat little Euclidean shapes. Nature is always poking out in some inexplicable, seemingly chaotic, yet patterned fashion. Similarly, we haven't been able to make market observations fit under the neat little probability curves on which financial professionals often rely. We haven't discovered the probability theory equivalent of fractal geometry to describe financial market behavior.

This book covers some of the original ways in which credit derivatives go beyond merely a system of combining derivatives and credit risk to become instruments that enable investors to question, theorize, and create a new framework for evaluating market credit risk.

The market doesn't reveal its secrets; it responds to a method of questioning. This book does not spend time on model theory. The value of credit derivatives is a mark-to-market, not a mark-to-model. The models currently in use have their value, but it is the assumptions used as inputs to these models that are the key and the focus of this book.

Many years ago, my advanced statistics professor, one of the world's most talented statisticians and statistical modelers, laughingly admitted to model hubris early in his career. He had been asked to participate in a study to model tree trunk wood volumes. He diligently measured the trees and recorded the wood yield data corresponding to the measured trees. He tabulated and graphed the data. He used a computer program and regression analysis. He applied modeling theory and came up with a formula that was closely correlated with tree wood yields. It was magic. Statistics worked. The formula looked very much like that for the volume of a cylinder—with a small fudge factor thrown in. Fudge factors are common. They make up for the fact that the world doesn't always behave the way we think it should behave. This was in the days before fractal theory. Euclidean geometry always leaves us with the need for fudge factors; we're used to it. We know the world isn't made up of squares, triangles, circles, and cylinders. Nonetheless, the model was a nice, neat, and intuitive little formula. It had a high correlation coefficient. When you plugged in the trunk width and the height of the tree, the wood volume was pretty much as predicted by the neat little formula. Statistics showed that the formula described the data and predicted future events pretty well. That—among other things—is what makes a statistician feel satisfied.

Everyone was happy. Statistics did just what it is supposed to do. A statistician collected historical data and found a mathematical formula, which described the relationship between measurable attributes of a tree and the potential wood yield. A measurement of attributes would now allow the statistician's employer to predict wood yield of a forest.

The formula was perfect.

Well, *almost* perfect.

Little things about the formula kept bothering the budding professor. For instance, a plot of the residuals didn't look random. The residuals, the unexplained data, appeared to have a pattern. Statisticians know that isn't a good thing. That usually means the neat little formula missed something. But it was so close. The minor error seemed negligible. The budding professor was tempted to ignore these pesky residuals and declare the job done. But he kept at it, laboring away, modifying the formula, trying to make the residuals disappear. The cylinderlike formula seemed so *right*. It made sense. Trees look like cylinders. The professor had a small problem. He couldn't see the formula for the trees.

Trees do indeed look very much like cylinders. But they look even more like cones. One of the foresters pointed this out one day to the budding professor. This is a moment statisticians and mathematicians both love and hate. They hate it because they get a churning feeling in the pit of their stomachs, which lets them know in their gut that they are wrong. They also love it because now they've hit on a better answer.

Sure enough, when the professor used the formula for the volume of a cone (with tiny modifications), those pesky residual patterns disappeared. The residuals were now random. A conelike formula was the better answer— not a *perfect* answer (we're still in the world of Euclidean geometry)—but good enough for what the foresters were trying to do. That's all we really want from mathematics: utility, not perfection.

The approach of this book is to help prevent market practitioners from getting baffled by jargon, equations, and diagrams. It is based on the belief that before one runs off and crunches numbers like crazy, stares at a computer screen for lengthy hours, and draws dozens of diagrams, one should step back and view the problem objectively. Ask a few questions. Bring your experience to bear on the problem. What would I reasonably expect the result to look like?

Afterward, it is easy to see that a tree trunk looks more like a cone than a cylinder.

Credit Derivatives Market Overview

ESTIMATED MARKET SIZE

Buyers and sellers enter into negotiated credit derivative contracts primarily for two reasons: to manage risk and to earn income. If there is a benefit to booking the transaction off balance sheet from a regulatory, tax, or accounting point of view, this is an added bonus. The buyers and sellers are called counterparties. The terminology can be confusing. A buyer can be a buyer of credit risk or a buyer of credit protection. A seller can be a seller of credit risk or a seller of credit protection. In this book I adopt a convention to avoid confusion. The protection buyer is the buyer of credit protection (a seller of credit risk). The protection seller sells protection (buys risk) and generally receives a fee for this protection.

The global size of this mainly privately negotiated market was estimated to be $100 billion to $200 billion at the end of 1996. The British Bankers Association (BBA) estimated the size of the London market to be $20 billion at the end of 1996. That didn't include transactions done by some Japanese securities firms, which included credit default puts imbedded in privately placed structures; one firm alone had done about $1 billion of this type of business. The BBA's estimate of year 2000 trading volume was $900 billion and the forecasted volume for 2001 is $1.6 trillion.

Because much of the credit derivatives market is off balance sheet and many of these negotiations are private, there is no way of knowing the size of the market unless participants volunteer that information.

The definition of what should be included in market size is also somewhat fluid. Some firms consider total rate of return swaps to be a form of financing. These may be handled in a department separate from the credit derivatives department, which handles credit default swaps. Credit spread puts may be in yet another department. Convertibility protection, if it is traded at all, may be part of yet another group within the same institution.

This is a very rapidly growing market. Many experts thought the market would double between 1996 and 1998. That projection appears much too low. The market probably doubled in the first six months of 1997 compared to the entire annual volume in 1996.

Banks typically increase volume from zero to more than $10 billion inside of one year and accelerate rapidly after that. Rabobank, a relative newcomer to the market, reported $5 billion notional in credit derivative transactions by July 1997. The notional principal amount, usually called the notional amount, is the amount against which fees, interest payments, price differential, and recovery values are based in a credit derivative contract. Union Bank of Switzerland (UBS) went from zero to $4.5 billion notional in transactions in their New York branch's loan group alone for the first half of 1997. UBS estimated total 1997 transaction volume at $15 billion. That figure did not include UBS's emerging market activities or London or Asian activities.

Collateralized loan obligations (CLOs) and collateralized bond obligations (CBOs) are queued in Moody's Investor Services's in box awaiting ratings. The number of deals has increased nearly 15-fold from 1996, although the number of viable deals has only tripled. Most of these deals have a credit derivative component, often equal in notional to the deal size. Synthetic securitization volume has increased 30-fold from the first deal in the fall of 1997.

Total rate of return swaps on loans have increased dramatically in volume as market participants have familiarized themselves with the documentation. Every month new entrants engage in their first transaction.

New participants have entered the credit default protection market in both Europe and the United States, and at least six brokers are now gearing up to service this new swell of business.

Credit derivatives are in high demand because they service an unfulfilled market need. At the moment, the products seem new and difficult to understand. But like the personal computer, it isn't a matter of whether the broader financial community will adopt the new product, it is merely a matter of how fast.

EVOLUTION OF THE MARKET

The concepts of portfolio theory and risk versus reward gained popularity early in the twentieth century, and various models were developed in that century to measure risk. The most important concept in investment theory is illustrated in Figure 1.1. This concept, developed by Jack Treynor, William Sharpe, and John Lintner, is known as the *capital asset pricing model*. It states that the expected risk premium varies in direct proportion to *beta*, the sensitivity of an investment's return to market movements. This concept can be and has been generally applied since human beings started thinking in terms of money and increasing their amount of money.

The simple graph in Figure 1.1 is the key to all financial management. I deliberately made it simple because, for all of the simplicity of this concept, it is violated time and again in the financial markets. Promoters of Ponzi schemes, "respectable" investment managers, and "sane" banking executives try to promote the idea that one can earn a high risk-free return without risking capital. That's nonsense, and I give limited examples of some of

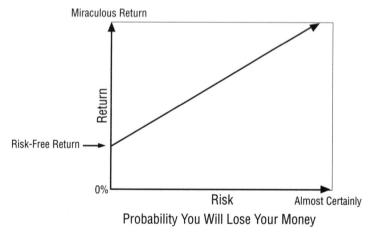

FIGURE 1.1 The Most Important Investment Graph

this nonsense and the undoing of a few of the participants in this nonsense in this decade in Chapter 2.

The key to investment management is to minimize risk while maximizing return. In theory, for every risk appetite there is an "efficient frontier" of returns. This is sort of the demilitarized zone (DMZ) of investment management. Below the DMZ one is safe—too safe to win the war against inflation. At the efficient frontier, one is taking the reasonable amount of risk for the desired return. Above the DMZ, the likelihood increases of having your investment shot down and taking a casualty to your principal.

Credit derivatives are a tool to help move the DMZ farther into risky territory without taking more casualties. Specifically, credit derivatives can help diversify the credit risk of a portfolio to dampen the volatility of potential returns. Credit derivatives can help portfolio managers diversify their portfolios. One of the key concepts in risk management developed in recent decades is the concept of diversification of assets. This includes classes of assets such as equities, bonds, real estate, and cash. It also includes diversification of the market risk of various assets through management of the sensitivity to interest rate or currency fluctuations. Recently, the focus of risk management has included management of credit risk in investment portfolios as well. Usually this means diversification through increasing the size of a portfolio, but it can also mean reducing exposure to an obligor while adding exposure to another obligor and keeping the size of the portfolio constant. In any case, the number of obligors or the number of assets increases, although the size of the portfolio itself need not increase.

When diversifying a credit portfolio, it is important to keep the correlation between assets as low as possible. This means that, to the extent possible, credit events should not affect assets in the same way. Credit-quality changes of the two assets should not be related. To the extent that they are related, the positive impact of diversification is diluted. The best assets of all would be assets that have negative correlation. If one asset is adversely affected, the other asset is positively affected by the same event. The covariance—a measure of the behavior of two random variables in relation to each other—should be as low as possible. As the number of assets in a portfolio increases, the portfolio variance approaches the value of the average covariance. Covariance matrices are used in many financial models. Sharpe's capital asset pricing model may be the most famous.

Rating agencies attempt to measure the ability of obligors to meet their obligations. The long-term ratings are based on ability to pay principal and interest and on the likelihood of not defaulting on an obligation. A chart of long-term credit ratings from highest to lowest is shown in Table 1.1. Ratings shown are from Standard & Poor's (S&P), Moody's Investors Service (Moody's), Fitch, Duff & Phelps (D&P), Best's, and Dun & Bradstreet (D&B).

A credit rating below BBB is considered noninvestment grade. In addition to the ratings in the table, the rating agencies sometimes give "+" and "–" or add numbers to indicate additional gradations within classes. For instance, Bank of America's long-term debt is rated Aa2 by Moody's (other choices are Aa1, the highest in this class, and Aa3, the lowest in this class) and AA– by S&P. Obligors rated D are in legal or technical default or have filed a bankruptcy petition. There are other rating services besides the ones listed in Table 1.1, but these are the most common in the United States and are usually a benchmark in the global markets. Japan, for instance, has its own rating agencies, which tend to rate Japanese institutions higher than Moody's or S&P does.

Rating of single securities is not enough to define credit risk. Opinions of ratings may vary widely. Banks, sensitive to credit after the foreign loan debacle of the 1980s, often have their own internal rating system for their clients. The internal rating systems of banks are often much different than those for Moody's and S&P. Furthermore, the rating of a single security doesn't tell us much about the risk of a portfolio of securities and doesn't tell us anything about the correlation of securities in a portfolio. As we shall see in the next section, there are ways to get around some of these deficiencies.

TABLE 1.1 Long-Term Credit Ratings from Selected Agencies

S&P	Moody's	Fitch	D&P	Best's	D&B
AAA	Aaa	AAA	AAA	A++	5A1
AA	Aa	AA	AA	A	4A1
A	A	A	A	B++	5A2
BBB	Baa	BBB	BBB	B	4A2
BB	Ba	BB	BB	C++	5A3
B	B	B	B+	C+	4A3
CCC	Caa	CCC	B	C	4A4
CC	Ca	CC	B–	D	4A4
C	C	C	CCC	E	3A
D	D	D	DD	F	NR

Credit derivatives are not new. Only the hype about them and their classification as a stand-alone product are new. The new crop of credit derivative specialists is quite young, some in their late twenties, which is perhaps why these products are often hyped as brand new. The risk/reward profile of the act may have changed recently, but the fundamentals are the same.

Humans have evaluated credit risk ever since they started bartering goods. Insurance companies have always looked at event and individual credit risks. Banks have evaluated credit risks for as long as they have been in business.

Even the "new" products aren't particularly new. Options on corporate bonds have been traded quite actively since the 1970s, even before there was an option methodology employed by the major Wall Street firms.

Salomon and others have offered total rate of return swaps on mortgage-backed securities since the mid-1980s. Merrill, Lehman, Salomon, and others have offered debt warrants on corporate debt since the mid-1980s. Merrill and others stripped U.S. government risk from Latin American sovereign debt in the mid-1980s.

Even the idea of structuring credit risk is not a particularly new concept. Banks have been doing this since the late 1970s. Some of the most savvy credit analysts went on to make fortunes for their banks with structured credit products in the late 1980s. In 1988 Stephen Partridge-Hicks and Nicholas Sossidas approached Citibank's clients with a unique proposal and launched the Alpha fund, soon followed by the Beta fund. Their management of credit risk was so successful that they left Citibank in the mid-1990s and started Sigma Finance Corporation. Gordian Knot Limited investment management, headed by the two gentlemen from Citibank, is responsible for day-to-day management. Sigma Finance is rated AAA by Moody's, S&P, and Fitch. The commercial paper program is rated A+.

The structure is deceptively simple. Sigma Finance is a corporation owned by institutional investors. The equity is privately placed with well-known institutional investors whose names are kept private. Sigma offers investors either equity (which pays dividends) or capital (which pays interest). These have equal rank. Investors can choose either a 7- or a 10-year maturity. The returns are paid out to investors every six months, and therefore investors hold an instrument that is identical to a floating rate note with a return over the London interbank offering rate (LIBOR). The return gradually builds up over a two- to three-year period and levels out. The equity is similar to subordinated debt. Returns are not volatile, and the equity has a finite maturity. The corporation itself does not have a finite maturity because it can continue issuing equity and/or capital. Sigma can expand to $5 billion in equity capital, if it so chooses.

The fund managers purchase a portfolio of AA assets (lower-rated investment-grade assets are allowed with more limited leverage and more constraints) and issue Aaa/AAA notes in the market. Through this method, Sigma earns a credit spread and takes no market risk. Sigma also uses leverage (8× for AA-rated assets) to accumulate more AA-rated (on average) assets. The investments and leverage are strictly controlled with an optimization program, which equally considers credit quality, maturity, portfolio diversification, asset-to-liability maturity gap, and liquidity eligibility.

Sigma invests in sovereigns, supranationals, general finance companies, high-credit-quality corporates, asset-backed securities, and other high-credit-quality assets. Sigma also buys assets with a monoline insurance wrap from Financial Security Assurance (FSA) and Capital Markets Assurance Corporation (Cap Mac), among others. The average credit quality is high AA.

Gordian Knot does not take market risk, currency risk, or credit risk outside of the fund preestablished parameters. They promise their clients they will do their best to preserve principal and to give them the highest returns possible. They do not promise magical returns either or no risk and high rewards. In fact, they aren't *guaranteeing* anything. They simply promise to do the best job of managing a portfolio according to well-defined risk parameters. They made good on that promise. The resulting returns allow their clients to sleep well at night while they continually grow wealthier.

Gordian Knot employs a structured credit play. Some of the "new" funds promise flashier returns. There is nothing wrong with higher returns. But they come with higher risks. There is nothing wrong with higher risk, if that is what you want and if you know that is what you are getting. Unfortunately, that isn't always what is represented. We examine some of these structures later in this book. The fundamental principles of credit structures apply. After all the models have had their say, after all the mechanics of the structure have been analyzed, after all graphs have been produced, after all the "guaranteed" returns have been published, the fundamentals still apply. *In an efficient market, if you are reaching for higher return, you will take more risk.* No matter how much evolution we see in credit derivatives, we have not evolved beyond this fundamental tenet.

There are a few exceptions, mainly in the cross-border credit and cross-border tax markets; but that is due to market or regulatory inefficiencies, and my caveat does not apply to those cases. Later, we examine these exceptions as well.

TECHNIQUES OF CREDIT RISK MEASUREMENT

Models proliferate for looking at credit risk measurement on a portfolio basis. It is a daunting task to try to model credit risk on a global scale.

One of the earliest models for looking at credit risk in the United States was the Altman Z score. A high Z score implied a low probability of default on the part of a potential borrower. The formula was very simple, and a conventional balance sheet held most of the information required. The following is the Altman formula:

$$
\begin{aligned}
Z = 3.3 \quad & \text{(Earnings before Interest and Taxes [EBIT]/Total Assets)} \\
+ 1.0 \quad & \text{(Sales/Total Assets)} \\
+ 0.6 \quad & \text{(Market Value of Equity/Book Value of Debt)} \\
+ 1.4 \quad & \text{(Retained Earnings/Total Assets)} \\
+ 1.2 \quad & \text{(Working Capital/Total Assets)}
\end{aligned}
$$

Much of this information is not available to foreign borrowers, particularly Asian borrowers, who may use different accounting methods and who do not disclose financial information as U.S. obligors do. For sovereigns, much of the information is not applicable. The Z score is mainly useful only for U.S. corporations.

JP Morgan hopes to define a new industry standard with its CreditManager software, which applies the CreditMetrics methodology developed to examine credit risk. The methodology is to compute the exposure profile of each asset in a portfolio. The model also computes the volatility of value caused by upgrades or downgrades in credit quality or volatility due to defaults. Long-term migration likelihoods are factored into the model. A key component of the model is to also compute the correlation between assets in the portfolio. These results are then boiled down to a one-year time horizon assessment of the value-at-risk due to credit in a portfolio using a mark-to-market framework.

The data are mainly taken from publicly available information. S&P and Moody's have calculated how credit quality is likely to move over time.

Table 1.2 shows an S&P transition matrix for corporate debt for a one-year time horizon. The numbers in the table do not necessarily add up to 100 percent because they exclude entities whose ratings were withdrawn or changed to "not rated" due to obligation payoffs or that had insufficient information after a merger or restructuring. Probability of default and re-covery rates are similarly estimated. The probability of default and assumed recovery values associated with various ratings are discussed further in the sections on pricing in Chapters 2 and 3.

Correlations between assets are estimated using equity price correlations, where available. Fundamental data analysis or the model user's own data are alternative sources of data for correlation calculations. Data, particu-larly data used for calculating correlations, are sparse. Data for Asian in-struments, emerging markets, and nonpublicly traded data are difficult to obtain.

In the end, the CreditManager software can help portfolio managers identify credit risks according to key parameters. Three of the most useful are absolute size, percentage level of credit risk, and absolute amount of risk. CreditManager has powerful report tools to enable portfolio managers to categorize risk. Figure 1.2 shows a typical CreditManager report.

CreditManager is able to determine the size of credit risk by maturity and by country. The power of this tool is that it also allows portfolio man-agers to change parameters and view by obligor industry, for instance. One of the more useful graphs shows exposure size versus risk (Figure 1.3). Risky assets and large exposures are quickly highlighted. Large-exposure–low-risk and small-exposure–high-risk assets are also highlighted, as these may be

TABLE 1.2 S&P One-Year Transition Matrix

Initial Rating	Rating at Year-End (%)							
	AAA	AA	A	BBB	BB	B	CCC	Default
AAA	88.46	8.05	0.72	0.06	0.11	0.00	0.00	0.00
AA	0.763	88.27	7.47	0.56	0.05	0.13	0.02	0.00
A	0.08	2.32	87.64	5.02	0.65	0.22	0.01	0.05
BBB	0.03	0.29	5.54	82.49	4.68	1.02	0.11	0.17
BB	0.02	0.11	0.58	7.01	73.83	7.64	0.89	0.98
B	0.00	0.09	0.21	0.39	5.98	72.76	3.42	4.92
CCC	0.17	0.00	0.34	1.02	2.20	9.64	53.13	19.21

Source: Standard & Poor's, February 1997.

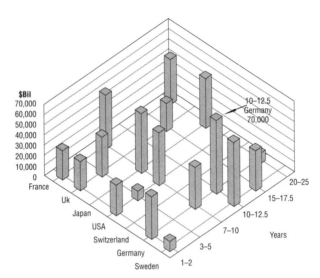

FIGURE 1.2   Value-at-Risk due to Credit
Source: JP Morgan CreditManager™

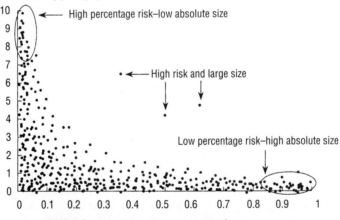

FIGURE 1.3   Exposure Size versus Risk
Source: JP Morgan CreditManager™

problem areas. Another feature of this graph is that it shows the portfolio data; and if one were to draw a curve that captures most of the data points (other than the high-risk and large-size exposures), one could define the boundary condition of credit risk for this portfolio. If that boundary is consistent with the risk philosophy of the portfolio manager, that is fine. If the boundary suggests that the portfolio manager assumes too little or too much risk relative to the investment philosophy, changes can be made to shift the portfolio risk boundaries.

CreditMetrics and CreditManager are tools, but they are not the answer. As a means of checking up on the status of a portfolio, they can be very useful tools indeed. But there are caveats.

Franklin Lee, head of the corporate bond proprietary-trading desk at Merrill Lynch, has this to say about CreditMetrics and statistical models in general:

> At first glance, it looks like they use the statistical method for risk control, which I don't feel very confident about. Statistical methods that have been used in the past have never worked. However, the section on transitional probabilities is relevant in valuing credit-spread levels.

Statistical models do have their shortcomings. We apply a model to describe data; and if it looks nice on the graph, we feel we have done our jobs. But when someone shows me a probability distribution of defaults or credit spreads, my first question is: "Says who?"

The key to CreditMetrics, as in most statistical models, is dealing with the probability distribution. *What is the best way to deal with skewed (asymmetry of data) distributions and kurtotic (bunching or dispersion of data relative to a normal distribution) irregularities?* Simply stated: How much is the credit and value of the security/securities really likely to change? Gaussian (normal) and even lognormal distributions are merely mathematical representations designed to attempt to answer this question. There is no magic about either of them. *If we know the exact probability for certain, we don't need to use a Gaussian or lognormal or other mathematical distribution. We could simply use the raw data as is. If we know the exact distribution for certain, we don't need a model.* Everything else in the model is mere mathematical manipulation of the result of the initial probability assumptions, and the model rises and falls on these initial assumptions.

When prepayment-probability distribution assumptions failed to reflect reality in the mortgage portfolio, Wall Street firms with sophisticated models took massive hits to their profit-and-loss statements (P&L). The memory needed to store historical data and programming code put the Pentagon's Cray computer to shame. The models were impressive and sophisticated, but the underlying probability distribution assumptions were fatally flawed. Mountains of historical data were precisely manipulated to give inaccurate results, on which people relied as if the models were a religion. Firms took massive losses to their mortgage-backed securities (MBS) trading portfolio as a result of inadequately hedged positions—a classic case of more precision than accuracy.

Nonetheless, historical data provide a good place to start; and with some bonds or loans, there will be more history than others. But what about the future? Historical data are not always good at predicting the future, historical data do not incorporate news of current events, and credit risk does not lend itself to a Monte Carlo–type analysis in the way that interest risk does.

There is a market instrument, however, that incorporates current information: options. Puts and calls on underlying securities incorporate views of the future credit–influenced price moves of securities. For instance, if we want to construct a probability distribution of the terminal value of a security due to interest rate and credit moves, we could canvas the market for a menu of puts and calls in, at, and out of the money for the relevant time horizon. From this we can not only back out implied volatilities, but also check the market view of the implied probability distribution of the payoff outcomes of the security and, from that, back out the market-implied probability of credit migration for the relevant time horizon. This method is a good "reality check" for the results coming out of a model that uses only historical data. Price discrepancies should be due to market views of the influence of current events on the credit migration of the security above and beyond that predicted by the historical data. In an efficient market, the market should price all of this information into the option premiums. Of course, the market is not really efficient, due to information and interpretation dislocations. So even the combined method won't be perfect. But that is true of any security we price, including U.S. Treasury bonds, albeit with one less factor—the credit factor. If there were enough options available, modelers could spend happy weeks using this sort of methodology.

More simply, knowing the spread of a "pure" floater would also be very valuable. If a floater resets instantaneously, the element of price fluctuations due to interest-rate moves drops from the equation. Longer resets incorporate larger interest-rate-influenced price effects. The price move of a floater incorporates a lot of credit information, but even this market has glaring inefficiencies and inconsistencies, especially with emerging market debt. In any case, it is much easier to examine the history and the current pricing in this market than it is to try to model spreads.

I am not suggesting here that portfolio managers should abandon models. In fact, I am a proponent of CreditMetrics and CreditManager. Although portfolio managers must use judgment inputting the data into CreditManager, JP Morgan has come up with an effective snapshot of portfolio credit risk in this model. JP Morgan doesn't claim or represent that the snapshot is a moving picture. Models are best when they are sorting, organizing, and manipulating data. Models cannot exercise judgment. JP Morgan's model does a good job of massaging the data so that portfolio managers can exercise better-informed judgment.

In 1989, Stephen Kealhofer, John McQuown, and Oldrich Vasicek founded KMV Corporation to focus on corporate credit-risk measurement and management. KMV Corporation's credit risk model is another valuable tool. KMV has done considerable fundamental analysis on credits and on correlations between credits. KMV defines the benefits of "cutting off" weaker credits (as defined by KMV) of same-rated securities. An investor can dramatically reduce the risk of default in a portfolio of same-rated securities. The strength of the KMV model is the enormous potential benefit to improvement in portfolio quality at no additional cost.

This doesn't violate the efficient market statement made earlier, however. KMV is successful because the market does not have access to this kind of detailed information because of the barriers to obtaining it. The methodology can be cumbersome, and skill and judgment are needed for some of the assessments of a corporation's balance sheet strength. The model also does not lend itself to the analysis of sovereign risk without the necessity for the modeler to make some crude assumptions. KMV is less accessible to portfolio managers other than large banks because it is very expensive. Despite these weaknesses, it is an impressive portfolio management tool for modeling credit risk and possibly the best technology and data currently available in the credit markets.

The ideas put forth by JP Morgan are not new. The concept of portfolio diversification has been around since the 1970s, with some of the best work being done by Roger Ibbotson and R. Sinquefield. The fundamental concepts remain exactly as they applied them. Diversification works because prices of different credit securities do not move exactly together. A decline in one credit may be partially or completely canceled out by a rise in another. The risk that can be potentially eliminated by diversification is called *unique risk*, or specific risk. This name stems from the fact that many of the risks that pertain to a specific credit are peculiar to that credit. There is risk that cannot be mitigated by diversification. That is market risk. No matter how many credits one holds, there are global economic risks that can threaten all credits or clusters of credits, and investors will always be exposed to market uncertainties.

Few models can combine credit risk and market risk. Neither CreditManager nor KMV attempts to do so. Algorithmics has developed a model, Regret, that provides a framework for risk management at the enterprise level. Algorithmics is the only company in the business to get three stars from Meridian Research. The model links market and credit exposure and has complex netting hierarchy. One can build an infrastructure to simulate a forward moment in time for the value of a portfolio. Regret prices the cost of a put option on the net portfolio exposure. It minimizes the price to hedge the net exposure.

KMV's models can be used within the Algorithmic framework. Algorithmics provides the infrastructure to stress test, create synthetics, and use the Regret option.

Regret and the models of a few other new firms, which plan to compete with Regret, are new on the scene. No one actually uses them as trading models yet. They are time-consuming and difficult to implement properly and not close to a near-term industry standard. As we shall see in Chapters 2 and 3, market professionals presently retreat to the fundamentals of relative value.

CHAPTER **2**

Total Rate of Return Swaps— Synthetic Financing

Total rate of return swaps (TRORS) are simply another form of financing. An example of a modified form of a car lease illustrates the concept. The investor, the receiver of the total rate of return (TROR), is the lessee, the one who leases the car. In this particular lease, the investor gets all of the benefits of the car without any of the hassle. The investor gets a chauffeur. The investor does not have to worry about parking the car, putting gas in the car, maintaining the car, or servicing the car. The investor does not pay luxury tax because the investor does not own the car. At the end of the lease, the investor must pay the lessor any depreciation in the value of the car. If the car has not depreciated in value, the investor pays nothing. If the car appreciates in value, the investor gets a payment from the lessor for the value of the appreciation of the car.

For all of this, the investor pays a lease fee. There is one catch, however. If the car is damaged as defined in the lease agreement, the investor must pay the difference between the original value and the damaged value, and the lease terminates. Alternatively, the investor can take ownership of the car and pay the original value of the car to the lessor. The definition of "damage" and the determination of the value of the "damaged" car are conditions the investor and the lessor negotiate at the beginning of the lease. In some cases, the lease agreement may allow the investor to purchase the car at the market value of the car at the end of the lease agreement. The method of determination of market value of the car is negotiated by the investor and the lessor before they sign the lease agreement.

A TRORS allows an investor to enjoy all of the cash flow benefits of a security without actually owning the security. The investor receives the TROR. At the end of the TRORS, the investor, the receiver of the TROR, must pay any decline in price to the TROR payer. If there is no decline in price, the investor does not make a payment. If the security appreciates in price, the investor gets the difference between the original price and the new, higher price. For all of this, the investor makes ongoing payments to the TROR payer. The payments are analogous to the lease payments we discussed earlier. In the credit derivatives market, this payment is referred to as the floating rate payment, the financing cost, or the funding cost of the investor.

TRORS are off–balance sheet transactions. They are the highest volume, the most popular, and the most widespread sector of the credit derivatives market. As we shall see, low-cost borrowers with large global balance sheets are naturally advantaged as payers in TRORS. Synthetic assets are created in the process.

A TRORS is a bilateral financial contract between a total return payer and a total return receiver. The total return payer pays the total return of a reference security and receives a form of payment from the receiver of the total rate of return. Often payment is a floating rate payment, a spread to the London interbank offering rate (LIBOR). The reference assets can be indexes, bonds (emerging market, sovereign, bank debt, mortgage-backed securities, corporate), loans (term or revolver), equities, real estate receivables, lease receivables, or commodities.

Total return swaps have been around since at least 1987 when Salomon Brothers offered the first mortgage swap agreement (MSA). Most of the total return swaps offered in the market are simpler than the MSA, which we look at later in more detail. The basic total rate of return swap transaction is shown in Figure 2.1.

The total rate of return payer is the legal owner of the reference asset, just as the lessor was the legal owner of the car in our initial example. The total rate of return payer holds the reference asset on its balance sheet. For the period of the transaction, the total rate of return payer has created a short position in the market risk (depreciation of the car) and a short position in the credit risk (potential damage) of the reference asset.

The total rate of return receiver, the investor, is not the legal owner of the reference asset, any more than the lessee was the legal owner of the car. The TRORS is an off–balance sheet transaction, and the reference asset does

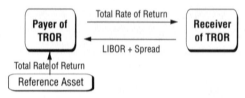

Total Return: Interest Flows + (Final Value – Original Value)
Reference Asset: Bond, Loan, Index, Equity, Commodity

Total Return Receiver is long both price and default risk of the Reference Asset.
Total Return Payer is the legal owner of the Reference Aset.

FIGURE 2.1   Total Rate of Return Swaps (TRORS)

not appear on the balance sheet of the receiver. For the period of the transaction only, the total rate of return receiver has a synthetic long position in
the market risk and a synthetic long position in the credit risk (damage) of
the reference asset. At the maturity of the transaction, the total rate of return receiver may choose, but is not obligated, to purchase the reference
asset at the then prevailing market price.

In the event of default of the reference asset prior to the maturity date
of the TRORS, the TRORS usually terminates, but it need not necessarily
terminate. We look at the case in which it does not terminate later; in most
cases of default, however, the TRORS does terminate. The total rate of return
receiver bears the risk in the event of default in either case.

If the TRORS terminates due to a default, the total rate of return receiver, the investor, makes the total rate of return payer "whole" for the
market risk and the credit risk of the reference asset. The investor may make
a net payment of the difference between the price of the reference security
at the beginning of the transaction and the price of the reference security at
the time of default. Alternatively, the investor may agree to take delivery of
the defaulted reference asset and pay the initial price of the reference asset
to the total rate of return payer. Once this has occurred, neither the payer
nor the receiver has any additional obligation to the other party, and the
TRORS terminates.

The following term sheet shows typical language for a total return swap
in which the reference asset is a par bond. At the swap termination date,
there is no physical delivery of the reference bond; the transaction is settled
with cash.

Total Rate of Return Bond Swap
Abbreviated Indicative Term Sheet

Total Return Payer:	U.S. bank.
Total Return Receiver:	European bank.
Reference Asset:	Reference bond.
Issuer:	U.S. corporate.
Coupon:	7.0%.
Interest Payable:	Semiannual, 30/360.
Final Maturity:	Five years.
Collateral Type:	Senior unsecured.
Settlement Price:	100.
Calculation Amount:	USD 10 million.
Trade Date:	Today (insert today's date).
Effective Date:	Five business days from today.
Termination Date:	The earlier of the effective date plus one year *or* the "early redemption date."
U.S. Bank Pays:	All cash flows of the reference bond on the same day the cash flows of the reference bond are paid.
European Bank Pays:	Three-month LIBOR + 25 basis points on a quarterly $A/360$ basis on the calculation amount, where A is the actual number of days in the period.
Termination Payment:	On the termination date, any accrued payments due by either the total return payer or the total return receiver will be paid. In addition, the following termination payment amount will be made:
	Calculation Amount × (Initial Price − Market Value)
	If positive, the TROR receiver will make this payment to the TROR payer.

	If negative, the TROR payer will make this payment to the TROR receiver.
Initial Price:	100%.
Market Value:	The market value of the reference bond, including accrued interest, on the termination date. A dealer panel will determine the market value using the market bid price.
Early Termination:	Two business days following notice of a credit event with a terminal payment being made.
Credit Event:	Occurs when the calculation agent is aware of publicly available information as to the existence of a credit condition.

Credit condition means either a payment default or a bankruptcy event in respect of the issuer.

Payment default means, subject to a dispute in good faith by the issuer, either the issuer fails to pay any amount due of the reference asset, or any other present or future indebtedness of the issuer for or in respect of moneys borrowed or raised or guaranteed.

Bankruptcy event means the declaration by the issuer of a general moratorium in or rescheduling of payments on any external indebtedness.

Publicly available information means information that has been published in any two or more internationally recognized published or electronically displayed financial news sources.

Calculation Agent:	Total rate of return payer.
Business Days:	Days on which commercial banks and foreign exchange markets settle payments in London and New York.

(continued)

| Documentation: | Standard master agreement and swap confirmation of the International Swaps and Derivatives Association, Inc. (ISDA). |
| Law: | As per the ISDA master agreement. |

Although the preceding term sheet is typical, there is no standard transaction in the market. Some TRORS may specify physical delivery of the reference asset as an option. Credit-event triggers may vary. Definitions may also vary. Additional clauses may be added to credit events. The sections "Defining the Event" in Chapter 3 and "Hidden Costs in Default Language" in Chapter 8 cover this in detail. Chapter 3's section "Termination Payments" offers detailed information on how to define final payments.

TRORS are often compared with repurchase agreements. Repurchase agreements allow an owner of a security, the "seller," to sell securities to an investor with the agreement to repurchase them at a fixed price on a fixed date. Repurchase agreements are financings. The seller of the security agrees to pay the buyer a negotiated rate of interest, the repurchase rate (repo rate). The buyer lends the seller money for the period of the agreement. The repo rate compensates the buyer for the financing. At the maturity of the agreement, the seller is obligated to repurchase the securities at the prespecified price. In a TRORS, the total rate of return receiver is not obligated to purchase the reference asset at the maturity of the transaction. There is no preagreed fixed price for the reference asset at the maturity of the transaction. The TRORS receiver is obligated only to exchange payments based on the market value of the reference asset at the maturity of the transaction.

MOTIVATION OF THE RECEIVER OF THE TOTAL RATE OF RETURN

In a very important sense, TRORS are not credit derivatives. TRORS, considered in their most basic form, are funding cost arbitrages. TRORS are applied in a variety of ways: balance sheet management, portfolio management, hedge fund leverage, and asset swap maturity manipulation. *Even though the overall effect of a TRORS may have very important credit implications for both the payer and the receiver of the TRORS, the use is primarily that of a financing.*

There are many reasons for both a payer and a receiver (investor) to enter into a total rate of return swap, and there is one overwhelmingly compelling reason for the *receiver* of the total rate of return swap. Many credit derivatives specialists who either miss the point or pander to the sensitivities of credit managers and regulators will cite reasons such as the following:

- Investors can create new assets with a specific maturity not currently available in the market.
- Investors gain efficient off–balance sheet exposure to a desired asset class such as syndicated loans or high-yield bonds, to which they otherwise would not have access.
- Investors may achieve a higher return on capital. TRORS are often treated as derivatives, or off–balance sheet instruments. Direct asset ownership is an on–balance sheet funded investment.
- Investors can fill in the credit gaps in their portfolios.
- Investors can reduce administrative costs via an off–balance sheet purchase (as opposed to buying loans on balance sheet).
- Investors can access entire asset classes by receiving the total return on an index.

I have been to presentations where these are the only reasons cited for the motivation of the receiver of the total rate of return. These above reasons are often true. But it is like saying the reason you are driving a Porsche Targa around a race track is that it gets you around faster than walking. Although it is true, it is not the point of what you are doing.

The key reason receivers of the total rate of return enter into this transaction is to take advantage of **leverage**. Investors make no initial cash payment. Cash flows are usually paid on a net basis. The investor's "payments" are subtracted in advance from the securities cash flows. The investor does nothing, yet receives a positive net payment. (This assumes that the funding cost of the investor remains less than the cash flows from the security. If the investor is receiving a fixed coupon and makes a floating payment, it could happen that in an inverted-yield-curve environment the investor would be in the position of having to make a net payment.)

The return on capital using leverage is compelling and significant. Let us look at an example of the power of leverage. Suppose three different investors wish to receive the total rate of return of a given asset. The asset is a BB– par asset with a coupon of LIBOR + 250 basis points (bps), or a current yield of around 8.30 percent. Two of the investors are hedge funds and must pay a funding cost of LIBOR + 100 bps. The third investor is a mutual fund, which pays cash for the investment. The first hedge fund, hedge fund A, gets better credit terms than the other fund, hedge fund B. Hedge fund A deals with a bank eager to do business and has to put up only 5 percent collateral up front; hedge fund B deals with a more cautious bank and must put up 10 percent collateral. The banks will both pay LIBOR flat as interest on the cash held as credit collateral for the total rate of return swap. Table 2.1 shows the net economic return for each of the investors.

Hedge fund A, which employs a 20:1 leverage, has a net return of 35.8 percent, whereas hedge fund B, which employs a 10:1 leverage, has a return of 20.8 percent after funding costs. The cash investor has a net return of only 8.3 percent, and that does not take into account any funding costs. It is reasonable to assume that an investor with cash has an implied funding cost. If we assume LIBOR as the funding cost, the cash investor's net return is only 2.5 percent versus the double-digit returns enjoyed by the hedge funds. This is the power of leverage.

Leverage is the reason that hedge funds are a primary target as counterparties in TRORS. The hedge funds are the receivers of the total rate of return. The primary motive of the hedge funds is to exploit leverage. The

TABLE 2.1 Net Economic Returns for Counterparties Employing Various Degrees of Leverage

	Hedge Fund A	Hedge Fund B	Cash Investor
Asset yield	8.30%	8.30%	8.30%
LIBOR yield	5.80%	5.80%	
Net asset spread	2.50%	2.50%	
Spread to LIBOR	−1.00%	−1.00%	
Net swap spread	1.50%	1.50%	
Collateral	5%	10%	
Leverage	20 to 1	10 to 1	1 to 1
Levered swap return	30%	15.00%	
Interest on collateral	5.80%	5.80%	
Net return	35.80%	20.80%	8.30%

participation of hedge funds and other shaky, albeit partially collateralized, credits is a critical, and not necessarily welcome, development in the credit derivatives market. Whereas the motive of the hedge fund counterparty is leverage, the motive of the payer of the total rate return in the TRORS is high earnings. We examine this transaction and the quality of these earnings in more detail in the section on hedge funds in this chapter.

For a creditworthy bank or other creditworthy receiver, generally no up-front collateral is required. The receiver puts up no cash. The spread earned is pure spread income—the interest income on the TRORS less the receiver's funding cost.

MOTIVATION OF THE PAYER

The payer in a TRORS creates a hedge for both price risk and default risk of the reference asset, although the payer in the TRORS is a legal owner of the reference asset. Investors who cannot short securities may be able to hedge a long position by paying the total rate of return in a TRORS.

The TRORS is an off–balance sheet transaction for the payer of the total rate of return. A long-term investor who feels that a reference asset in the portfolio may widen in spread in the short term but then recover may enter into a TRORS that is shorter than the maturity of the asset. The structure is flexible and does not require a sale of the asset. In this way the investor can lock in a return, yet take a temporary short-term negative view on an asset.

In some accounting regimens, an investor who has an unrecognized loss in a bond position can defer the loss without risking even further losses on the asset. The investor can pay the total rate of return on the asset for the period of time required to defer the loss. At the maturity of the TRORS— if it is not the same as the maturity of the asset—the investor can sell the asset and recognize the loss. An investor with a gain in a security can employ the same method to defer a gain while simultaneously protecting the value of the reference asset. Although this method may work for certain accounting scenarios, U.S. taxpayers will find that paying the TROR on an asset will be evaluated as a true sale. Treatment for accounting and tax purposes varies by country, and investors must consult their own accountants and tax experts.

REGULATORY CAPITAL AND BANK MOTIVATION

Regulatory capital treatment of credit derivatives is unclear (see also the section on regulatory capital in Chapter 7). Nonetheless, understanding the fundamental issues is important to both bank and nonbank participants in the credit derivatives market because banks make up most of the driving force of this market.

The Bank for International Settlements (BIS) issued a framework for setting minimum capital requirements for international banks in July 1988. Since that time, each country has set up its own capital guidelines for banks, often applying inconsistent interpretations of the BIS guidelines.

After December 31, 1992, all banks were expected to meet a minimum ratio of qualifying total capital to BIS risk-weighted assets of 8 percent. The amount of capital reserved against a risk-weighted asset is not necessarily 8 percent, however. The amount of capital reserved against an asset will depend on its BIS risk weighting. This risk weighting has very little to do with credit quality or the risk-weighted asset; it has very much to do with often arbitrary capital standards set up for the international market by regulators who thought they were creating a framework to strengthen and stabilize the international banking community.

The well-intentioned regulators had a quaint idea. The end result is that the international banking community lives with the shortcomings of an inflexible and arbitrary system. Inflexible and arbitrary rules also create perverse incentives to "optimize" according to the letter of the rules, even if common sense says otherwise. In its mildest form, a bank may enter into an economically neutral transaction to gain a regulatory capital advantage. But the rules sometimes force banks to behave like Radar O'Reilly in *M*A*S*H*, making the best of a crazy system. A bank may enter into an economically disadvantageous transaction because it improves the bank balance sheet with respect to regulatory capital treatment. Manipulating regulatory capital is not the sole motivation of most healthy banks, but it is an important motivation. It is an even more important motivation for less healthy banks that are barely able to meet regulatory capital requirements. The game every bank plays, to a greater or a lesser degree, is to optimize return on regulatory capital.

The risk weight of a reference asset in a credit derivative transaction will generally be referred to as the "BIS risk weight." The risk weight of a reference asset may vary by jurisdiction, however. This further complicates matters because central banks and ministries of finance have the right to set local standards for assets, which aren't clearly addressed by BIS. In general, however, it is useful to employ the following assumptions throughout this book:

- The sovereign debt member countries of the Organization for Economic Cooperation and Development (OECD) will receive a zero percent risk weight. This means that they are as good as cash. A bank does not need to reserve any capital against these assets.
- The senior debt obligations of OECD banks receive a 20 percent BIS risk weight. The amount of capital a bank must hold against this asset is 20 percent of 8 percent, or 1.6 percent. This means that for a $10,000,000 investment, a bank would hold $0.016 \times \$10,000,000$, or $160,000, in capital against this asset.
- Unfunded revolvers for corporate credits have a 50 percent BIS risk weight. Banks hold 50 percent of 8 percent, or only 4 percent, capital against this asset.
- If the revolver funds, the bank would assign a 100 percent BIS risk weight to the funded amount and hold 8 percent capital against this amount.
- For corporate debt and non-OECD sovereign debt, an OECD bank would assign a 100 percent risk weight to these assets and hold 8 percent regulatory capital in reserve.

Risk weightings aren't always logical, however: The debt of the Republic of Argentina, a non-OECD country, receives a 100 percent BIS risk weight. The debt of Mexico, an OECD country, receives a 0 percent BIS risk weight. The Federal National Mortgage Association (FNMA) in the United States receives a local 20 percent BIS risk weight. Germany assigns FNMA a 100 percent risk weight.

I don't make the rules, I just live by them. These rules remind me of a card game in which each card has its own intrinsic value based on its hierarchy in the deck. For a reference asset, intrinsic value is creditworthiness; integrity of cash flow structure; and timing, magnitude, and certainty of cash flows. When I am dealt a hand of cards, I know the value of each of the cards and I know the value of my hand. I place my bets accordingly. But regulatory capital is like assigning a wild card value to certain cards in the hand. The wild card value may not agree with the intrinsic value of the card.

When the wild card value agrees with a card's intrinsic value, my behavior in the card game will be the same. When the wild card value doesn't agree with the intrinsic value of the cards in my hand, I will modify my playing strategy accordingly.

To summarize, some of the key issues that affect bank regulatory capital with respect to credit derivatives are:

- In June 1997, the Bank of England, and shortly thereafter the U.S. Federal Reserve Board (known as the Fed), agreed that credit default swaps and options can be held on the trading book instead of on the bank book. (Total return swaps had already been given trading book treatment.) Capital can potentially be offset for risk assets and hedges.

- Unless a position is perfectly hedged, capital adequacy rules will not recognize offsets for credit derivatives. This means that if there is basis risk between the reference asset for the credit derivative and the asset being hedged, no risk and no capital netting will be allowed. Potentially, a bank could be charged capital for counterparty risk on an imperfect hedge and also be charged capital for the reference asset being hedged. The end result for an imperfect hedge could be a *greater* capital charge after hedging.

- The Bank of England, the U.S. Federal Reserve Board, and the Office of the Comptroller of the Currency (OCC) are leaning toward revised capital treatment. For example, after January 1, 1998, the Fed allowed certain banks to treat credit derivatives held on the bank's trading book the same as other derivatives in the trading book. Instruments held in the banking book are risk weighted at 8 percent of notional value, and trading book positions are usually held at much lower percentages of their notional value, so this would result in a drastic reduction of required capital. Banks would have to demonstrate that they have internal models that accurately describe the risk and add-on capital to account for counterparty risk.

The regulatory capital guidelines for credit derivatives are in a state of flux. Capital requirements for credit derivatives depend on whether the credit derivative is held on the trading book or on the bank book and whether the bank can use a mark-to-market treatment. If mark-to-market is not allowed, hedging is not recognized. This means that hedging a position with a credit derivative can attract a higher capital charge than if it were not hedged. This is a dreadful state of affairs. The entire point of using credit derivatives is to recognize a hedging benefit of exposure. On a regulatory capital basis, a bank can be punished for using credit derivatives if they are booked in the banking book and not in the trading book.

The issue of recognizing hedging is an important one, but it is not the only one. Banks must currently reserve capital according to the risk weight of the reference assets (and sometimes take into account counterparty risk) whether a trade is booked in the bank book or in the trading book. The 1988 accord applies. If a bank sells credit protection, the credit risk is treated as a guarantee or as a letter of credit (LOC). A credit derivative is not treated as other derivatives are treated.

This makes the BIS risk weight of the reference asset all the more important. Figure 2.2 shows the effect of selling credit protection in the form of a TRORS. The bank receives the TROR on two different assets with a notional value of $10 million on the reference asset. The bank has a funding cost of LIBOR flat, and both assets have coupons of LIBOR + 50 bps. The reference asset for one transaction (shown diagrammatically on the left in Figure 2.2) has a BIS risk weight of 100 percent. The reference asset for the other transaction has a BIS risk weight of 20 percent.

The net spread earned on the assets is identical. The net spread is unaffected by the BIS risk weight for regulatory capital purposes. If one looked at net spread alone, it appears the bank should be indifferent to selling credit protection by receiving the total return of either asset. The balance sheet analysis in Table 2.2, however, tells a different story.

Even though the return on the asset is identical in each transaction, the

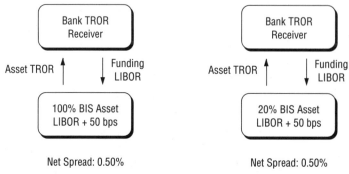

FIGURE 2.2 TROR on 100% versus 20% BIS Risk-Weighted Asset

TABLE 2.2   Bank Balance Sheet Comparison: Bank Receives TROR, 100% versus 20% BIS Risk Weight

Risk-Based Capital Calculation			
100% Risk-Weighted Asset		**20% Risk-Weighted Asset**	
Asset Book Value	100.00%	Asset Book Value	100.00%
× Category Risk Weight	100.00%	× Category Risk Weight	20.00%
= % Risk-Weighted Asset	100.00%	= % Risk-Weighted Asset	20.00%
× Capital Requirement	8.00%	× Capital requirement	8.00%
= **% Risk-Based Capital**	**8.00%**	= **% Risk-Based Capital**	**1.60%**
Notional	$10,000,000	Notional	$10,000,000
Net Income 50 bps	$50,000	Net Income 50 bps	$50,000
Capital:	$800,00	Capital:	$160,000
Return on Capital:	**6.25%**	**Return on Capital:**	**31.25%**

return on regulatory capital is dramatically different. The asset with the 20 percent BIS risk weight has a return on capital five times greater than the asset with the 100 percent risk weight. This result has nothing to do with the creditworthiness of the assets and nothing to do with the market risk of the transaction, but everything to do with the skewed effect of regulatory capital requirements.

Note that in these examples I assume my cost of regulatory capital is roughly the same as the return from investing in Treasury bills (T-bills). The cost of regulatory capital and return on investment of regulatory capital nets to zero.

The effects of the use of leverage in these examples are due to changes in economic capital and affected return on assets (ROA). The effect of differences in regulatory capital is less apparent. Actual cash inflow has not changed for a trade with the same notional amount. What has changed is the return on capital (ROC), based on an arbitrary reserve of capital.

Currently, the regulatory capital treatment for credit derivatives is the same whether the transaction is booked on the bank book or on the trading book. As we saw earlier, banks already care where a transaction is booked because hedging can be recognized only if a transaction is booked in the trading book. After January 1, 1998, however, it mattered a great deal more to banks whether a transaction is booked on the bank book or on the trading book. The capital regime will change for the trading book, and credit derivatives will be treated like other derivative transactions. Under the new market-risk proposal, there will be three components of risk:

1. *Counterparty risk*, which is the mark-to-market exposure for the credit derivative due to the possibility that the counterparty may default on its obligation or potential obligation under the terms of the credit derivative transaction.
2. *Market risk*, which is the net exposure to interest rates, foreign exchange rates, commodity prices, and equity prices.
3. *Specific risk*, which is an adverse change in price from factors related to the issuer of the reference asset due to nonmarket movements.

One example of specific risk would be changes in the credit risk of the reference asset. This can be accounted for by scaled risk weightings of 0 percent for government risks, 3 to 20 percent for investment-grade risks, or 100 percent for noninvestment-grade and other risks. Banks have the alternative of using standard specific-risk add-on factors from models such as KMV Corporation's market-risk models from Chapter 1.

Only banks that can prove that they have models to calculate exposures in a reproducible and consistent manner will be allowed to use this new capital treatment for credit derivatives. Much is at stake. The potential reduction in regulatory capital is great.

Consider, for example, a transaction in which an OECD bank with a funding cost of LIBOR – 25 bps buys credit protection on an asset with a 100 percent BIS risk weight by paying the total rate of return on an asset to another OECD bank. The protection seller, the receiver of the TROR, is willing to pay LIBOR + 20 bps in this transaction. The transaction is represented as shown in Figure 2.3.

If the bank's model can show that the combined maximum exposure to the asset and to the payer of the TROR is only 30 percent of the notional amount of the transaction, the bank would get a much more favorable return on capital under the new regime. This would apply only to the trading book, however. The balance sheet summary in Table 2.3 shows the effect of buying protection under the current regime versus the capital charges under the proposed new regime.

The trading book return on capital is potentially much greater under the proposed new capital regime. Return on capital for the transaction jumps

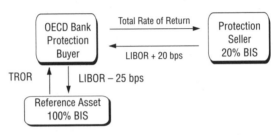

FIGURE 2.3 Buying Protection: Paying TROR

from 28.13 percent to 93.75 percent. This assumes that the bank has a model that can demonstrate the counterparty exposure as represented in Figure 2.3. If a bank does not book this transaction in the trading book or if the bank does not have a suitable model for credit derivatives, the bank will not be eligible for this potentially very favorable capital treatment.

TABLE 2.3 Bank Balance Sheet Comparison under New Regime: OECD Bank Pays TROR to OECD Bank

Risk-Based Capital Calculation			
Current Treatment		**New Regime**	
Asset Book Value	100.00%	Mark-to-Market Exposure	25.00%
		Counterparty Credit Equivalent	5.00%
Total Exposure	100.00%	Total Exposure	30.00%
× Category Risk Weight	20.00%	× Category Risk Weight	20.00%
= % Risk Weight Asset	20.00%	= Relevant % Risk Weight	6.00%
× Capital Requirement	8.00%	× Capital Requirement	8.00%
= **% Risk-Based Capital**	1.60%	= **% Risk-Based Capital**	0.48%
Notional	$10,000,000	Notional	$10,000,000
Net Income 45 bps	$45,000	Net Income 45 bps	$45,000
Capital:	$160,00	Capital:	$48,000
Return on Capital:	28.13%	**Return on Capital:**	93.75%

CREATING SYNTHETIC ASSETS

There are several different structures beyond the plain vanilla one in which the TRORS maturity matches that of the underlying asset. The following list summarizes some of the most common features:

- Investors can receive the total rate of return for a shorter period of time than the maturity of the reference asset.
- For the first time, a financial institution can short credits even in maturities for which no reference asset exists.
- The return of the underlying asset can have a cap or a floor.
- The financing can be capped or floored to better control the financing cost on the floating rate payment.
- Investors can lock in a market level for the underlying asset or for the financing rate by specifying a forward start date. This is particularly useful for investors who will have cash to put to work in the future.
- Investors can receive the total rate of return on a basket of assets and can possibly reduce collateral requirements and net financing costs.

MISMATCHED MATURITIES

The most significant development, besides financing, in the TRORS market is the ability to change the maturity of the credit exposure. This is touted as a tremendous benefit to the TROR receiver, the investor, but I offer some very important caveats to this structure. The term sheet shown earlier for the bond total return swap referenced a five-year maturity, fixed-coupon asset, but the term of the swap was for only one year. The returns for total return swaps are generally greater than for a credit default swap with the same maturity. This is because the return to the protection seller incorporates compensation for a combination of default risk and price risk. Price risk is particularly important when the maturity of the reference asset is greater than the term of the TRORS.

When the maturity of the TRORS is less than that of the fixed-coupon reference asset, the receiver of the TROR has a great deal of price risk at the end of the transaction. Many protection sellers—investors who are receiving the TROR on a fixed-coupon reference asset—do not like to engage in unmatched maturity transactions. The benefit to the investor of the unmatched maturity is the ability to invest in a reference asset for a period of time that is shorter than what is available in the market. The risk to the investor now includes an additional element of market risk.

The TRORS will end before the maturity of the reference asset, even if there has been no default event on the reference asset. This means that the price of the reference asset may fluctuate due to market interest-rate moves. If interest rates rise relative to the start of the transaction, the price of the reference asset may decline. The receiver of the TROR must pay the difference between this new market price and the price at the start of the TRORS transaction. This price may have declined purely due to interest-rate moves, even in the absence of any deterioration in the credit quality of the reference asset. It is even possible that the reference-asset credit quality can improve while the final market price declines due solely to a general rise in interest rates.

How much can this price risk be? Consider the case for a one-year period in which the price of the reference asset declines by one point. The total rate of return on the transaction will decline by 100 basis points. If the net spread earned by the investor for the one-year time period is only 50 basis points, the investor must now make a termination payment of one point, or 100 basis points, to the total rate of return payer. This means the net margin on the trade is now a *negative* 50 basis points for the investor, the total rate of return receiver.

TRANCHED ASSET SWAP VERSUS TRORS

Tranched asset swaps look very similar to mismatched maturity TRORS, but there are some important differences. Tranched asset swaps have been around for several years, but only recently have they been classified by some market professionals as credit derivatives.

A tranched asset swap is an asset swap package, which can be put back to the asset swap package "seller" provided the reference bonds are not in default. The put is usually a European put, exercisable one time only, on the specified put date. The investor purchases the asset swap package. This consists of the reference asset combined with a swap of the fixed coupons for floating rate (or floating coupons net of the investor's funding cost). The investor usually pays par for the shorter maturing asset swap position and earns a reduced spread relative to the longer asset swap position from which it was tranched. The investor is the legal owner of the asset swap package.

If there is no default on the reference asset and if the investor exercises the put, the seller of the asset swap package is obligated to purchase the asset swap package at par. The seller is immunized from the default risk of the reference asset, but the seller has the market-price risk and credit-spread-widening risk of the reference asset if the put is exercised under adverse market conditions. Figure 2.4 shows the cash flows of this transaction.

The net asset swap return is determined by the spread over LIBOR paid on the investment less the funding cost of the investor. The *tranched* asset swap return is further determined by the relative maturity of the tranche to the longer underlying asset swap. The spread difference between the underlying asset swap and the shorter tranche is similar in concept to a loan facility fee.

A TRORS with a shorter maturity than that of the reference asset is economically different than a tranched asset swap. In this case, the seller—the TROR payer—is the legal owner of the reference asset. The seller passes the cash flows of the reference asset to the investor, the receiver of the TROR. The investor has the market risk and the credit risk of the reference asset as if the investor owned the asset, albeit the investor does not own the asset.

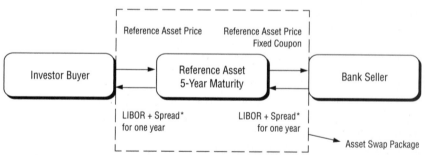

At the end of one year, the Investor Buyer has the right to put the Asset Swap Package back to the Bank Seller at Par, provided the Reference Asset has not defaulted. The Investor Buyer receives a spread near the one-year asset swap spread, not the five-year asset swap spread.

*Any discount or premium to par of the Reference Asset is incorporated in the spread.

FIGURE 2.4 Tranched Asset Swap: Five-Year Maturity Asset, One-Year Maturity Tranche

The seller is immunized from price risk and credit risk—including default risk—of the reference asset.

Unlike the asset swap, a TRORS *is* sensitive to the investor's credit quality. If the reference asset experiences a credit event, the investor (the TROR receiver) must make an uncollateralized payment to the TROR payer. The credit rating of the investor and the correlation of the investor to the reference asset being hedged are key considerations in determining the spread to the investor. For OECD banks, the investor BIS risk weight is also important. This spread is determined by the contingent payment, so calculation of this spread is not always straightforward, as we shall see in Chapter 4. Simplifications abound, and for publicly well-traded assets with investment-grade-rated counterparties, simple assumptions, usually related to the funding cost, and broad guesses of correlation between the investor and the reference asset usually suffice to make a market level.

FUNDING ARBITRAGE AND JOINT PROBABILITY OF DEFAULT

One of the primary reasons that total return swaps are so popular is that they are a form of financing and thus banks can employ a perceived funding cost arbitrage. A higher funding cost bank can receive the total rate of return on an asset from a lower funding cost bank and take advantage of a favorable financing rate. The lower cost bank benefits from the lower joint probability of default from the combination of the reference asset and the receiver of the total rate of return.

Consider the case for an AA rated bank with a funding cost of LIBOR – 15 bps and an A– rated bank with a funding cost of LIBOR + 30 bps. If each bank were to purchase a BBB rated asset with an asset swap coupon of LIBOR + 65 bps for a five-year maturity outright, the net investment might be as shown in Figure 2.5.

If the AA rated bank enters into a TRORS with the A– rated bank, the AA rated bank may be able to give the A– rated bank a slightly more favorable funding cost. If both banks are OECD banks, the AA rated bank hedges the market risk—the credit risk (both the default risk and the credit-spread-widening risk)—and can reduce the capital charge of the transaction from 100 percent to 20 percent. The AA bank can offer more favorable funding terms to the A– rated bank and still be better off. If the AA bank offers a

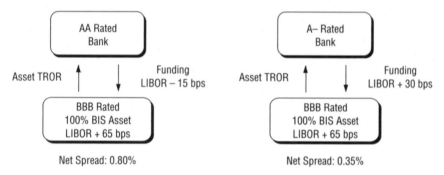

Net Spread: 0.80%   Net Spread: 0.35%

This is an On–Balance Sheet Transaction for Both Banks.

FIGURE 2.5   Outright Purchase: 100% Risk-Weighted Asset

five-year financing cost to the A– rated bank of LIBOR + 15 bps—a 15-basis-point reduction in its normal funding cost—the transaction flows will be as shown in Figure 2.6.

The AA bank benefits from the lower joint probability of default between the A– rated bank and the BBB rated reference asset. Based on Standard & Poor's (S&P) tables, if there is no correlation between the A– rated bank and the BBB rated reference asset, the implied rating on the effective credit risk to the AA rated bank is a rating of A+. S&P and Moody's publish

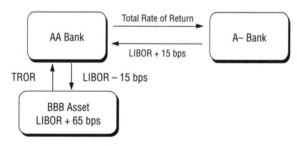

The maturity of the TRORS matches the five-year maturity of the BBB Asset. If the Asset defaults, the A– bank makes a payment to the AA rated bank.

The A– rated bank has the same risk as if it purchased the BBB asset outright and locks in a five-year funding cost of LIBOR + 15 bps versus a funding cost of LIBOR + 30 bps.

FIGURE 2.6   TRORS Transaction Flows

jointly supported ratings for noncorrelated assets and guarantors. Table 2.4 shows S&P's jointly supported ratings.

The AA bank has created a *synthetic* asset with an implied credit rating of A+, a 20 percent BIS risk weight versus the 100 percent risk weight before the TRORS, and is able to reduce credit-risk and market-risk exposure to the reference asset on its books. In fact, both institutions are economically better off after the transaction, although the A– rated institution is in exactly the same regulatory situation as when it purchased the asset outright as opposed to receiving the TROR.

The A– rated bank locks in a favorable financing rate for five years. The A– rated bank does not have to put up any economic capital and receives net flows on the transaction off balance sheet. The A– rated bank is able to leverage its position even if it is temporarily short of investment cash. The new position of both banks after doing the TROR is as shown in Figure 2.7.

Even if the AA bank found a counterparty, such as a 100 percent BIS risk-weighted investment banking firm, the AA bank still benefits from the lower joint probability of default, even though the regulatory capital charges will remain the same. All other things being equal, however, the AA bank will prefer to do this transaction with another OECD bank.

Notice that this transaction works because of the difference in the funding costs of the two institutions. For some assets, and for some institutions where the funding cost differential is less, the funding cost arbitrage may not look as good, and it is sometimes impractical to structure this sort of trans-

TABLE 2.4   S&P Jointly Supported Ratings as of August 1997

	AAA	AA+	AA	AA–	A+	A	A–	BBB+	BBB	BBB–
AAA	AAA	AAA	AAA	AAA	AAA	AAA	AAA	AAA	AAA	AAA
AA+	AAA	AAA	AAA	AAA	AAA	AAA	AAA	AAA	AAA	AA+
AA	AAA	AAA	AAA	AAA	AAA	AAA	AAA	AA+	AA+	AA+
AA–	AAA	AAA	AAA	AA+	AA+	AA+	AA+	AA+	AA+	AA
A+	AAA	AAA	AAA	AA+	AA+	AA+	AA+	AA	AA	AA–
A	AAA	AAA	AAA	AA+	AA+	AA	AA	AA–	AA–	A+
A–	AAA	AAA	AAA	AA+	AA+	AA	AA–	A+	A+	A
BBB+	AAA	AAA	AA+	AA+	AA	AA–	A+	A	A	A–
BBB	AAA	AAA	AA+	AA+	AA	AA	A+	A	A–	BBB+
BBB–	AAA	AA+	AA+	AA	AA–	A+	A	A–	BBB+	BBB–

Note: The way to read this table is to choose either the row or the column for the A– bank and the other for the BBB rated reference asset. Reading across and down, they intersect at A+, the implied effective credit risk for the joint credits.

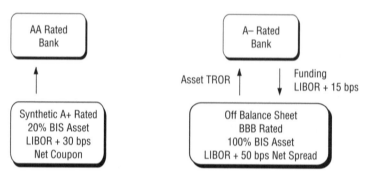

FIGURE 2.7 Net Position after TRORS

action. This is particularly true because of the current compression in credit spread differentials.

BALANCE SHEET MANAGEMENT

Besides using TRORS for financing and for gaining the benefits of leverage, there is another key use for TRORS. Financial institutions often use TRORS as a balance sheet management tool. For example, an institution with a relatively high cost of funds, such as the U.S. branch of a Japanese bank, Lehman Brothers, or Salomon Brothers, will want to get assets off its balance sheet. It may want to do this for a long period of time or for a short period of time. Most of these transactions are thinly disguised balance sheet dressing when done for short periods of time, such as two weeks to three months. Nonetheless, the higher funding cost institutions wishing to get assets off of their balance sheet by using this technique have a true economic risk as if they own the asset for the term of the transaction.

For example, suppose a BBB rated securities firm with the higher cost of funds sells securities to an AA rated bank with a lower cost of funds. The AA rated bank pays the TROR on the securities to the securities firm, and the securities firm simultaneously pays LIBOR plus a spread to the bank. The bank in essence finances the position for the securities firm. From the point of view of the securities firm, this is a true sale of securities as long as the securities firm is not obligated to repurchase the securities. The securities firm will take the mark-to-market risk at the end of the transaction and may actually repurchase the securities; but the key is that it is not *obligated* to do so. The bank earns the income from the short-term transaction. At the end of the transaction, it can sell the securities in the market at the market price without taking price risk on the securities. The bank earns income, which is immunized from price risk. The gain or loss in price at the maturity of the TRORS is borne by the securities firm.

ADVANCED BALANCE SHEET MANAGEMENT

Many banks have set up conduits as fee-earning vehicles to accommodate balance sheet transactions. One creative use of these conduits is as a vehicle to pass through risk. Banks enter into a Sale/TRORS transaction with the conduit. The conduit purchases the bonds and funds this purchase via its commercial paper (CP) program. The conduit then transfers the risk. If the risk is merely being passed through the conduit, it must eventually end up somewhere. It usually ends up back where it started. The conduit pays the total rate of return on the assets to the derivatives trading desk internal to its mother bank. The derivatives trading desk then passes the risk by paying the total rate of return on the assets to a subsidiary of the bank that originally sold the assets to the conduit in the first place. This circular transfer of risk sounds confusing at first. The basic transaction is illustrated in the following scenario:

> You run the corporate bond trading desk for Bank A. Bank A has a variety of subsidiaries and other entities. Your trading desk has taken down a $100 million position of very illiquid bonds, and you are having no success in selling them. You want to get these bonds off the trading book balance sheet for a period of at least one year. It would be ideal if you could get rid of the bonds altogether. Bank A is willing to continue to bear the market risk and the credit risk of the illiquid bonds, which have a highly positive carry; but you don't want the risk to appear in the trading book. For all intents and purposes, you want it to appear as if you sold the bonds to a customer.

Figure 2.8 shows the cash flows of the transaction. You sell $100 million of bonds to Bank B's conduit. Notice that by setting up a conduit for this purpose, Bank B avoids having the bonds hit its balance sheet. Bank B's conduit pays you the market price for these bonds. Bank B's conduit obtains $100 million in funding from the CP market in order to purchase the bonds. The conduit lays off the market risk of the bonds for one

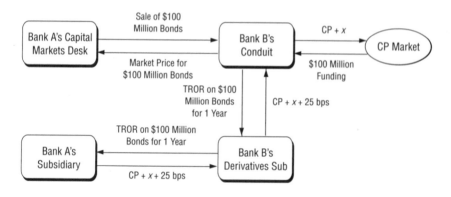

FIGURE 2.8 TRORS for Balance Sheet Management

year by paying the TROR to Bank B's derivatives subsidiary. Bank B's derivative subsidiary lays off the market risk by paying the TROR on $100 million notional of the bonds to Bank A's subsidiary. Bank A's subsidiary pays Bank B's derivatives desk CP plus a spread plus a fee. The spread is denoted in Figure 2.8 as "x." This spread is equal to the spread required for the conduit to fund itself. The fee is consideration for the use of Bank B's conduit and the derivatives subsidiary to pass through the risk. Bank B's derivatives subsidiary pays CP plus the spread plus the fee (minus a small consideration) to the conduit. The net cash flow to the conduit is the fee. Fees vary. This is a negotiated market. In 2000, banks charged 12.5 to 26 bps and more to allow other banks to rent their balance sheet in this fashion.

At the end of the year, how does Bank B make sure that the bonds are sold? Because these bonds may still be very illiquid, they want to be sure to have a way of disposing of these bonds. Furthermore, the bonds may have deteriorated in value, and that is the scenario that most concerns Bank B. Documentation usually calls for an average of several dealer quotes to determine the market value of the bonds at the end of the one-year TRORS. Bank B can ask for a bid on these bonds. If the bid price is too low, Bank A has an incentive to buy the bonds because they have to pay the difference between the original market price and the current market price at the end of the TRORS. If the TRORS called for a mark-to-market on a periodic basis, the final exchange of value would be based on the market price at the beginning of the period, versus at the end of the year. Some documents have a provision that if they cannot get a dealer bid at the end of the TRORS, the assumed mark-to-market price of the bonds is zero. The language is careful not to require Bank A to repurchase the bonds in this scenario, but the economic incentive of Bank A to make a bid is overwhelming. Naturally, this documentation is controversial, and one must check with accountants and lawyers to make sure that Bank A gets the required true sale treatment while Bank B gets its required flexibility at the end of the TRORS.

RELATIVE PERFORMANCE TRORS

Two investors may manage the balance sheet by paying the total rate of return of one asset in exchange for receiving the total rate of return of another asset. This is essentially a relative performance TRORS and theoretically should help investors diversify credit risk using an off–balance sheet tool. In practice it is not seen often in the market. Most banks, for instance, want to pay the total rate of return as a means of getting credit protection, but they are less eager to take on credit risk. It is also difficult to get two institutions to agree on the proper ratios of payment for the relative performance of two different credits.

Nonetheless this underused transaction may become more popular in the future among low funding cost banks wishing to free up overused credit lines of investment-grade credits. Banks may become more willing to swap low-margin returns to free up lines for the opportunity to book higher-margin business with targeted clients. This transaction is a means of expanding credit lines. This concept has been slow to grow among banks, but for transactions in the banking book, the favorable capital treatment enjoyed by some banks supports continued exponential growth.

HEDGE FUNDS AND LOAN TRORS

Until recently, most financings were done through repurchase agreements. Most repurchase agreements are short term, but some can be longer. In the United States, mortgage-backed securities dealers, eager to sell risky inverse floaters combined with interest-only tranches ("inverse/IO" product) in the early 1990s to drive collateralized mortgage obligation (CMO) deals, offered repurchase agreements for as long as two years to buyers. Buyers eagerly sought leveraged financing for their already very risky purchases. The financing rate is known as the "repo rate." The repo rate took into account the creditworthiness of the repurchase agreement "seller" as well as the creditworthiness of the "buyer." The repo rate also took into account the riskiness of the asset. In this case the riskiness of the asset arose from its prepayment sensitivity to interest rates. Therefore, the dealers asked for up-front collateral, usually 10 percent or 20 percent of the initial value of the securities. This up-front collateral compensated for the unusual price volatility of these securities.

The up-front collateral was also meant to compensate for the fact that many of the institutions buying these "high yielding" risky assets were risky institutions. The reason for the financing, of course, was leverage. Most of the institutions asking for financing were either hedge funds or lower-rated Japanese trading and leasing companies.

In the early 1990s, David J. Askin managed a fund of very risky CMO tranches. Askin thought he had a model that could predict an unknowable unknown—the prepayment behavior of the U.S. mortgage holder. His firm, Askin Capital Management, bought these securities using dealer-provided financing on margin. Unfortunately, the prices predicted by his models did not agree with the market quotes he got from the dealers who sold him those securities. As buyers for esoteric mortgage-backed securities withdrew from the market, liquidity disappeared. Market prices diverged even farther from model prices as fundamentals gave way to supply-and-demand forces in the market. As prices dropped, Askin was asked to put up more collateral. Askin, with insufficient liquidity (and some said insufficient solvency), was unable to meet margin calls. He was forced to liquidate fund positions at distressed prices and finally to file for bankruptcy protection. Askin Capital Management's losses caused Kidder Peabody, which had financed sales of many of these CMO tranches to Askin, to lose about $25 million.

How did this happen? It is the old story. If the returns seem miraculously high, the probability that you will lose your money is just about as high. Askin reportedly promised his investors a return of *15 percent on their money with no risk*. The *New York Times* quoted one regretful investor: "Maybe this sounds too easy to say now: If it looks too good to be true, maybe it is." The investment banks were eager to extend financing because they wanted to get rid of the "nuclear waste" tranches of CMOs. Once the risky piece was sold, investment banks could underwrite more transactions and book attractive underwriting fees. When liquidity for these instruments dried up, risk managers started asking tough questions, but much too late.

David Askin was purported to be a presentable, articulate, well-educated investment manager. The models, the graphs, and the investment literature he developed all seemed to support his claim that he could deliver well above market returns with no risk. Clients suspended their disbelief in the face of dazzling models and detailed graphs. This is intellectual slight of hand. "Garbage in" equals "garbage out," even if the garbage is wrapped in gold foil. Forget the glitz, forget the hype, and forget the intellectual bullying of people who want your money. Remember the "most important investment graph." If it sounds too good to be true, it is.

The Askin experience is just one of many examples in the history of the market. Investors want high returns, and they borrow money to buy CMOs, tulip bulbs, Tokyo real estate, or shares of stock. The lenders "know" their client is good for the money because prices are rising and will continue to rise. In the end everyone learns the lesson for the umpteenth time. The only sure thing is that there is no such thing as a sure thing.

What do market professionals learn from these experiences? Not a great deal.

Today's TRORS market shows interesting parallels with the hedge fund/mortgage debacle in the early 1990s. Today several banks are falling over themselves to provide financing for hedge funds. Hedge funds are purchasing highly leveraged transactions (HLTs). These are loans coming from bank loan origination groups eager to open up a new investment base for their products. Banks are offering to pay the total rate of return on these loans to hedge funds.

It is only recently that hedge funds and mutual funds have access to the bank loan market. This is because banks syndicate and underwrite loans, and most of the loans are held in bank portfolios, and because of the higher recovery rates on loans and the high returns available relative to similar risks in the bond market. Banks, eager to broaden HLT market liquidity, found yield-hungry investors. By receiving the total rate of return in a loan swap, an investor creates a synthetic lending facility (SLF). The maturity of the SLF may not match that of the reference loan. SLFs may use either an investment-grade loan or an HLT as a reference asset. Hedge funds, with their high implied funding costs, participate in TRORS using HLTs as the reference asset. The appealing features of a TRORS referencing HLTs include the following:

- Loans are senior secured assets for the most part with high estimated recovery rates, which contributes to low price volatility.
- The transaction is off–balance sheet.
- HLTs are floating-rate instruments, so the netting is simple to calculate.
- Investors avoid the high administrative costs associated with direct management of a loan portfolio, such as tracking funding of revolving credit facilities or prepayments and amortization on term loans.
- As an investor books a collection of transactions, overall risk may decline. Diversified loan portfolios tend to have low volatilities.
- The TRORS structure enables investors to use *leverage*.

LOAN TRORS MECHANICS

The hedge fund investor receives all loan payments, including interest, commitment fees and all pro rata amortization (subject to adjustment for price changes). Fees may be split between the total return payer and the investor, however. The hedge fund pays LIBOR plus a margin on the notional principal. As the loan amortizes, any period gain in price on the amortized amount relative to the initial loan price is paid to the investor. The investor pays the decline from the initial price on the amortized amount. This price adjustment may be netted with amortization, interest, and fee payments. At maturity or default, the reference loan is marked to market. Any gain in price on the remaining notional amount is paid to the investor. The investor pays any decrease in price.

The SLF or TRORS on loans is similar to an investment in a subparticipation in a loan while funding the purchase on a LIBOR basis. The bank payer of the total rate of return is the legal owner of the loan. The investor receiving the total rate of return does not have voting rights and, therefore, does not have a say in potential loan restructuring. This can be a disadvantage; therefore some banks have a "gentleman's agreement" that they will consult and vote according to the wishes of the total rate of return receiver. An advantage to the investor is that this is an off–balance sheet transaction.

The terms of loans are different from those for bonds. Periodic amortization, tranching of loan maturities, and the combination of revolvers and term loans in a loan syndication can be confusing to novices. The following term sheet is a generic example of a one-year-maturity total return swap on all of the tranches of a newly syndicated loan for one-fourth of the entire loan. In this case, a bank is paying the total rate of return to an investor. The investor essentially takes the risk on this package for one year, a period of time shorter than the term of the underlying loans. This idea can be adapted for just the revolver or for any of the tranches of a term loan, whether newly syndicated or traded in the secondary market.

This term sheet is for an investor with a high cost of funds. The spread of 100 basis points required as payment by the investor may be reduced if the investor agrees to give the payer of the total return swap up-front collateral. If the investor were more creditworthy and had a lower cost of funds, then the required spread might be greatly reduced and no collateral required. For more information on credit events and definitions, see also Chapter 7.

TOTAL RATE OF RETURN SWAP
Loan Reference Asset Indicative Term Sheet

Transaction Overview:	The bank will pay the total rate of return on 25 percent of the full commitment amount on the following basket of high-yield loans (the reference asset[s]) to the total rate of return receiver as consideration for receiving the payments shown below.
Reference Obligation(s):	
Type of Borrowing:	High-yield borrower senior bank facilities.
Credit Agreement Dated:	To be determined.
Senior Bank Facilities:	Collectively, the revolving credit facility, a term loan A facility, a term loan B facility, a term loan C facility, and a term loan D facility.
For Each Loan Facility:	
Principal:	Up to USD XXX million as in credit agreement.
Interest Rate:	1. Contract rate plus x.xx% per annum, or
	2. LIBOR plus x.xx% per annum.
Final Maturities for Each Loan Facility:	
Revolving Credit Facility:	Six years from closing date.

Term Loan A Maturity:	Six years from closing date.
Term Loan B Maturity:	Seven years from closing date.
Term Loan C Maturity:	Eight years from closing date.
Term Loan D Maturity:	Nine years from closing date.

Initial Prices for Each Loan Facility:

Revolving Credit Facility:	Par.
Term Loan A:	Par.
Term Loan B:	Par.
Term Loan C:	Par.
Term Loan D:	Par.
Total Return Payer:	The bank.
Total Return Receiver:	Investor hedge fund.
Closing Date:	As soon as practical.
Trade Date:	Today.
Effective Date:	Closing date (usually within five business days).
Termination Date:	The earlier of:

1. one year from the effective date; *or*

2. date of cancellation and payment in full of principal and interest on the revolving credit facility, term loan A, term loan B, term loan C, term loan D; *or*

3. the nonscheduled termination date, if any.

Investment Participation:	25%.
Notional Amount:	The sum of the average daily funded commitment amount of the reference loan times 25 percent (the investment participation) times the initial price, where the funded commitment amount as of any date is the total amount of borrowings, the principal amounts of any drawings, outstanding under the reference loan. The notional amount may be reduced by mandatory and voluntary prepayments as outlined in the credit agreement.

(continued)

Prepayments: Mandatory and voluntary prepayments may
                                    exist on the senior bank facilities as discussed
                                    in the credit agreement.

Amortization based on full commitment (the investor receives 25 percent of full
commitment):

Year	Term Loan A	Term Loan B	Term Loan C	Term Loan D
1	$0	$0	$0	$0
2	$6,000,000	$780,000	$780,000	$780,000
3	$30,000,000	$780,000	$780,000	$780,000
4	$36,000,000	$780,000	$780,000	$780,000
5	$36,000,000	$780,000	$780,000	$780,000
6	$36,000,000	$780,000	$780,000	$780,000
7	—	$74,100,000	$780,000	$780,000
8	—	—	$73,320,000	$780,000
9	—	—	—	$72,540,000
Totals	$144,000,000	$78,000,000	$78,000,000	$78,000,000

The Bank Total Rate of Return Payments:

On the payment date, the bank will pay the investor an amount equal to:

25% x (Sum of Any Interest Amounts, xx% of all Commitment Fees, on the unfunded portion of the revolving credit facility and letter of credit fee on the unutilized
letters of credit for each reference loan accrued and paid during the period).

Additional Amounts: On each payment date, the bank shall pay to
                                    investor the positive amount, if any, equal to
                                    the sum of each reference loan of:

                                    (Period Principal Prepayment for Each Refer-
                                    ence Loan) × 25% × (Par – Initial Price for the
                                    Reference Loan)

Investor Payments:

Floating Payment: On the payment date for each period, investor
                                    pays an amount equal to:

                                    (Notional Amount – All Prepayments) × (Float-
                                    ing Rate Index **plus 100** bps) × A/360, where
                                    A is the actual number of days in the period.

Additional Amounts:	On each payment date, investor shall pay to the bank the positive amount, if any, equal to the product of:
	(Period Principal Prepayment for each Reference Loan) × 25% × (Most Recent Mark-to-Market − 100%), if positive.
Floating Rate Index:	Identical to reference obligation interest rate.
Spread:	**100** basis points per annum.
Period End Dates:	Reference obligation period end dates.
Payment Dates:	Two business days after period end date.
Compounding Rate:	Investor floating rate index plus **100 basis points** for the appropriate accrual period.
Final Termination Payment:	Two New York banking days after the termination date; at the option of the bank, the final exchange will consist of either:

1. Physical Settlement:

   The bank makes physical delivery of the reference obligation equal to the notional amount to investor.

   Investor pays the sum of:

   (Notional Amount of Each Reference Loan) x Initial Price

or

2. Cash Settlement:

   Investor pays the bank the sum of the amount for each reference asset calculated as follows:

   Notional Amount (Most Recent Mark-to-Market − Initial Price), if positive

   or

   The bank pays investor the sum of the amount for each reference asset calculated as follows:

(continued)

	Notional Amount (Initial Price – Most Recent Mark-to-Market), if positive.
Nonscheduled Termination:	
Date:	Two business days following the notification date, if any.
Payment:	As described in final termination payment.
Notification Date:	If a credit event or a merger event occurs during the term of this transaction, the agent shall have the right to designate a nonscheduled termination date by delivering notice (even if such notice occurs after the maturity date) to investor of the occurrence of such credit or merger event. Such notice must contain a description, in reasonable detail, of the facts giving rise to the credit or merger event. Total return payment accruals shall terminate on such notification date, if any.
Credit Event:	With respect to the issuer of the reference obligation (reference credit), any of the following that occurs on or prior to the maturity date:

1. A failure by the reference credit to make when due any payment under any financial obligation.

2. A default, event of default, or other similar condition or event that occurs on the part of the reference credit under any financial obligation.

3. A waiver, deferral, restructuring, rescheduling, exchange, or other adjustment occurs in respect of any financial obligation, and the effect of such adjustment is overall materially less favorable from a credit-and-risk perspective to the relevant creditor.

4. Bankruptcy.

5. Any violation of the credit agreement.

6. Downgrade.

7. Credit event upon merger.

8. Repudiation.

Merger Event:	An actual or publicly announced intended consolidation, amalgamation, substantial transfer of assets, or merger of the reference credit with another entity.
Financial Obligation:	With respect to the reference credit, any senior unsecured financial obligation incurred by the reference credit in any capacity.
Market Value:	On any day, with respect to the relevant reference obligation, the percentage equal to the unweighted arithmetic mean of the firm USD denominated bid prices (exclusive of any accrued but unpaid interest and expressed as a percentage of principal amount) for such reference obligation provided to the calculation agent on such day by not less than one and not more than five referenced dealers, including the bank, as such prices are available.
Suitability:	This transaction will be executed with an investor having such knowledge and experience in financial and business matters that he or she is capable of evaluating the merits and risks of the transaction.
Documentation:	Standard ISDA master agreement and swap confirmation.
Liquidity:	There may be no, or only a limited, secondary market for a transaction of this type.
Firm Unwind Prices:	The bank may quote (but is not legally obligated to quote) a firm price that the bank would pay or charge to unwind the transaction prior to maturity. A firm unwind price for a transac-

(continued)

	tion of this type will be affected by the then-current level of the market, but it may also be affected by other factors. A firm unwind price for a transaction of this type can change significantly from day to day over the life of the transaction.
Periodic Pricing:	It is the current practice (but not a legal obligation) of the bank to provide to its client in a transaction of this type information in writing about the value of such transaction, upon request of the client.
Calculation Agent:	The bank.
Business Days:	Days on which commercial banks and foreign exchange markets settle payments in London and New York.

The preceding term sheet is not a confirmation. Confirmations are up to 30 pages long and are modeled after the ISDA standard. The ISDA does not actually have a current standard for total rate of return swaps or for loans as reference assets. Therefore documents are negotiated in the spirit of ISDA guidelines. The confirmation is the document to which counterparties look as their legal agreement. These are usually couched in language much more precise and technical than the language in the term sheet. The confirmation will usually contain information not referenced in the term sheet. Detailed credit terms, including required up-front collateral, are generally included in the confirmation, not the term sheet.

The TRORS is a convenient and efficient way for financial institutions to lay off the risk of existing loan portfolios. The borrower need never know that the bank is laying off its risk, and the bank can continue to have a profitable relationship with the borrower. In the event of an actual borrower default, if the TROR receiver takes delivery of the loan, the borrower would know at that time that the bank no longer held its loan. In that event, however, the bank will probably not be as concerned about the relationship implications of laying off the borrower's credit risk.

HEDGE FUNDS AND LEVERAGE

TRORS open up distribution in the loan market, and the TROR receiver continues to be an important element in the structure. When a bank lays off the credit risk of a loan by paying the total rate of return to a hedge fund, how much risk does the bank reduce?

Figure 2.9 shows a total return swap using a B+ rated loan as the reference asset for a hedge fund investor. Let us look at potential one-year returns for a hedge fund that puts up 10 percent collateral to receive the total rate of return of a $10 million principal amount of an HLT. The initial price of the HLT is par (100). Let us assume that the collateral is invested at 6 percent per annum. Table 2.5 shows the one-year total rate of return for different loan prices ignoring potential margin call adjustments to the up-front collateral. The coupon amount shown in the table is the net spread earned by the hedge fund after financing costs. The gross coupon is assumed to be LIBOR + 325 bps, and the hedge fund is required to pay LIBOR + 75 bps with 10 percent up-front collateral. The total rate of return for the hedge fund is calculated based on the actual cash collateral amount posted, $1 million. The hedge fund enjoys the positive effects of leveraged high returns when the asset performs well or increases in value. When the asset declines in value, however, the hedge fund returns feel the negative effects of leverage.

Credit managers face a dilemma. Banks are in the business of providing finance and generally want to lay off risk in a cost-effective manner. Credit

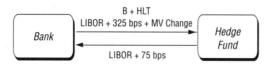

Total Return* = Net Interest + % *of Commitment Fees* + (Final Value** – Original Value)

Hedge Fund posts 10% collateral on a $10,000,000 loan balance.

*Total Return is paid on remaining balance.
**Final Value at amortization is the current Market Value (MV) calculated on the amoritized amount.

FIGURE 2.9   TRORS: Reference Asset Is a Loan

TABLE 2.5   HLT TRORS: Rate of Return Scenarios after One Year, $10,000,000 Notional, 10% ($1,000,000) Collateral

Loan Price in One Year	Loan Coupon LIBOR + 250 bps	Gain (Loss) on Loan	Interest on Collateral (at 6% per annum)	Rate of Return (% per annum)
102	$250,000	$200,000	$60,000	51.0%
100	$250,000	0	$60,000	31.0%
96	$250,000	($400,000)	$60,000	(9.0%)
92	$250,000	($800,000)	$60,000	(49.0%)
88	$250,000	($1,200,000)	$60,000	(89.0%)

derivatives traders, eager to book income, want to lend money to hedge funds because the spread of LIBOR + 75 basis points, and sometimes as high as LIBOR + 100 basis points, is a greater spread than the banks can get from other counterparties, such as U.S. banks, insurance companies, or investment banks.

There is a reason for the high funding cost demanded of the hedge funds, however. Hedge funds do not disclose other assets on their balance sheets. The credit manager evaluating the credit of a hedge fund has nothing to go on. There is no way of knowing how many of these transactions have been done by the hedge fund. On the one hand, more transactions imply greater diversification. On the other hand, the credit manager has no way to determine how much leverage the hedge fund employs.

Some hedge funds are required to put up only 5 percent up-front collateral. Banks demanding 20 percent up-front collateral often find that hedge funds will do the TRORS with another bank who will give more favorable collateral terms. Banks will often require a daily mark-to-market on the underlying asset, and often there is a "cure" period, which allows the hedge fund time to come up with additional collateral. Not every bank requires a daily mark-to-market, however.

If a bank enters into a transaction with a hedge fund, what benefit, if any, does the bank get from a reduced joint probability of default? Is there a reduced probability? Does the up-front collateral suffice to enhance the credit quality of the hedge fund counterparty to compensate the bank in the event of default? If the HLT defaults, is the price volatility low enough so that the up-front collateral will cover the decline in value?

A hedge fund counterparty seems to be a perversion of the concept of credit derivatives. Do I view the hedge fund as a single A? Most banks would emphatically say not. Do I view the hedge fund as BB+? The problem is, no one really knows. Hedge funds do not disclose enough information to make this evaluation.

If I want to lay off risk in the portfolio, to what degree am I hedged when the counterparty is a hedge fund? What sort of assumption can I make for a jointly supported rating?

I believe that there is no benefit from a jointly supported rating when a hedge fund is the "guarantor." The protection provided by the hedge fund is phantom protection. The only benefit is from the up-front collateral, which reduces my exposure in the event of a default on the underlying asset. If a hedge fund puts up only 5 percent collateral, that is not much of a reduction in my overall exposure. The unfortunate truth is that in the event of default of the reference asset, I do not know whether the hedge fund will be in a position to come up with the additional money. Will the hedge fund seek comfort in bankruptcy?

The fact that banks are willing to do this business with hedge funds illustrates how difficult it is for banks to generate income from their traditional investment-grade loan business. Investment-grade loans show a dismally low return on capital. Unlike the CMO scenario, banks do not need to provide financing in order to find buyers for their loans. There is high demand for HLTs from investors and banks seeking collateral for collateralized loan obligations. The primary goal isn't increased distribution. The primary goal is to book higher spread income. The question remains whether the enhanced spread income of LIBOR + 75 bps and more that hedge funds are willing to pay as a funding cost is enough to compensate banks for the credit risk.

HEDGE FUNDS AND LEVERAGED EXPOSURE TO SPREADS

Sandy Sloane, a principal in Global Derivative Products and head of marketing to Professional Trading Accounts at Bank of America, points out that there is another use for TRORS. When hedge funds engage in fixed-income arbitrage transactions, they often attempt to create leveraged exposure to asset swap spreads by buying an asset, financing the asset, and paying fixed in an interest-rate-swap transaction. The combination of the long position (buying the fixed-coupon asset) and the short position (paying fixed in an interest-rate swap to receive floating) creates a market-rate, asset swap package. By financing the asset, the hedge fund then creates a leveraged exposure to asset swap spreads.

Let's look at an example of this transaction. A hedge fund buys a 30-year German-government Bund and pays fixed in a 30-year Euro swap. If interest rates increase, the hedge fund will have a gain in the swap position and an equivalent loss in the bond position, the difference being the gain or the loss on the swap spread. The fixed coupon on the bond offsets the payment of the fixed leg of the swap. The floating leg of the swap offsets the financing cost of the bond. The financing of the bond could be done with term repurchase agreements or a bond forward; but because we are concerned with TRORS, we'll assume that that is how the hedge fund will finance the asset. The hedge fund will usually obtain funding at some discount to EurIBOR, which I'll define as Y. Figure 2.10 illustrates the cash flows.

The bank's credit exposure to the hedge fund on the 30-year Euro swap is huge. Many banks will decline to do this swap even with a collateral agreement and mutual termination provision. The TRORS seems to mitigate most of this credit risk. Because TRORS are usually executed under an ISDA master, this transaction can be combined in one confirm. The credit risk on both the long and the short sides of this transaction offset each other.

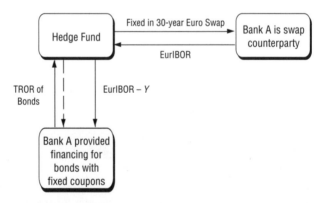

Example for rising-rate scenario: If rates rise, the price of the Bunds declines, but the market value of the swap increases. The hedge fund would owe the bank Final Value − Initial Value on the bonds for the TRORS (represented by dashed arrow), but this credit risk is offset by the hedge fund's gain in swap market value.

FIGURE 2.10 Hedge Fund Spread Play

The bank would take further steps to ask for frequent mark-to-market periods on the asset swap package (often daily, but at a maximum of every three months), for initial margin on the asset swap package, and for a one-day "cure" period on the collateral to further minimize risk.

This is a risky transaction from an operational point of view. The bank has risk if the hedge fund tries to unwind any leg of this transaction. This is known as "fire hydrant" risk, or the risk of "lifting a leg." For instance, if the hedge fund lifts the TRORS leg of the transaction, the bank will have no offset for the credit risk on the swap. The bank should attempt to get the hedge fund to agree that the entire transaction must unwind in entirety. This condition should be explicitly spelled out in the confirm, and risk management must have a means of monitoring and enforcing this condition.

RELATIVE VALUE AND BALANCE SHEET MANAGEMENT

Often a mispricing exists between loans and debt markets. In the mid-1990s, for instance, banks lent money to Italy at a rate of LIBOR + 45 bps, whereas Italian government dollar-denominated debt traded at LIBOR + 25 bps. This is a dislocation in the pricing of capital structure.

Often subordinated debt may trade at a tighter spread than loan yields do. Subordinated debt is generally more volatile than loan pricing. It is generally nonamortizing and has a much longer maturity than loans do. The price of subordinated debt will therefore be much more volatile than that of a loan. It is possible, however, to construct an asset swap from subordinated debt to make this debt a synthetic floating rate note (FRN). The synthetic FRN has much less price volatility than a fixed rate bond because the coupon resets frequently and the price hovers near par. In the absence of a general change in market credit spreads and in the absence of a change in the credit spread of the issuer, the synthetic FRN will have the same price characteristics as a par floater. Counterparties interested in receiving the total rate of return on subordinated debt will probably be much more willing to do this if the price volatility due to a change in market interest rates is dampened by the creation of the synthetic subordinated debt FRN.

If an investor, such as an insurance company, owns subordinated debt trading at spreads tighter than the same issuer's bank loans, the insurance company can arbitrage the credit risk. The transaction to do in this case is to pay the total rate of return on the subordinated-debt, asset swap package.

The insurance company lays off the subordinated credit risk of the issuer. The insurance company then simultaneously receives the total rate of return on a bank loan to the issuer. The credit quality of the bank loan is higher than that of the subordinated debt, and the insurance company can therefore receive the total rate of return on a higher notional amount. For instance, for every $20 million of subordinated debt, the insurance company may be willing to receive the total rate of return of $30 million of the bank loan debt. The insurance company may view the net credit risk position as equal; however, the insurance company can enjoy a pickup in income.

Figure 2.11 shows a transaction in which an insurance company pays the total rate of return to a high-credit quality bank, which funds at LIBOR – 20 bps. The bank receives the total rate of return on the $20 million subordinated-debt, asset swap package and receives a payment stream of LIBOR + 200 bps until the maturity of the transaction, if there is no default on the subordinated debt. The insurance company then agrees to pay LIBOR + 25 bps to the loan desk of another bank and receives the total rate of return on a term loan with an initial balance of $30 million. The insurance company receives a payment stream of LIBOR + 300 bps until the maturity of the transaction if there is no default on the bank loan.

Although the insurance company pays a higher cost to receive the bank loan total returns, the higher spread of the bank loan more than makes up for this. In addition, the insurance company levers the return by receiving

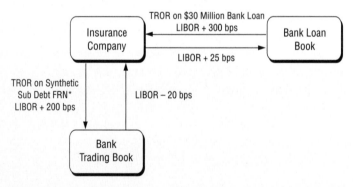

*This is the total rate of return on a par asset swap package consisting of the subordinated debt and a swap of the fixed coupons for floating.

FIGURE 2.11   Subordinated Debt/Bank Loan Arbitrage

the total rate of return on a higher notional amount. In this case, before taking into account the higher notional amount of the bank loan, the insurance company has a net positive spread of 55 basis points. Taking into account the notional of the bank loan, which is 1.5 times higher than that of the subordinated debt, the insurance company earns a net spread of 192.5 basis points.

Bank loans are prepayable, amortized, and often have final maturities and average lives shorter than the remaining maturity of subordinated debt. The insurance company can mitigate this maturity mismatch if it is willing to accept a reduced payment from the bank trading book in order to have the right to periodically adjust the notional of the TRORS on the subordinated-debt synthetic FRN.

Total rate of return swaps also give investors the ability to take views on entire sectors of the market. Investors can receive the total rate of return of an equity index, the technology sector of an equity index, a high-yield bond index, or any sector of the market for which an index is available and a counterparty is willing to pay the total rate of return.

Investors can take views on the relative value of different sectors of the market as well. Figure 2.12 illustrates how an investor can short the 10-year constant maturity treasury (CMT) and go long a broad-based high-yield index to take a view on the relative performance of the high-yield index and the U.S. 10-year treasury. The investor has the view that the high-yield index will outperform the 10-year CMT. The bank payer of the high-yield index may want to reduce exposure to the high-yield market or may be laying off the other side of a transaction in which it receives the high-yield index.

The bank in the above example may have used the TRORS as a balance sheet management tool. In general, TRORS are underused as balance sheet tools when banks swap credit risk. Banks are more than happy to offer bonds

Investors can increase exposure to high-yield spreads and benefit from a tightening versus the 10-year U.S. treasury by paying the 10-year Constant Maturity Treasury and receiving the total rate of return on a high-yield bond index.

FIGURE 2.12   Spread Play: High Yield versus 10-Year Treasury

for purchase to another bank and then receive the total rate of return on the swap. This is a method of financing a position and getting bonds off the balance sheet. Banks are less willing to swap risks, however, as there is no permanent net reduction in credit exposure for a transaction that is shorter than the maturity of the reference assets. Nonetheless, this method of cooperating to diversify credit exposures is a transaction that makes sense for banks. Figure 2.13 illustrates an underused market transaction in which a European bank reduces credit concentration to a low-yielding investment-grade European corporate bank loan and a U.S. bank reduces exposure to a low-yielding investment-grade U.S. corporate bank loan.

The market is not as willing to recognize the value of transactions in which no money changes hands but portfolio risk is diversified. One of the barriers to this recognition is that on a portfolio basis, it is difficult for banks to see the small incremental benefit. The interest in the case-by-case transaction from banks is almost exclusively a one-sided sale of exposure to gain relief from a full credit line.

CREDIT EXPOSURE AND THE CONDITIONAL PROBABILITY OF DEFAULT

If a bank owns a reference obligation on the bank book, it might use a TRORS to reduce both market risk and credit exposure to an underlying obligor. The internal debate will usually center around how much credit exposure the bank has after doing the TRORS. In addition, the bank must determine to whom the bank has this credit exposure. This is not obvious to the internal credit-and-risk committees of many banks. In particular, management of

Banks can reduce overconcentration of credit risk by swapping exposures off–balance sheet. Notional may or may not be one-to-one depending on perception of credit risk and compensation for credit exposure.

FIGURE 2.13   Balance Sheet Exposure Management

the credit exposure lines of the bank book and recognition of the benefit of the conditional (also sometimes erroneously called the "joint") probability of default are still debated among banks that rank among the top five in size in their respective countries.

I will digress for another word on market terminology, although nontheoreticians may want to skip this paragraph. Consider the purchase of credit default protection in which Bank A buys credit default protection from Bank B on the loan obligation of Reference Obligor, R. If only R defaults, Bank A is still protected by Bank B. If Bank B defaults but R has not defaulted, Bank A can theoretically replace the credit default protection with another protection seller. Bank A is concerned about the scenario in which R defaults, given that Bank B has defaulted. It may be a source of annoyance to statisticians that the credit derivatives market often refers to the former scenario as the *joint* probability of default when in reality we mean the *conditional* probability of default. Throughout this book, I've generally adopted the market terminology. The JP Morgan CreditMetrics Monitor published in the third quarter of 1998 gave tables of joint credit transition probabilities and conditional probabilities. Assume Bank B has a probability of default of 0.04 percent. The probability that R migrates to default is the marginal probability of default of 0.17 percent. For a correlation of 0 percent, the joint probability of default is 0.0001 percent. For a correlation of 30 percent, the joint probability of default is 0.0011 percent. The conditional probability given a default of Bank B for zero correlation is 0.17 percent. For 30 percent correlation, the conditional probability is 2.69 percent. The conditional probability is higher than the joint probability for a given correlation. The bank book assumes that 100 percent of the loan value is applied against a credit line, so applying credit for the lower conditional probability of default is a tremendous benefit versus the current bank book treatment.

Although there is still no market standard, I sense a trend. Most banks for bank book purposes will show $100 million of credit exposure for a loan to a reference obligor. How much should a bank reduce this exposure when a bank buys credit default protection on a loan to the reference obligor? I believe most banks will eliminate the entire exposure for the $100 million loan from the credit line of the reference obligor. The credit line of the counterparty, which receives the TROR, is then reduced by the amount of credit exposure resulting from the TRORS. But this credit exposure is significantly lower than the original $100 million credit exposure charged to the line of the reference obligor who issued the original reference obligation. This is due to the fact that many banks recognize a much-reduced credit exposure because the conditional probability of default between the reference obligor and the counterparty is much lower than one.

The challenge of calculating the conditional probability of default is finding data that are acceptable to all the internal committees who want to have a say in your calculation method. While you may never reach an agreement, if you did have the data, the following approach is usually viewed as reasonable.

Let's review some of the features of a TRORS that will affect any calculation approach. First and foremost, you can decide either to accept the counterparty and the underlying credit risk, the obligor, or to reject the transaction. This means you must have some view on the default probability of the reference obligor, on the default probability of the counterparty, on the correlation of the default probability of the reference obligor and the counterparty, and on the market risk or market volatility of the reference obligation. Considering a basket of reference obligors instead of a single asset can further complicate the transaction. If you choose to do a basket transaction, correlation is a very important consideration, and you will try to create the most diverse basket possible to minimize specific risk.

Besides your choice in doing the transaction at all, you have further input to the structure of the transaction. You can minimize credit exposure and risk by increasing the frequency of the mark-to-market periods in the TRORS. This increase in frequency will decrease the joint probability of default, the event risk, and the market risk, or price risk, of the transaction.

The joint probability of default describing the event risk is defined by the following equation. Note that we are actually calculating the conditional probability of default of the asset, given the probability of default of the counterparty. It is only under this scenario that risk exists. If the counterparty alone defaulted, you could replace the counterparty with another—at least that is the theory.

$$P_{(u|c)} = P_{(u)} + \rho_{(u,c)} \sqrt{\frac{(P_{(u)})(1 - P_{(u)})(1 - P_{(c)})}{(P_{(c)})}}$$

where $P_{(u|c)}$ = Conditional default probability of underlying asset dependent on default probability of counterparty

$P_{(u)}$ = Probability of default of underlying asset
$\rho_{(u,c)}$ = Correlation of default between asset and counterparty
$P_{(c)}$ = Probability of default of counterparty

This formula is easy to understand, but coming up with formulas isn't the main issue in determining the value of credit risk. The main issue is the data. Where do you get the data for the default probability of the assets, the default probability of the counterparty, and the default correlations between the assets (also between assets if it is a basket structure) and the counterparty?

As we stated before, ratings agencies such as Moody's and S&P provide default probabilities per ratings class, though they lack firm specific data. Alternatively you can use estimates provided by experts in your own institution. That presupposes you can get experts to agree on the treatment of the data, itself a major undertaking.

Data from the firm founded by Stephen Kealhofer, John McQuown, and Oldrich Vasicek (KMV) is gaining wide acceptance. KMV has data on more than 17,000 firms. KMV generates default probabilities and default correlations by modeling asset values against the relative level of debt for a firm. KMV assumes that when the asset value falls below that debt level, the firm defaults. The distance away from that point is measured and expressed as the expected default frequency (EDF; we'll discuss this further when we address capital issues).

If you get to the point that your data are accepted and your institution adopts a formula such as the one given for $P_{(u\,|\,c)}$, you have another decision to make. For what time period is the formula valid? Most default frequency data are available for periods no shorter than six months or one year. Is it proper to scale this by the square root of time? Should you use a different time factor, depending on the frequency of resets of your TRORS? There is no evidence to support scaling by the square root of time. Indeed for credits below investment grade, scaling with the square root of time can be very misleading because noninvestment-grade credits near bankruptcy may actually improve with time if their credit difficulties were due to factors that resolve with business success and time. Nonetheless, for investment-grade credits the temptation is great to scale with the square root of time, and several banks currently do this. Once you've decided on your calculation of the joint probability of default, you will want to calculate the credit exposure. The following equation describes the credit exposure one would apply to the notional amount of the swap. This is the event risk associated with the swap. Because you've already calculated the conditional probabilities and default correlations across all the assets and the counterparty, you can use these results to compute the exposure of the swap.

$$UL_{(u,\,c)} = \sqrt{\sum \rho_{i_j} n_i n_j \sqrt{\frac{(P_{(u_i|c)})(1 - P_{(u,\,c)})(P_{(u_j|\,c)})(1 - P_{(u,\,c)})}{(1 - P_{(c)})}}}$$

where $UL_{(u,\,c)}$ = Unexpected loss or credit event risk (default)

$\quad\quad P_{(u_i\,|\,c)}$ = Probability of default of asset i

$\quad\quad P_{(u_j\,|\,c)}$ = Probability of default of asset j

$\quad\quad P_{(u_p,\,c)}$ = Joint probability default of asset i and counterparty

$\quad\quad P_{(u_p,\,c)}$ = Joint probability default of asset j and counterparty

$\quad\quad P_{(c)}$ = Probability of default of counterparty

$\quad\quad \rho_{(i,\,j)}$ = Correlation of default between asset i and asset j

$\quad\quad n_i$ = Asset i's weight in the portfolio

$\quad\quad n_j$ = Asset j's weight in the portfolio

Now that you've calculated the exposure, you can multiply the exposure by the notional amount of the swap. You have now established the credit exposure for the swap with respect to event risk.

Market Risk/Price Risk

Although market price risk is the other credit exposure component, it is often tracked separately and reported for regulatory and internal management purposes as value-at-risk (VaR). We need the volatility of the asset or the basket of assets in order to calculate VaR.

Let me generalize this approach for a fixed-income asset and then address the special case of the TRORS, which can be viewed as a collateralized FRN. First you must choose the time horizon over which you want to calculate the volatility and the VaR. These time horizons are drastically different. For the volatility calculation, you need a time series of data for the calculation. We'll get back to that in a moment. You also need to decide the confidence level for your VaR. Notice we are talking not about confidence *intervals* but confidence *levels*. Furthermore, we generally make the assumption that we are using a lognormal distribution, an assumption that may cause you further unease. After you determine the volatility and the confidence level, you plug them into the following equation:

$$Confidence\ level\ percentile = e^{-\sigma\sqrt{t}*c} -1$$

where σ = Volatility of assets
$\quad t$ = Time between resets
$\quad c$ = Factor corresponding to the chosen confidence level

For the 95th percentile (1.645 standard deviation[SD]), the result implies that your price movement would exceed this value on the loss side only 1.645 times, or twice if you round up, for every 100 trading days. Your formula would look as follows:

$$95th\ percentile = e^{-\sigma\sqrt{t}*1.645} -1$$

where σ = Volatility of assets
$\quad t$ = Time between resets

For the 99th percentile (2.33 SD), the result implies that you expect that your price movement on the loss side would exceed this value no more than once for every 100 trading days. Your formula would look as follows:

$$99th\ percentile = e^{-\sigma\sqrt{t}*2.33} -1$$

where σ = Volatility of assets
$\quad t$ = Time between resets

We still haven't calculated the volatility of the assets, however. There are several good resources on the complicated issues surrounding the calculation of volatility. If I can recommend only one, I usually recommend *Option Volatility and Pricing* by Sheldon Natenberg. To keep myself humble, I review an article written for the February 1, 1991, *Risk* by Kenneth Leong: "Estimates, Guesstimates, and Rules of Thumb." While there are many ways to calculate the volatility, it is probably a good idea to step back for a moment and review the general approach. Your specific approach will depend on the amount and the frequency of the data available to you and on the application.

Volatility as a Measure of Total Market Risk

We tend to retreat to familiar mathematics when trying to describe risk. Because variance and volatility are such key concepts in any discussion of risk, it may be useful to step back and review a general method for calculating these risk parameters. Variance of an asset's or a portfolio's return or price change is usually used to describe the price risk of a portfolio. You may recall that *variance* is simply a statistical measure of the dispersion of a return from its average return level for a specific period of time. We generally make an assumption about the probability distribution. Most practitioners assume a normal distribution because the mathematics is well known.

For a given probability density function *f(x)*, variance is defined as follows:

$$\sigma^2 = \int_{-\infty}^{+\infty} (x - \mu)^2 f(x) dx$$

where μ is the distribution's mean. If I had all of the data and the actual distribution, I wouldn't have to approximate the distribution. I could just examine the actual distribution and draw my conclusions from that. Of course, we usually never have the actual distribution *f(x)*, so we must use that actual sample data to try to approximate the distribution.

For some time series of returns $\{R_1, \ldots, R_n\}$, sample variance is:

$$s^2 = \frac{1}{n-1} \sum_{i=1}^{n} (x_i - \mu)^2$$

where μ is now the sample mean, or the average return over time periods 1 to n. The square root of the variance is the standard deviation of the returns. The market usually refers to this as the volatility. This is most properly symbolized as σ, but we will use the more common symbol for volatility, σ.

TABLE 2.6 Weekly Prices

Week	Underlying Price	$\ln(P_i/P_{i-1})$	Mean	Deviation from Mean	Deviation Squared
0	102.00		0.0009756		
1	103.00	0.0097562		0.0087806	0.0000771
2	100.00	−0.0295588		−0.0305344	0.0009324
3	100.50	0.0049875		0.0040119	0.0000161
4	100.70	0.0019881		0.0010125	0.0000010
5	104.00	0.0322451		0.0312695	0.0009778
6	99.00	−0.0492710		−0.0502467	0.0025247
7	99.50	0.0050378		0.0040622	0.0000165
8	99.90	0.0040120		0.0030364	0.0000092
9	104.00	0.0402212		0.0392456	0.0015402
10	103.00	−0.0096619		−0.0106375	0.0001132

Example: You have 10 weeks of bond price data and want to calculate the annualized price volatility. (In practice, you would have much more data and probably use daily closing prices, but I'm using a small sample to make this example easier to follow.) How would you determine the annualized price volatility?

You might first calculate the natural log of the daily price changes. If your current price is P_i, and the previous week's price is P_{i-1}, the natural log of the daily price changes is $\ln(P_i/P_{i-1})$.

From these price changes, you calculate the mean, or μ. For n observations, this is simply:

$$\mu = \frac{1}{n}\sum_{i=1}^{n} x_i$$

Now you calculate the square of the deviation from the mean and the variance from the formula for variance stated earlier. Table 2.6 shows the results you will get for the weekly prices given in the table.

The sum of the squares of the deviation from the mean is 0.0062082. The variance is simply 0.0062082/9, or 0.0006898. The standard deviation, or volatility, is the square root of the variance, or 0.02626399. We recall that annualized volatility is simply the standard deviation times the square root of the time period. Because we used weekly prices, the time interval between prices is 7 and the time interval is 365/7, or 52.14. The annualized volatility is $0.02626399 \times (52.14)^{0.5}$. Therefore, the annualized volatility is 0.1896, or 18.96 percent. Some assets, such as investment-grade floating rate loans, will generally have lower annualized implied price volatilities because volatility for periods shorter than a year can be calculated from annualized volatility by multiplying by the square root of time. For instance, if the mark-to-market is weekly, we would use 0.02626399, or 2.6 percent. This is why frequent mark-to-market periods are often used for TRORS.

Now that you have all of the components, you can calculate the credit exposure due to both price risk and event risk using the following formula:

$$\text{Credit Exposure} = \text{Notional Amount} \times$$
$$(\text{Price Risk}_{\text{at your chosen confidence level}} + \text{Event Risk})$$

This is the amount of credit exposure one would apply to the line of the counterparty, which is the credit protection provider.

The reduction of credit line for the assets in the basket is another matter. Many banks apply a credit exposure reduction to the worst credit in the basket only. If one is using investment-grade credits, however, it is often difficult to distinguish the "worst" credit in the basket. Banks have a lot of discretion on how they handle their internal credit lines with respect to basket transactions, and as yet there is no market consensus.

The preceding analysis does not take into account the possibility of credit spread migration. You may have the view that the market prices the possibility of credit spread migration into the price risk. Currently, most practitioners do not seem to share this view. They feel that models such as CreditManager account for this possibility over a time horizon of three months or more, but market price volatilities do not seem to imbed this information in short-term price moves. Most practitioners are willing to ignore this problem for regulatory reporting purposes that typically have a one-day or a ten-day time horizon for reporting VaR. For credit exposure purposes, if the reset of the TRORS is monthly, the possibility of credit spread migration is usually ignored. For longer reset periods, some practitioners attempt to account for credit spread migration, but many do not.

MATURITY MISMATCHES: LOANS AND SYNTHETIC CLOs

When financial institutions begin using credit derivatives, they often claim that they do not have maturity mismatches when they do a TRORS or a credit default swap. While that may be the intent, maturity mismatches may occur due to the structure of the underlying reference obligation. For instance, if a bank buys two years of protection in the form of a credit derivative against a two-year loan, in the beginning the reference asset and the credit default hedge are matched in maturity. After one year, it is remembered that the issuer of the reference asset has the option to extend the loan for an additional year. If this is done, the final year of the loan will not have credit default protection. The loan originally had a two-year maturity, but now the loan has a three-year maturity. The credit default protection had no feature to allow extension of the protection. A maturity mismatch is the result. This poses a problem for credit line managers. Do you credit the remaining first year (originally the second year) with credit protection knowing that you have default risk in the final year? How do you reserve capital for this credit risk? Could you look at this as a forward credit obligation? None of these questions have been satisfactorily resolved by most financial institutions. It is worth addressing these issues early on as the issues become even more pressing later. Once an institution engages in a synthetic CLO, it may find that protection is provided for a fixed period of time; but credit obligations may be added that exceed the maturity of the original protection.

A side effect of the issue of the structural issue mentioned earlier in the case of the extendable loan is that banks are starting to think more seriously about how they price these imbedded options in their loans. Today, most lenders do not attempt to rigorously price these features, albeit they have real economic value. The cost of purchasing credit protection shines a bright light on the value of the ability to extend a loan. This may force banks to use option pricing models to justify the costs they assign to the imbedded options in loan documentation. Although it is not an accounting require-ment, there is a growing trend to mark to market loan portfolios. JP Mor-gan currently marks its loan portfolio to market, and many U.S. banks are attempting to follow suit. In a very short period of time, this will be deemed a bank best practice. But what do we mean by marking to market? To do this properly, one must be able to assign a price to the imbedded options in loan documentation. I predict increased demand for quantitative skills and for better models in loan portfolio pricing and in loan syndications.

CHAPTER 3

Credit Default Swaps and Options

A credit default swap or option is simply an exchange of a fee for a payment if a credit default event occurs (see Figure 3.1). Credit default swaps differ from total rate of return swaps (TRORS) in that the investor does not take price risk of the reference asset, only the risk of default. The investor receives a fee from the seller of the default risk. The investor makes no payment unless a credit default event occurs.

If the fee is paid up front, which may be the case for very short dated structures, the agreement is likely to be called a credit default option. If the fee is paid over time, the agreement is more likely to be called a swap. Unless two counterparties are actually swapping and exchanging the credit default risk of two different credits, I prefer to call the former structure a credit default "option." Cash flows paid over time are nothing more than an amortization of an option premium. Because the documentation references International Swaps and Derivatives Association, Inc. (ISDA) master agreements, however, swap terminology has crept into the market. Because the credit derivatives business at many commercial and investment banks is often run by former interest-rate-swap staff, the tendency to use swap terminology persists. Therefore, I most often refer to these transactions as credit default "swaps."

The credit default premium is usually paid over time. For some very short dated structures, the credit default premium may be paid up front. In fact, professionals new to this market often ask if the premium should be

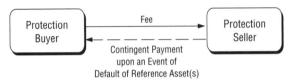

FIGURE 3.1   Credit Default Swap

paid up front, instead of over time. After all, if the credit defaults, the default protection seller will get no additional premiums.

The credit default option or swap is a contingent option and not to be confused with an American option. A termination payment is made only if a credit event occurs. If the credit event does not occur, the default protection seller has no obligation. The premium can be thought of as the credit spread an investor demands to take the default risk of a given reference asset. If the investor bought an asset swap, the investor would earn a spread to his funding cost. This spread represents the compensation, or the premium, the investor needs in order to take the credit default risk of the reference asset in the asset swap.

For an American option, the premium is paid up front (or over time with the proviso that the total premium is owed, even if exercise occurs before the expiration date). The American option can be exercised any time that it is in the money. The holder of the option does not have to exercise, however, and can wait and hope the option will go further in the money. If the market reverses direction, the American option can again become out of the money, and the holder who failed to exercise the option when it was in the money cannot then exercise it. With a credit default option, once the trigger event has occurred, the holder must exercise and the option stays exercisable.

Default protection can be purchased on a loan, a bond, sovereign risk due to cross-border commercial transactions, or even credit exposure due to a derivative contract such as counterparty credit exposure in a cross-currency swap transaction. Credit protection can be linked to an individual credit or to a basket of credits.

At first glance, a credit default swap or option looks structurally simpler than a total return swap. We already know that a total return swap is simply a form of financing. In this chapter, we explore the complex, various, and interesting features of the credit default swap and the credit default option market. *Complex? Various?* Wait a minute. Didn't I mention that a total return swap already has a credit default swap imbedded in its structure? After all, if my counterparty is taking the default risk of a bond or a loan, I have reduced my credit exposure to that reference asset. We understand everything there is to know about credit default swaps already, don't we?

Those are the questions most practitioners ask themselves the first time they enter into a credit default contract. The first key difference is that although the price or premium of a credit default swap or option may increase, it is never actually in the money until a credit default event as defined by the confirm language has occurred. That seems like a knock-in option or a knock-in swap, which is a type of barrier option. Knock-in options have been around since the 1960s. When a market price reaches a predetermined strike price—the barrier—the knock-in option comes into existence. But *this* "knock in" is not linked to traditional market factors, but rather to either credit default or a credit event. If the option "knocks in," then and only then is the option in the money. The termination payment is usually not binary or predefined, and we explore exceptions in this chapter. The termination payment is usually linked to a recovery value or a recovery rate for the reference credit or credits involved.

The terminology is further complicated by the U.S. market's use of the word *swap* to refer to an exchange of one bond for another (usually accompanied by a cash payment to make up for any discrepancy in relative values) and the U.K. market's use of the word *switch* for the same transaction. U.S. market practitioners are often mystified when they first hear of "asset swap switches," an exchange of one asset swap package risk for another asset swap package risk. We discuss this product later in this chapter.

As we see in this chapter, a variety of structures have evolved in this market. The risk characteristics of these structures are different from the structures discussed so far and merit close scrutiny. One structure, known by such names as digital, binary, all-or-nothing, and the zero-one structure, has a substantial amount of risk. The investor loses the *entire notional amount*—not merely coupon and some principal loss—if there is a default event.

Other structures, such as the par value minus recovery value structure, can leave a position of premium bonds partially unhedged or can overhedge a position of bonds trading below par. Exposure management officers evaluating the suitability and the appropriateness of such deals must be fully aware of the total exposures implied in these transactions.

The credit swap becomes even more interesting when one realizes that the term *default event* does not even apply to many credit agreements. The event, which triggers a termination payment under the terms of the credit default swap confirmation, is negotiable. The event may be defined as a spread widening, an event in a foreign country that may cause its sovereign debt to decline in price, or just about any event on which the two parties can agree and define a price. Even the termination payment is negotiable. It may be preset at a fixed amount or based on the recovery value of a reference asset, to mention only two structures.

Some credit "default" options, those linked to spread widening, for instance, sound suspiciously like put options that are struck out of the money.

> *Example:* A German bank's emerging-markets trader discovered he had exceeded his Russia position limit, an offense for which he could have been fired. He approached a large U.S. bank and asked to buy credit protection on Russia for one month. To accomplish this, the German bank's trader paid a high premium for a one-month, 35-point, out-of-the-money put on Russian Vanesh. The U.S. bank happily pocketed the fat premium for an option it considered virtually worthless. There was no pricing model, no calculation of recovery values, and no analysis of asset swap spreads. The price the German bank's trader was willing to pay was an obvious windfall for the U.S. bank. The need defined the price.

Was this transaction a credit derivative, or was this merely a bond option? This question often stymies people who are new to this market. It reminds me of a commodity conference attended by a number of bright derivative specialists who were relatively unfamiliar with the commodities market. It was the end of a very long day marked by a series of speakers who had worn down the stamina of their audience. One of the last speakers of the day stood up. Louise Rowsell Crean, a petite British oil trader, bounded up to the podium trailed by a veil of long brown hair. She briefly paused, looked at her mainly male audience, and said, "All right chaps! Who knows the difference between a future and a forward?"

She paused again. "Let me find a volunteer." Louise Rowsell Crean picked up a seating chart and began examining it.

Philip Basil, a structuring specialist at Royal Bank of Scotland in London, recalled a sense of panic and dread as he came to attention and hurriedly sifted through his notes.

Mrs. Crean called out to a "volunteer" (actually a prepared colleague planted in the audience) and asked again, "You there, in the second row at the left aisle, what is the difference between a future and a forward?"

The answer, of course, is that a future is an exchange-traded contract and a forward is an over-the-counter contract. Of course. Everyone in the room probably intuitively knew the answer. Nonetheless, when confronted with an unfamiliar product, we tend to be thrown by unfamiliar terminology.

The credit derivatives market has adopted similar over-the-counter versus exchange-traded terminology, which makes it difficult to define the size of the credit derivates market. Virtually any credit-related, over-the-counter option could be defined as a credit derivative. Generally, however, credit derivative contracts are further distinguished from other over-the-counter options on bonds by the fact that they are negotiated transactions.

Was the Morgen Grenfell trade a credit derivative? It certainly helped a bank free up credit lines. It was a negotiated transaction. I would say, yes, the transaction was a credit derivative, albeit the circumstances created an urgent and odd negotiation, which suited both parties.

This chapter examines the not so plain "plain vanilla" structures and explains in greater detail the difficulties of defining credit events, hedging default risks, basis risk between the reference asset and the risk, and mutually agreeable methods of exchanging payments if a credit event occurs. It investigates the difference between par and reference asset price-adjusted structures. The chapter also covers the basic building blocks of complex structures: knock-in options, first loss–protected options, asset swap switches, geared default options, options on credit spreads, callable step-up structures, basket default options, and pro rata default structures.

TRADITIONAL CREDIT DEFAULT SWAP

The traditional, or plain vanilla, credit default swap is a payment by one party in exchange for a credit default protection payment if a credit default event on a reference asset occurs (see Figure 3.2). The amount of the payment is the difference between the original price of the reference asset and the recovery value of the reference asset.

Let us look at an example in which the reference asset is a bond. If the issuer of the bond fails to make coupon interest payments when due and

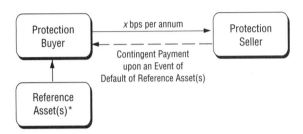

*Seller receives a fee in return for making a Contingent Payment if a predefined Credit Event occurs to the Reference Asset(s). Underlying exposure can be single credits, baskets of credits, or indexes.

FIGURE 3.2   Plain Vanilla Credit Default Swap

other conditions of a default event exist, then the buyer of the credit default protection option has the right to notify the seller of the option to make a payment.

As we shall see, even for plain vanilla credit default protection, there are a variety of choices in creating a credit default protection agreement. The following term sheet presents an example of one of the most common structures in the credit default protection market.

ONE-YEAR BRAZIL CREDIT DEFAULT SWAP
Indicative Term Sheet

Default Protection Buyer:	Default protection buyer.
Default Protection Seller:	Default protection seller.
Transaction Type:	Credit default swap.
Trade Date:	As soon as practical.
Effective Date:	Three days after the trade date.
Maturity:	One year after the trade date.
Early Termination Date:	With three business days' notice following a credit event with a terminal payment being made.
Calculation Amount:	USD 25 million.

Payments of the Default Protection Buyer:

Payment Amount and Dates:	XXX basis points on a semiannual A/360-day basis (where A is the actual number of days in

the period) calculated from the effective date to the earlier of:

1. one year after the trade date, *or*
2. the early termination date.

Payments of the Default Protection Seller:

Termination Payment:

The default protection seller pays to the default protection buyer the following amount:

(Calculation Amount × Par − Market Value) + Accrued but Unpaid Interest on the Reference Obligation

where a dealer panel using the market bid price will determine market value.

Credit Event:

When the calculation agent is aware of publicly available information as to the existence of a credit condition and at the same time materiality exists.

Credit Condition:

Either payment default or a bankruptcy event in respect of the issuer.

Payment Default:

Subject to a dispute in good faith by the issuer, either the issuer fails to pay any amount due of the reference asset when due; or any other present or future indebtedness of the issuer for or in respect of moneys borrowed or raised or guaranteed, in an amount in aggregate of not less than USD 25 million (or its equivalent in other currencies), becomes due and payable prior to its stated maturity otherwise than at the option of the issuer, or any such amount of indebtedness is not paid when due or, as the case may be, within any applicable grace period.

Bankruptcy Event:

The declaration by the issuer of a general moratorium in or of a rescheduling of payments on

(continued)

	any external indebtedness in an aggregate amount of not less than USD 25 million (or its equivalent in other currencies).
Materiality:	The price of the reference asset after price adjustment is 90 percent or less relative to the initial price as reasonably determined by the calculation agent.
Publicly Available Information:	Information that has been published in any two or more internationally recognized published or electronically displayed financial news sources. Nonetheless, if either of the parties or any of their respective affiliates is cited as the sole source for such information, then such information will be deemed not to be publicly available information.
Price Adjustment:	The price of a reference U.S. Treasury security on the valuation date less the price on the effective date. The reference U.S. Treasury security will be selected by the calculation agent to match, as far as possible, the maturity and other features of the reference asset.
Market Value:	On any day, with respect to the relevant reference security, the percentage equal to the unweighted arithmetic mean of the firm USD-denominated bid prices (exclusive of any accrued but unpaid interest and expressed as a percentage of principal amount) for such reference security provided to the calculation agent on such day by at least two but not more than five referenced dealers.
Dispute:	If there is a dispute between the parties as to the occurrence of a credit event unresolved on the maturity date, a credit event will be deemed to occur on that date.
Notification Date:	If a credit event occurs during the term of the transaction, the default protection buyer shall

	have the right to designate a protection seller payment date by delivering notice (on the notification date) to the default protection seller of the occurrence of such credit event. Such notice must contain a description in reasonable detail of the facts giving rise to the credit event.
Business Days:	Days on which commercial banks and foreign exchange markets settle payments in London and New York.
Business Day Convention:	Modified following.
Calculation Agent:	Default protection seller.
Documentation:	Per the existing ISDA master agreement between the default protection seller and default protection buyer.
Law:	Per ISDA master agreement.
Suitability:	The notes will be sold to an investor with such knowledge and experience in financial matters to assure capability of evaluating the merits and risks of the prospective investment.
Default Protection Buyer Risk:	The default protection buyer is exposed to the default protection seller for its payment if there is a credit event for the Republic of Brazil. The maximum amount of this payment is the calculation amount.

Reference Obligation:

Issuer/Borrower:	Federative Republic of Brazil ("the Republic").
Rating:	B1 Moody's, B+ Standard and Poor's.
Type:	Global.
Currency Denomination:	USD.
Coupon:	8 7/8 percent payable semiannually.
Maturity:	November 5, 2001.
Reference Issue Date:	November 5, 1996.

(continued)

Reference Amount Issued:	USD 750 million.
Substitution:	If the amount of the reference asset (or a substitute) is materially reduced, the calculation agent shall reasonably select a substitute issued or guaranteed by the reference name that is of the same credit quality as the reference asset and with a maturity at least that of the reference asset and shall notify the counterparties. If no substitute can be found, the swap will terminate with no further payments on either side.

Notice that, except for the definition of the credit event and some additional defined terms, there is really not much to this term sheet. One counterparty agrees to pay the other a fee in exchange for a payment equal to the par amount minus the market value of the reference asset plus accrued interest due on the reference asset in the event of a default. In actual practice, the negotiation of all of these terms can be a drawn-out and protracted process. Each of these terms potentially has an economic value to the buyer and the seller of default protection; we examine them in more detail later in this chapter.

IMPORTANCE OF THE DEFAULT PROTECTION SELLER

If an investor is purchasing credit default protection, what kind of credit default protection seller is most desirable? If prices were the same, a default protection seller with a triple A credit rating and a zero percent correlation with the asset that the investor is trying to hedge would be the most desirable. But as we saw in the sections on TRORS in Chapter 2, a default protection seller with these characteristics will probably sell very expensive protection. Therefore, it is beneficial to relax the criteria and find another provider. The investor should be aware that there are unsuitable providers, however.

There are unsuitable applications, too. One must ask the right questions before trying to apply a solution. Credit derivatives are sometimes seen as the panacea, the answer to any finance problem that cannot be solved by conventional market strategies. Although this is often true, the following example shows an instance in which a "credit derivative" is not the answer.

> *Example:* In the summer of 1997, a newly hired salesman in Bank Arranger's Asian office wanted to get cheaper funding for one of his customers. One of the top Korean commercial banks, Hanil Bank (BBB), wanted to raise USD 100 million to 200 million one-year money in the floating rate note (FRN) market at a rate below six-month London interbank offering rate (LIBOR) plus 40 basis points (bps).
>
> Unfortunately, Hanil Bank's outstanding issues traded at around six-month LIBOR + 45 bps. This was at least 5 bps cheaper than the new issue market. Further, Hanil Bank did not want to issue an interest-rate-related structured note to lower its cost of funds.
>
> The salesman was positive that a credit derivative could lower the cost of funds for Hanil Bank. He suggested that Bank Arranger's Asian office should underwrite USD 100 million at around six-month LIBOR + 45 bps. He further suggested that Bank Arranger do a credit default swap with the issuer, Hanil Bank. Bank Arranger would pay a premium of 10 bps at the end of one year, *only if Hanil Bank repaid its principal.* With the 10-basis-point rebate, Hanil Bank would achieve a funding cost of six-month LIBOR + 35 bps.
>
> The salesman thought that by buying credit default protection in the form of a credit default swap from the issuer, he could transfer underwriting credit risk from Bank Arranger's Asian syndicate group to the swap book. The salesman discussed this concept with his managers and sent e-mail to Bank Arranger's credit derivatives group. Everyone with whom the salesman spoke agreed this was a good idea. No one challenged the salesman's assumptions for two weeks. Finally, one of the credit derivative specialists carefully read the e-mail and debunked this notion.
>
> What was wrong with the salesman's logic?

Ignoring credit derivatives for a moment, consider if a bank offered an after-the-fact rebate to *any* issuer who performed under the terms of their agreement to pay back principal and interest as promised. The bank could pay a rebate to a credit-card holder who pays the entire balance on a credit card. The bank could pay a rebate to an auto-loan holder who pays back the entire auto loan. The bank could pay a rebate to an issuer who pays back the entire amount of principal borrowed plus interest.

Why stop at a measly 10 basis points? After the borrowers have actually paid back the entire amount of principal and interest, they are better credit risks than a *proposed* AAA borrower.

Why is this?

It is due to the fact that after the borrower has actually repaid principal and interest, the bank has 100 percent *certainty*. Value is based on the timing of cash flows, the magnitude of cash flows, and the certainty of cash flows. Even a proposed AAA borrower cannot give a bank 100 percent certainty *before* the AAA borrower has repaid the obligation.

Following that logic, why not give Hanil Bank a rebate of 65 basis points. At the time, an AAA issuer had a proposed funding level of around LIBOR – 20 bps. Hanil Bank's funding level of LIBOR + 45 bps versus LIBOR – 20 bps would have suggested a 65-basis-point rebate. It seems only fair in the calculation of crazy rebates. As we saw earlier, after repayment Hanil Bank is *better* than an AAA proposed issuer.

The reason banks do not hand out rebates is that in advance the bank does not have the certainty, so the bank needs to be compensated for the uncertainty, for the risk. It is these risk premiums that over time compensate a bank for the occasions when one of the issuers actually does default. Therefore the bank doesn't give back any part of these risk premiums.

Perhaps an easier way to come to this conclusion is to notice that the joint probability of default of Hanil Bank versus Hanil Bank is 100 percent, so no one should pay a premium for credit default protection for Hanil Bank to Hanil Bank. *The whole point of using credit derivatives is to diversify credit risk.*

Asset swap spreads are independent of the credit quality of the investor. A market asset is swapped to a LIBOR-based floating coupon, for instance. The market is indifferent to the credit quality of the investor, who pays cash up front for the asset swap package. Unlike an asset swap, the premium paid to the investor—the credit default protection seller—is sensitive to the credit quality of the investor. The premium is further sensitive to the correlation between the investor and the reference asset on which one is buying the credit default protection. Depending on the structure, the credit default swap contract may require an uncollateralized payment by the investor if there is a credit default event.

Around three months after I fielded the question about Hanil Bank, but before the fall 1997 crisis, I took a call from a trader at a securities firm formed by a French bank. The trader told me that several Korean banks were willing to offer credit default protection on other Korean names. In order to bolster up their own credit perception, they were willing to post 30 to 40 percent of the notional amount with G7 (Group of Seven) collateral. One bank was even willing to post 100 percent G7 collateral if it went below investment grade. That sounded mildly interesting, although I had no interest in taking on more Korean credit risk. The trader then went on to tell me that Commercial Bank of Korea would sell credit default protection on bonds issued by the Commerical Bank of Korea.

"That's very interesting," I countered, "but that credit default option is worthless."

"But people are doing it," persisted the trader.

"That's because they don't know what they are doing," I affirmed. "The correlation between Commercial Bank of Korea and itself is 100 percent. I would pay nothing for that credit protection. It is worthless for this purpose."

The trader mustered his best grammar, chilliest tone, and most authoritative voice: "There are those who would disagree with you."

That is what makes a market.

Example: An investor has a choice of buying credit default protection from one of two counterparties to hedge a single-A rated asset. One counterparty is rated BBB with a zero percent correlation with the A credit. The second counterparty is rated single A but is 90 percent correlated with the single-A rated asset, which I'm trying to hedge. Which counterparty is the better choice?

Counterintuitive as it may seem, *it is better to buy credit default protection from an uncorrelated lower-rated credit default protection seller than from a credit protection seller that is highly correlated with the reference asset one is trying to hedge.* Again, the benefits of diversification, as we saw in the Standard & Poor's (S&P) table earlier, weigh in favor of the BBB counterparty. The joint probability of default between the A rated asset and the BBB counterparty might merit an implied credit rating of AA for the credit default protected asset. The combination of the 90 percent correlated A rated names would probably merit a rating no higher than A.

Determining correlation, then, would seem key. CreditMetrics has useful information for a variety of credits. The data break down when we look at sovereign credits and at foreign credits, however. For example, let us look at a U.S. commercial bank that hedges a Hyundai (Korean corporate) asset-swapped position with credit default protection purchased from Korea Exchange Bank (see Figure 3.3). Notice that the U.S. commercial bank may pick up some benefit from protecting the credit default risk of Hyundai with credit protection from Korea Exchange Bank. But the question is: "How much additional protection?" What is the correlation between these credits? The difficulty is that no one knows. The U.S. commercial bank in this example assumed a low correlation. That is why the U.S. commercial bank was willing to pay 40 basis points for the credit protection. But the degree of correlation is debatable. I personally feel the correlation is high—at least 50 percent. Political risk, restructuring risk, and the risk of possible future war merit a number at least that high for a two-and-one-half-year period.

Why not just purchase an asset swap on Korea Exchange Bank? At the time of this transaction, the U.S. commercial bank could have saved itself a lot of paperwork and earned LIBOR + 45 bps. How much does the reduction in the joint probability of default enhance the value of the synthetic Korea Exchange–Hyundai package? Remember the Moody's and S&P credit-rating enhancement tables? They assumed that the correlation of the rated assets was zero. If there is a 100 percent correlation, there is no rating enhancement benefit. If the correlation is high, the enhancement will be very slight. Does this enhancement justify the reduction in spread of 15 basis points versus the stand-alone purchase of Korea Exchange Bank?

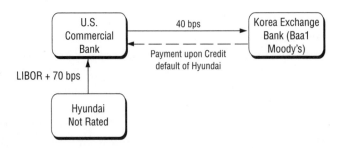

Net Spread to the U.S. Commercial Bank is LIBOR + 30 bps. Korea Exchange Bank at the time traded at LIBOR + 45 bps.

FIGURE 3.3   Korean Bank Corporate Credit Default Swap, 2.5-Year Maturity

The head of one U.S. bank's New York Emerging Markets Derivatives Group thinks not. "I've heard about those trades, but I don't do them. It is a little crazy to do a trade like that." He feels the correlation between Korean banks and Korean corporates is extremely high.

The head of a U.S. bank's London office credit derivatives department sees this differently. He feels that the international banking community could not tolerate an upset in the Korean banking community and would step in to see that there was not a series of defaults in Korea. The reflection and panic in the international banking community would be too horrible to contemplate if Korea were allowed to sink. Korea is viewed as part of the mainstream global banking network. He argues that Korea presents a much different situation from Latvia, for instance, where a default domino effect wiped out debt obligations in a series of defaults.

An emerging markets economist feels that the first tier of Korean banks won't have a problem. The merchant banks, however, have zero free capital of their own. Their funding costs reflect this at levels of LIBOR + 100 bps to LIBOR + 120 bps. He points out that in Vietnam, state-owned banks have defaulted. There have been defaults on private market debt service.

I personally would feel much better if the default protection seller were a European bank, for instance. I think European banks and Korean corporates have a very low correlation.*

This is why we rely on other experts, economists, and traders who closely follow the markets, and we rely on our own staff close to credit situations

---

*This section was written in the summer of 1997. By October 1997, Thailand's midsummer decision to allow the baht to float severely weakened several Asian currencies, among them the South Korean won, resulting in a severe dollar crunch. The sinking won mushroomed foreign debt. Interest rates soared and banks curtailed lending. At least nine Korean corporations declared bankruptcy in 1997. At the end of 1997, other major Korean corporations, the chaebol, indicated they might have problems repaying debt. The Korean Composite Stock Price Index closed down 42 percent for 1997, and banks and corporations neared default on their debt. The International Monetary Fund (IMF) announced a $57 billion bailout for South Korea in December 1997 and imposed restrictions, which may further dampen the Korean economy. By the end of 1997, the United States and the IMF announced $10 billion in new credit (part of the bailout plan) for South Korea. Major banks in the United States, Europe, and Japan were exploring ways of rolling over Korean debt rather than attempting to force repayment on loans that could likely default. At the end of 1997, Moody's lowered Korea's rating to junk bond status.

to provide guidance. The more information one has on correlation and credit risk, from whatever the source, the better. In the end, the differences in interpretation of information make a market.

Nonetheless, correlation and credit quality of the credit default protection seller are the key issues. One head trader's biggest concern is that the credit default protection seller has a zero or low correlation with the reference asset. Often this trader does deals in which an Asian bank provides credit default protection for a Latin American credit risk. If the credit default swap economics move more than USD 3 million to 4 million in exposure against the protection seller, Bankers Trust exercises a collateral call against the default protection seller.

Credit default swaps are negotiated transactions, and although there is some agreement on what is a plain vanilla structure, there is very little agreement on anything else. No standard practice exists in the credit derivatives market, so just about any contract imaginable can be created. The key issues in the credit default swap market revolve around the following parameters:

- Defining the event.
- Determining the default protection fee.
- Determining the reference asset.
- Determining the default payment.

The issues may vary by structure, and as we continue through this chapter, we encounter these issues in many forms.

DEFINING THE EVENT

The plain vanilla credit default market ceases to appear vanilla after we deviate from the most basic definition of credit default. Defining the event for a sovereign debt denominated in dollars, for instance, seems pretty straightforward. One reasonable way to define the default event would be to look at the language in the prospectus. The following language from the prospectus for the 100,000,000 British sterling (GBP)–denominated Federative Republic of Brazil, 9.75 percent due June 11, 1999, is typical of default language. Default, or acceleration of maturity, occurs if any of the following events occurs:

(a) Default in any payment of principal or interest on any of the Notes and the continuance of such default for a period of 30 days; *or*

(b) Default that is materially prejudicial to the interests of the Noteholders in the performance of any other obligation under the Notes and the continuance of such default for a period of 30 days after written notice requiring the same to be remedied has been given to the Fiscal Agent by any Noteholder; *or*

(c) Acceleration of in excess of USD 25 million (or its equivalent in any other currency) in aggregate principal amount of Public External Indebtedness of the Republic by reason of any event of default (however described) resulting from the failure of the Republic to make any payment of principal or interest thereunder when due; *or*

(d) Failure to make any payment in respect of Public External Indebtedness of the Republic in an aggregate principal amount in excess of USD 25,000,000 (or its equivalent in any other currency) when due (as such date may be extended by virtue of any applicable grace period or waiver) and the continuance of such failure for a period of 30 days after written notice requiring the same to be remedied has been given to the Fiscal Agent by any Noteholder; *or*

(e) Declaration by the Republic of a moratorium with respect to the payment of principal of or interest on Public External Indebtedness of the Republic that does not expressly exclude the Notes and that is materially prejudicial to the interests of the Noteholders; *or*

(f) Denial by the Republic of its obligations under the Notes.

Then each Noteholder, so long as such event is continuing, may, by written demand given to the Republic and delivered to the specified office of the Fiscal Agent, declare the principal of and any accrued interest on the Notes held by it to be due; and such principal and interest shall thereupon become immediately due and payable, unless prior to receipt of such demand by the Republic all such defaults have been cured; *provided that*, in the case of any event described in subparagraph (a), (e), or (f) entitling holders to declare their Notes due has occurred and is continuing, become effective only when the Fiscal Agent has received such notices from the holders of at least 10 percent, in principal amount of all Notes then outstanding. Notes held by the Republic or on behalf of the Republic shall not be considered outstanding for purposes of the preceding sentence.

If any event described in subparagraphs (a) to (f) gives rise to a declaration that is effective and such event ceases to continue following such declaration, then such declaration may, in the case of any event described in subparagraph (a), (e) or (f) be rescinded and annulled by the Noteholder that has made such declaration and, in the case of any event described in subparagraph (b), (c), or (d), (unless at the time any event described in subparagraph (a), (c), or (f) has occurred and is continuing) may be rescinded and annulled by an affirmative vote of the Noteholders in accordance with the procedures set forth in Condition 13.

In short, if there is a credit default event as defined in the prospectus and if 10 percent or more of the noteholders notify the Republic in writing that they want their principal and interest back, the Republic must pay it, unless it already did so before receiving the written notification. If the Republic has already agreed to pay back principal and interest as reflected in the prospectus, then why buy credit default protection?

The answer has to do with the joint probability of default discussed in Chapter 2. Let us take as an example Oresundskonsortiet, rated AAA by S&P. This is the entity responsible for building a bridge between Copenhagen and Stockholm. Oresundskonsortiet's debt obligations are jointly guaranteed by the Kingdom of Denmark (Aa1/AA+) and the Kingdom of Sweden (Aa3/AA+). Note that Oresundskonsortiet enjoys a triple A rating from Moody's. Neither the Kingdom of Sweden nor the Kingdom of Denmark has triple A ratings, however. The reason Oresundskonsortiet achieves a rating higher than either of its guarantors is because *both* the Kingdom of Sweden and the Kingdom of Denmark would have to default before an investor holding an obligation issued by Oresundskonsortiet would fail to get paid. The benefit of the joint probability of default can be represented schematically by the Venn diagram in Figure 3.4.

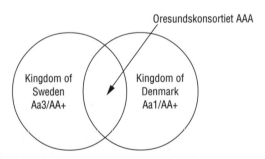

FIGURE 3.4   Benefit of Joint Probability of Default

If an investor purchases debt of the Federative Republic of Brazil (B1/ BB–) and wants added credit protection, the investor can purchase a credit default swap from a default protection seller. If that default protection seller is not in default, the investor has added protection in the event that the Federative Republic of Brazil defaults. The investor can demand a cash "make whole" payment from the default protection seller. Alternatively, the investor can deliver the defaulted bonds to the default protection seller and demand the principal plus accrued interest from the default protection seller. The default protection seller would then try to recover the maximum possible amount on the defaulted bonds. Payment calculations and methods of settlement are discussed later in this chapter.

DEFAULT LANGUAGE FOR NONSOVEREIGN DEBT

Corporate default language varies considerably from sovereign credit default language. The following term sheet is typical of structures offered where the reference obligation is corporate debt.

CREDIT DEFAULT SWAP
RJR Nabisco, Inc.
Indicative Term Sheet

Default Protection Buyer:	Default protection buyer.
Default Protection Seller:	Default protection seller.
Reference Obligation:	
Issuer:	RJR Nabisco, Inc.
Coupon:	8.625%.
Interest Payable:	Semiannual.
Maturity Date of the Reference Obligation:	December 1, 2002.
Moody's/S&P:	Baa3 / BBB–.
Cusip Number:	74960LAX4.

(continued)

Initial Price:	To be determined.
Calculation Amount:	USD 50 million.
Trade Date:	To be determined.
Effective Date:	Trade date + two business days.
Maturity Date of the Credit Default Swap (CDS):	The earlier of:
	1. the reference obligation maturity date, *or*
	2. the nonscheduled termination date, if any.

Default Protection Buyer:

Payment Date:	Each reference obligation coupon payment date.
Payment Amount:	XX basis points per annum.
Day Count Convention:	Payments are made in USD based on a semi-annual 30/360 day count.
Payment Calculation:	Calculation Amount × Payment Amount × Day Count Convention

Nonscheduled Termination:

Date:	Two business days following the notification date, if any.
Payment:	At the option of default protection buyer, either:

1. Default protection buyer makes physical delivery of the reference obligation with face value subject to this transaction to default protection seller. Default protection seller pays default protection buyer the calculation amount plus accrued but unpaid interest. Default protection buyer pays default protection seller the accrued payment amount up to the date of the earliest credit event, at which time the credit default swap is terminated with no further obligation to either counterparty.

or

2. Default protection seller makes a cash settlement payment to default protection buyer in an amount equal to:

Calculation Amount $\times$ (Initial Price – Market Value)

Default protection buyer pays default protection seller the accrued payment amount up to the date of the earliest credit event, at which time the credit default swap is terminated with no further obligation to either counterparty.

Notification Date: If a credit event or a merger event occurs during the term of this transaction, the default protection buyer shall have the right to designate a nonscheduled termination date by delivering notice (even if such notice occurs after the maturity date) to the default protection seller of the occurrence of such credit or merger event. Such notice must contain a description, in reasonable detail, of the facts giving rise to the credit or merger event.

Credit Event: Shall include, with respect to the issuer of the reference obligation (reference credit), any of the following, which occurs on or prior to the maturity date and at the same time materiality exists:

1. Bankruptcy.

2. Credit event upon merger.

   A default, event of default, or other similar condition or event occurs in respect of such reference credit under any financial obligation that has resulted in such financial obligation becoming, or being capable at such time of being declared, due and payable be-

(continued)

fore it would otherwise have become due and payable.

3. Cross-acceleration or cross-default.

   A waiver, deferral, restructuring, rescheduling, exchange, or other adjustment occurs in respect of any financial obligation, and the effect of such adjustment is overall materially less favorable from a credit-and risk-perspective to the relevant creditor.

4. Downgrade.

5. Failure to pay.

6. Repudiation.

7. Restructuring.

   Such reference credit (a) is dissolved; or (b) becomes insolvent or is unable to pay its debts; or (c) makes a general assignment, arrangement, or composition for the benefit of its creditors; or (d) institutes a proceeding seeking a judgment of insolvency or bankruptcy; or (e) has a resolution passed for its winding up, official management, or liquidation; or (f) seeks or becomes subject to the appointment of an administrator; or (g) has a secured party take possession of substantially all of its assets. (See also Chapter 7, "Hidden Costs in Default Language.")

Merger Event: An actual or publicly announced intended consolidation, amalgamation, or merger or a transferal of all or a substantial amount of assets from the issuer to another entity.

Financial Obligation: With respect to the reference credit, any senior unsecured financial obligation in an aggregate amount of not less than the threshold amount incurred by the reference credit in any capacity.

Materiality:	The price of the reference obligation less the price adjustment is 90 percent or less relative to the initial price as reasonably determined by the calculation agent.
Price Adjustment:	The price of a reference U.S. Treasury security on the notification date less the price on the effective date. The reference U.S. Treasury security will be selected by the calculation agent to match, as far as possible, the maturity and other features of the reference obligation.
Market Value:	On any day, with respect to the relevant reference obligation, the percentage equal to the unweighted arithmetic mean of the firm USD-denominated bid prices (exclusive of any accrued but unpaid interest and expressed as a percentage of principal amount) for such reference obligation provided to the calculation agent on such day by not more than five referenced dealers as such prices are available.
Business Days:	Days on which commercial banks and foreign exchange markets settle payments in New York and London.
Business Day Convention:	Modified following.
Calculation Agent:	Default protection buyer.
Documentation:	This transaction will be documented on a confirmation linked to the existing ISDA master agreement between the default protection seller and the default protection buyer.
Early Termination/Assignment:	An over-the-counter derivative transaction of this type may not be assigned, transferred, or terminated prior to its stated termination date by either party without the consent of the other party except as stipulated in the terms of the transaction.
Liquidity:	There may be no, or only a limited, secondary market for a transaction of this type.

Transactions of this type are not standardized or fungible. A seemingly identical transaction with another over-the-counter party will not automatically act as a perfect hedge for an existing transaction.

It is impossible to cover every contingency. Deteriorating creditworthiness can be a continuous process. A holder of default protection can watch in frustration as the value relentlessly yet slowly slides to credit default. Sometimes payment default is a minor problem compared to other potential problems. The manufacturer of aircraft carriers can be current on debt but fail to make a delivery of the carriers under the terms of a trade agreement. An automobile manufacturer can be current on debt but forced to recall a line of automobiles for safety reasons. A drug company may be current on debt but find that a newly launched flagship sedative causes birth defects. A chemical company may be current on debt but face class action lawsuits when the silicon implants it manufactured are leaking material into the chest cavities of thousands of women. An investment banking firm may be current on debt but fail to deliver bonds following the exercise of an option. An investment bank may be current on debt but suddenly face trading scandals enmeshing its management, which cause the exodus of its most productive employees.

None of the suggested events is commonly provided for in the standard credit default agreements in the market. Language referring to possible restructuring, bankruptcy, judgment of insolvency, and mergers is common. Common, too, is language referring to a secured party taking possession of substantially all assets. This language is absent from sovereign credit default language. On the other hand, one rarely sees war referred to as an event in corporate default language, although the example in the following section provides an exception.

REDEFINING THE CREDIT DEFAULT EVENT AS A CREDIT EVENT

All is well and good when the event of default is easily agreed on, as when trade counterparties are referencing a prospectus. But what about situations in which the default event is not as well defined? One U.S. corporate client, a producer of technology products, was interested in providing a hedge for its investment in a $100 million-factory in Mexico. The corporation was concerned that political risks, such as war, hostilities, labor strikes, confiscation of nonlocal assets, or a coup d'état, might disrupt business. Insurance seemed too expensive. A tax-advantaged lease-leaseback structure would take a long time to evaluate. Credit derivatives seemed less expensive and could be executed more quickly.

One solution was to reference a USD-denominated United Mexican States global bond (Ba2 by Moody's) 9.75 percent of 2001. Then the U.S. corporation defined the default conditions to include war, hostilities, and confiscation of nonlocal bank assets. The following abbreviated term sheet reflects those changes. Future term sheets will be abbreviated to illustrate key points with the assumption that term sheets will have the key definitions, subject to dealer variations, shown in earlier term sheets.

UNITED STATES OF MEXICO CREDIT DEFAULT SWAP
Abbreviated Term Sheet

Default Protection Buyer:	U.S. corporation.
Default Protection Seller:	Seller.
Calculation Amount:	USD 100 million.
Reference Credit:	United Mexican States (Ba2).
Reference Security:	United Mexican States, global bond.
	Maturity: February 2001.
	Currency Denomination: USD.
	Coupon: 9.75%.
Trade Date:	As soon as practical.
Effective Date:	One week from trade date.
Maturity Date:	The earlier of:
	1. one year from effective date, *or*
	2. the default protection seller payment date, if any.
Default Protection Buyer:	Default protection buyer.
Payment Dates:	Every reference security coupon payment date.
Payment Amount:	75 basis points for one year.

(continued)

Day Count Convention:	Payments are per annum paid on a semiannual $A/360$ basis, where A is the actual number of days in the period.
Nonscheduled Termination Date:	With five business days' notice (even if this date is after the maturity date) following a credit event with a termination payment being made.
Termination Payment:	Seller pays *only* upon a credit event: Calculation Amount $\times$ (Par − Market Value). where Market Value means the USD-denominated market value of the reference security on the notification date determined by the calculation agent with reference to a dealer panel.
Credit Event (abbreviated):	Credit condition means either a payment default or a bankruptcy event in respect of the issuer; any war, revolution, insurrection, or hostile act that interferes with foreign exchange transactions; or the expropriation, confiscation, requisition, or nationalization of nonlocal banks, the declaration of a banking moratorium, or suspension of payments by local banks. Payment default means . . . issuer fails to pay any amount due of the reference asset . . . of not less than USD 10 million. Bankruptcy event means . . . declaration by the issuer of a general moratorium . . . amount of not less than USD 10 million.

Notice that each of the term sheets presented so far differs in several details. This is typical of the proposals circulating in the credit derivatives market and is a reflection of the lack of standardization in the market. Notice that this term sheet uses a termination payment formula based on par instead of on initial price. Market value is determined by at least two but not more than five reference dealers. These terms are negotiable. The RJR Nabisco term sheet allowed for either physical delivery of the defaulted security or a payment calculated on the initial price. The RJR Nabisco term sheet also allowed a net cash settlement. The term sheet for Mexican risk is cash settle only, based on a payment calculated using par, not initial price. For the first time, we see a section allowing substitution of the reference obligation. We examine the issues surrounding calculation of the termination payment using par versus initial price and also examine substitution later.

Even if the bond has not defaulted according to the terms of the prospectus, if any of the credit events as defined clearly in a final confirmation has occurred, the U.S. corporation has remedies. The U.S. corporation must notify the default protection seller in writing that one of the credit default events has occurred. Once that happens, the U.S. corporation has the right to receive a payment according to the formula:

$$\$100 \text{ Million} \times (1 - \text{Market Value at the Time of the Occurrence of the Credit Event})$$

Notice that the U.S. corporation never actually purchases the global bonds issued by the United Mexican States, the 9.75 percent due 2001. The reasoning is that if such a credit event has occurred, even though the global bonds of the United Mexican States may not be in default, the bonds will probably decline in value. The potential payment under the terms of the credit default swap agreement would then partially hedge the loss in asset value of the Mexican factory.

BASIS RISK: IMPERFECT CORRELATION BETWEEN THE REFERENCE ASSET AND RISK

Once again we are plagued by correlation. One cannot write all of the desired terms into the contract. In a perfect world, the U.S. corporation could specify a termination payment as follows: "If the credit event occurs, pay me the decline in value of my Mexican operations due to depreciation in the value of my factory and interruption in income stream due to lost production." Credit derivatives are not designed to protect against this kind of risk. In the absence of a better hedge, it is not unreasonable to take some basis risk to get cash payment, which has some correlation to a drop in asset value in the face of a credit event.

A better hedge might be to reference bonds issued by a Mexican subsidiary of a U.S. corporation. If business of the referenced subsidiary is disrupted due to a credit event, the debt of the subsidiary should trade down in sympathy, reflecting a decline in the value of the subsidiary assets. This would apply only if the subsidiary were highly correlated with the original U.S. corporation seeking the hedge.

Coca-Cola Femsa, a subsidiary of Coca-Cola Bottlers in Mexico, issued 10-year maturity bonds in 1996 (see Figure 3.5). The number of bonds outstanding is only $200 million, and it is difficult to get a market price on these securities because bonds are rarely seen trading in the market. Unfortunately, the lack of liquidity and the lack of ability to fix a reference price make this bond unsuitable as a reference asset. Even if these bonds were relatively traded in the market, however, is this reference asset highly correlated with a producer of technology products? What if a credit event occurs, a national strike in midsummer, for instance, and Mexicans buy more Coca-Cola as an inexpensive source of consolation?

The questions must come before the model. The U.S. corporation must satisfy itself that the price of the protection justifies the residual intangible correlation risk. All events cannot be hedged, just the major events in this case. Because the sovereign debt is more liquid, the U.S. corporation concluded it is the more suitable benchmark for this application.

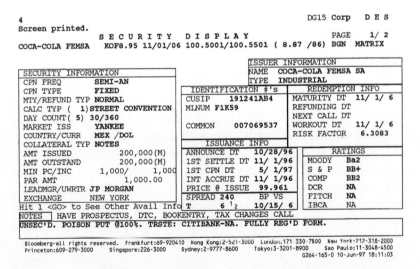

FIGURE 3.5 Security Display for Coca-Cola Femsa

VARIATIONS IN SOVEREIGN DEFAULT LANGUAGE

The definition of credit events for sovereign names is not standard, even though sovereign default language is readily available from the prospectus. All terms are negotiable. The investor also needs to be aware that aside from negotiated nonprospectus language, the prospectus language itself may vary for two different sovereigns.

The language used in the prospectus for the United Mexican States global bonds differs very slightly from the language shown earlier for Brazil. The threshold amount for nonpayment is $10 million for Mexico, whereas for Brazil the threshold amount is $25 million. As we see next, for high-credit-quality sovereign borrowers in the loan market, the language describing credit conditions is much less stringent than that for less credit-quality sovereigns.

The higher an issuer's credit rating, the more aggressively it can push to have favorable credit event language in its prospectus. A single issuer could have significant differences in credit default language, depending on when the debt was issued.

It is even possible for a single issuer to use different language when issuing different instruments. A private placement loan placed in the Japanese market may have different language than a Euro medium-term note intended for the European market. The following is an excerpt of a September 1996 loan agreement for loans from Japanese insurance companies to the Riksgaeld-skontoret, the Swedish National Debt Office (the Kingdom of Sweden) rated Aa3/AA+.

11.1 Occurrence of Events of Default

Subject to Clause 11.2, it shall be an Event of Default if:

(1) the Borrower fails to pay on the due date any principal, interest, or other sum due and payable . . .
(2) the Borrower commits any breach of or omits to observe any of its obligations or undertakings under this Agreement . . .
(5) the Borrower declares a general moratorium on its External Indebtedness.

Notice that language referring to negative pledges and cross default is absent from this loan agreement. The Kingdom of Sweden as borrower is in demand in Japan. Sovereign debt and long-dated debt are very popular with Japanese insurance companies, who are content with the credit risk and with the sparse language.

In general, loan documentation is even less standardized than bond documentation. Each bank and legal firm has developed its own favorite clauses. Loans are "inside debt," defined as a loan for which the lender has access to information about the borrower that is not otherwise publicly available. This is true for the interbank loan market in particular. Bank officers may be on the board of directors of a corporation, for instance. For loans privately placed into another country, a loan may not be classified as inside debt and may appear to be like any other senior-secured obligation of the issuer. Bond private placements are loanlike transactions with a limited number of investors. "Outside debt," on the other hand, would be publicly traded instruments such as bonds or commercial paper.

In the United States, corporations borrow primarily in the commercial paper market and in the commercial and industrial loan market. The commercial paper market is usually limited to the large, well-known corporate borrowers. Most medium-size and smaller corporates rely on the commercial bank loan market. Borrowers are subject to periodic review by the lenders. This brings into focus the issue of "information asymmetry." Bank relationships with the borrower frequently result in a greater variation of terms and conditions than in the publicly traded bond market.

If one is using a credit derivative to hedge a loan or a bond, the protection buyer is using the credit derivative to protect against the breach of the terms of the original credit document. Documentation asymmetry can occur if the terms are not matched.

If a protection buyer is using a commoditized credit derivative purchased in the broker market to hedge a bond or a loan position, there will very likely be basis risk. This basis risk arises from documentation differences. We see later how commoditized credit derivatives can also result in price risk. This seems to be a compelling reason to avoid the broker markets and to directly negotiate terms and conditions with the direct provider of the credit default protection.

How important are these language differences? When the market thinks the default probability is low, there is very little focus on these differences. When a credit event occurs, swarms of lawyers pore over nuances in the language. Loans can be delinquent for years without being called into default. The need to declare default is usually obviated by intermediate steps such as rescheduling and restructuring. The key is to understand the references in advance and negotiate any additional terms and conditions desired for the final default protection. The price for these additions or deletions may change, but the investor will pay the agreed price for the agreed conditions.

An additional caveat is that there is debate over disclosure issues when banks offer total rate of return swaps and when banks purchase credit default protection, in the form of credit default swaps and options, on loans. How much financial information is the bank required to disclose to its counterparties in these transactions? Does the lending bank have insider information that unfairly advantages it in these transactions? Does the lending bank have an obligation to the original borrower to keep confidential its knowledge of the corporation's nonpublicly disclosed financial information?

When a bank pays the total rate of return on a loan or when a bank buys credit default protection on a loan, the voting rights remain with the bank. There is usually a "gentleman's agreement" that the bank will vote according to the wishes of the total rate of return buyer, or the credit default protection seller. If the bank cannot contact the counterparty, however, it is usually assumed that the bank will vote with the majority of the other lenders. This may not be in the best interests of the bank's counterparty in the credit derivative transaction, however. There is the further issue that the lenders may have better information than the credit derivative counterparty, which may influence the majority vote.

These are all difficult issues and, as of this writing, have not been satisfactorily resolved. There is no standard in the market. For this reason, it is wise to carefully choose a counterparty based on reputation, expertise, grasp of the issues in the credit derivatives market, and willingness to negotiate terms.

MATERIALITY, PRICE ADJUSTMENTS, AND SUBSTITUTION: MORE POTENTIAL SOURCES OF BASIS RISK

Imbedded in the preceding term sheets were some clauses referring to materiality and price adjustments. Let us examine these clauses more closely:

Materiality: The price of the reference asset less the price adjustment is 90 percent or less relative to the initial price as reasonably determined by the calculation agent.

Price Adjustment: The price of a reference U.S. Treasury security on the notification date less the price on the effective date. The reference U.S. Treasury security will be selected by the calculation agent to match, as far as possible, the maturity and other features of the reference asset.

Materiality clauses are often inserted into credit default swaps to ensure that the credit event is indeed linked to a potential default of the reference bonds. The intent is to prevent exercise of the option merely because of a temporary negative view on the credit or a temporary market dislocation in the price of the bonds due to supply-and-demand factors.

As we see later, materiality clauses are absent from knock-in credit spread default options because a price decline due to a credit spread event is meant to trigger the option. A general increase in interest rates could cause a decline in the price of the bond. For bonds of the same issuer and the same maturity, the coupon makes a difference in the potential price move of the bond. The higher the coupon on the bond, the less sensitive it will be to this price decline. The lower the coupon of the reference bond, the more sensitive it will be to a change in interest rates.

To illustrate why this is the case, it is useful to quickly review what we know about duration. Duration is a short-hand method in the bond market for evaluating the change in the full price of a bond as interest rates rise and fall.

A noncallable bond trading at par has a MacCaulay duration of 4.0 and a yield of 10 percent. If interest rates rise so that the bond is repriced to yield 10.1 percent, we can use a quick duration calculation to estimate the new price of the bond. To do this, however, we need to use modified duration, not the MacCaulay duration.

$$\text{Modified Duration} = \text{MacCaulay Duration} / \{1 + (\text{Yield}/2)\}$$

$$= 4.0 / \{1 + (0.1/2)\}$$

$$= 3.809$$

What does this 3.809 represent? It represents the percentage price change in the price of the bond for a 100-basis-point move in rates. As rates move up 100 basis points, the price of the bond will move down approximately 3.809 percent, ignoring convexity effects. On a par bond, this represents 3.81 points. Therefore, the repriced bond will have a price of approximately 96.19.

Another security with a coupon of 8 percent, a full price of $70, and a modified duration of 8 would have a very different sensitivity to a change in interest rates. For this bond, the price move for a 100-basis-point increase in rates would be $70 × 0.08 = 5.6 points. This means the new price of the bond would be $64.40.

The relative difference in the price change in these two bonds for a 100-basis-point move in rates is 1.79 points. The bond trading at a discount with a lower coupon and a longer duration has a larger percentage price change than the bond trading near par with the higher coupon.

If the materiality clause did not have a price adjustment feature, the reference asset price could be 90 percent of the initial price due just to a general shift in market interest rates. For a security that is more sensitive to rate moves, this effect would be seen more quickly. The price move could be entirely unrelated to a credit event.

The price adjustment feature attempts to correct for this effect. Although it is impossible to find a Treasury security that will exactly match the price characteristics of a reference asset as interest rates move, a Treasury security with the closest possible characteristics is chosen. The price move of the Treasury security is then used to normalize, or adjust, the price of the reference asset. If the reference asset moved 7 points downward in price and the Treasury security moved down 7 points in price, the adjusted price would be exactly the same as the initial price. This is because the negative 7-point price move of the Treasury security is subtracted from the downward price move of the reference asset. This negative subtraction results in a positive price adjustment to get back to the initial price. Every effort is made so that market price factors do not trigger a credit event.

If the price of the reference asset drops 20 points and the price of the Treasury security drops 4 points, the normalized price of the reference asset would be deemed to have declined 16 points. If the original price was par, this 16-point price decline would constitute materiality. If a credit condition has not occurred, however, there would be no trigger of a termination payment. Only if a credit condition has occurred and materiality exists will a termination payment be triggered under the terms of an agreement that includes a materiality clause.

There are several other issues involving materiality that won't be obvious in a term sheet but should be specified in the confirmation. The market can use an averaging method in which the average price for a period of 10 days must be 90 percent of the initial price or lower for materiality to exist. Another method is the simple method in which materiality exists if on any one day the price is 90 percent of the initial price or lower. This is a matter of personal preference. Not surprisingly, the default protection buyer may want a simple test, and the default protection seller may want an averaging method.

Another issue may crop up when a credit condition exists but the materiality test is not met. How long must one go on testing before rejecting the credit condition as a credit event? This is entirely negotiable. Most default protection sellers will want a limited time period, such as 10 days. A default protection buyer may wish to insist on an unlimited number of days.

Even the frequency of evaluation to determine materiality is negotiable. One can evaluate daily or weekly, for instance. Because materiality is a necessary but not sufficient condition to determine whether a credit event has occurred, it is not necessary to make calculations to determine materiality until notification of a credit condition has occurred. After the notification, however, a default protection buyer may want a daily evaluation as opposed to a weekly evaluation. A default protection seller, on the other hand, may wish to have the longest possible time period between evaluations.

None of the preceding may be obvious from the term sheet. As we saw from the earlier term sheets, length of testing time, average versus simple determination, and frequency of evaluation are usually absent from term sheet language. These features are usually negotiated in the confirmation and there is no standard. Credit default protection buyers and sellers must negotiate the final document together.

BASIS RISK AND SUBSTITUTION

Substitution is another clause that may be present in some term sheets and absent in others. Going back to the plain vanilla, or traditional, term sheet earlier in this chapter, let us take another look at the substitution language:

Substitution: If the amount of the reference asset (or a substitute) is materially reduced, the calculation agent shall reasonably select a substitute issued or guaranteed by the reference name that is of the same credit quality as the reference asset and with a maturity at least that of the reference asset and shall notify the counterparties. If no substitute can be found, the swap will terminate with no further payments on either side.

If the reference asset is no longer priceable in the market, if the reference asset can no longer be produced, or if the reference asset has been paid down, then it makes no sense to have that specific security as a reference asset. In that case one would want to substitute another reference asset while keeping the credit risk identical. Often the maturity of the reference asset and the maturity of the credit default swap differ, but the maturity of the reference asset must be as long as or longer than the maturity of the credit default swap.

The maturity of the reference asset may make a difference in the determination of the termination payment in the event of default. If the agreement calls for physical delivery of a reference asset, the maturity can make a difference as well. A U.S. investment bank gave an Israeli bank a proposal that called for delivery of either a short-dated bond with a maturity near the maturity of the credit default swap or a long-dated bond with a maturity five years longer than the maturity of the credit default swap. This optional delivery was separate from the substitution clause, and the reason for it may have been different.

A bond-trading house may want to hedge more than one security, but the credit default protection seller should not be indifferent. In the event of default, bond prices typically become depressed. In the early 1980s, Latin American debt traded at severely depressed levels, and bonds of different maturities traded at different levels. The payment in the event of default for two bonds with maturities five years apart could very well trade at different levels, with the longer maturity bond likely to trade at a default market price well below the shorter-dated bond.

There is nothing wrong with the Israeli bank agreeing to this proposal, but the cost of the perceived difference between this proposal and a proposal that suggests delivery of a bond with a maturity near the maturity of the credit default swap should be factored into the decision-making process.

TERMINATION PAYMENTS

There are several different methods of calculating credit default swap termination payments. Counterparties should know the differences among the methods. In a February 1997 cover story article of *Emerging Markets Investor*, the following definition was given for a *credit default swap*:

> A transaction where a protection-buyer pays an upfront or annual premium to a protection-seller (an investor willing to take that exposure at the right price), in return for protection against default of some underlying reference credit. If default occurs during the life of the swap, *the protection seller pays the par value of the asset, minus recovery value.* (Italics mine.)

This is the structure with which most newcomers to the credit derivatives market are most comfortable. This structure has been touted in numerous articles published on credit derivatives over the past couple of years. But it is only one of several structures in the market. In some instances, the structure is actually inappropriate for certain reference assets.

There are three common types of credit default termination payments in the market and a fourth type that is being employed by counterparties who want to hedge nonpar assets:

1. Digital cash payment.
2. Par minus post-default price method.
3. Initial price minus post-default price method.
4. Normalized price minus post-default price method.

Digital Cash Payment

The digital cash payment structure has a termination payment based on a fixed percentage of the notional principal. Usually there is no physical delivery of the reference asset to the default protection seller. The default protection seller, however, makes the preagreed payment in the event of default. There are also two types of preagreed termination payments.

The first is a binary payment equal to the entire notional amount. For instance, if the notional amount of the credit agreement is $50 million, the payment if a credit event occurs is $50 million. This digital payment carries a great deal of risk to the default protection seller. The probability of default is combined with an *all-or-nothing* payment on the notional amount. The premium for giving this type of protection should be greater. The default protection seller should consider whether this structure makes sense for the application. These structures are also known as *zero-one structures*. I do not recommend them. The risk is not strictly related to credit default risk. Rather a credit default event is an event trigger, which causes the investor to lose the entire investment.

Although credit derivatives are not insurance products, perhaps an insurance analogy would be useful here. Would you write a fire insurance policy that allowed you to recover the entire cost of a home if the fire damage were limited to the kitchen? If it appears that I am not a fan of the all-or-nothing termination payment structure, it is because I am not. I encourage investors to avoid this structure. I see very little need to offer credit protection on the entire notional amount when recovery rates are usually greater than zero.

The second type of preagreed termination payment requires a fixed cash payment in the event of default. This might be set at 50 percent of the notional amount in the event of default, for instance. Many of these structures seem arbitrary but may be linked to a percentage recovery rate to credit enhance another piece of a complicated structure. If the structure is linked to historical recovery rates for the reference asset credit, the preagreed payment method may make sense. The determination of which method to use, however, is up to the default protection seller.

Another case in which the preagreed fixed cash payment makes sense is one in which the buyer of the default protection estimates a recovery value or a default price for a security but feels that market volatility after a default event may cause the reference asset to temporarily trade below its true value. Daily price volatility can be enormous. As most credit default contracts look for settlement within a month of an event, a daily price fluctuation can work against the default protection buyer. If the protection buyer wants protection against this possibility, it can make sense to agree in advance on a fair default payment.

Par Minus the Market Value of the Reference Asset

The most common termination payment calculation in the market today uses the following formula:

$$\text{Calculation Amount} \times (\text{Par} - \text{Market Value})$$

where the calculation amount is equal to the face value of the reference asset. This method was used in the vanilla term sheet at the beginning of this chapter. The market value is the postdefault price of the reference asset and is usually determined by a dealer poll. This method may be fine when there is no physical delivery involved and the default protection buyer is merely trying to hedge a country risk or a general credit risk, as opposed to a specific asset. This method may not be acceptable, however, when the reference asset is trading well above or well below par. When the credit default protection buyer is trying to hedge an actual position and the reference asset is trading above or below par, this method is simply incorrect.

Initial Price Minus the Market Value

The third common type of structure is a payment of the initial price of the reference asset minus the postdefault price. The credit default protection buyer receives this payment and, in return, must make physical delivery of the reference asset. If the credit default protection buyer does not own the asset, the asset theoretically can be purchased in the market at the postdefault price, which should be equal to the market value.

But what if the credit default protection buyer does own the asset? What if the asset is trading above par? What if the asset is trading below par? The initial price minus the postdefault price method was meant to somehow make up for this. That structure is shown in the abbreviated indicative term sheet on page 111.

Notice that the structure in the term sheet does not take into account accrued interest on the coupon of the reference asset. But if the credit default protection buyer owns the reference asset, the buyer should naturally want to hedge the loss of this potential coupon as well. The potential accrued coupon loss will vary. For instance, three bonds with the same credit and the same maturity will have different prices for different coupons. For higher-yielding bonds, the difference can be significant, as shown by the different

UNITED STATES OF MEXICO CREDIT DEFAULT SWAP
Abbreviated Indicative Term Sheet—
Initial Price Is Used to Calculate Payment

Calculation Amount:	USD 10 million.
Reference Security:	United Mexican States, global bond. Initial price of the security: **105.**
Nonscheduled Termination Date:	With five business days' notice (even if this date is after the maturity date) following a credit event with a termination payment being made.
Termination Payment:	Default protection seller pays *only* upon a credit event:

Calculation Amount × (Initial Price – Market Value)

where market value means the USD-denominated market value of the reference security on the notification date determined by the calculation agent with reference to a dealer panel.

initial prices and coupons for three different bonds with the same assumed credit and maturity.

Initial Price	Coupon
105	10.90%
100	9.75%
95	8.60%

Nonpar bonds pose a problem. If the bond is trading above par, the default protection seller doesn't want to receive the same premium as for a bond trading at par. The default protection buyer wants a termination payment linked to the above-par initial price of the bond and should also ask for accrued but unpaid coupon interest at the time of the credit event. The problem with making a termination payment based on the initial price is that as the bond approaches maturity, the bond decretes to par. The default protection seller is actually paying out more than the loss on the reference asset.

One bank's credit derivatives desk in New York said that they don't try to make an adjustment for the price of the bond because that is "too complicated." Rather, they adjust the calculation amount of the transaction. This compensates the default protection seller for the additional termination payment because the default protection buyer pays a fee based on a calculation amount adjusted to reflect the initial price of the bond. The following term sheet shows how the calculation amount is adjusted to $10,500,000 to account for a bond with $10,000,000 face amount trading at a price of 105.

UNITED STATES OF MEXICO CREDIT DEFAULT SWAP
Abbreviated Indicative Term Sheet—
Adjusted Calculation Amount above Par Price

Calculation Amount:	USD 10.5 million.
Reference Security:	United Mexican States, global bond.
	Initial price of the security: 105.
Nonscheduled Termination Date:	With five business days' notice (even if this date is after the maturity date) following a credit event with a termination payment being made.
Termination Payment:	Default protection seller pays *only* upon a credit event:
	Calculation Amount × (Par − Market Value)
	where market value means the USD-denominated market value of the reference security on the notification date determined by the calculation agent with reference to a dealer panel.

With bonds trading below par, the par minus postdefault price method will overstate the termination payment for the bond if the bond defaults prior to the bond's maturity date. Yet this is the way most of the credit default agreements are written for bonds trading a few points below par. Furthermore, for bonds trading below par, the initial price minus postdefault price method understates the termination payment for a default protection buyer trying to hedge a bond position.

These methods have led to much confusion. One large U.S. commercial bank underhedged a position in an Argentine bond trading at a price of 110. The bond was asset swapped using a par asset swap package. The U.S. commercial bank then purchased credit default protection on the Argentine bond from another bank using the par minus postdefault price calculation method for the termination payment.

What if the bond defaulted after day one? What would have happened? Assuming interest rates had not moved, the U.S. commercial bank would have a defaulted Argentine bond and would have an open swap position. The U.S. commercial bank's swap position would be 10 points under water because the 10-point bond premium was to have been paid over time as an above-market fixed coupon on the swap. The credit default premium calculated based on par, rather than on the actual 110 price of the reference asset, would leave the U.S. commercial bank with a 10-point loss after the credit event.

Normalized Price Method

To be fair to both the default protection buyer and the seller, one should account for the initial price of the reference asset and recognize that the price of the reference security will change over time. The price will decrete to par if the reference asset is initially trading above par. The price will accrete to par if the reference asset is initially trading below par. Naturally, the reflected price should be adjusted to screen out price changes due to market moves and changes in the term structure of credit spreads.

Creating a fictitious asset with the same maturity and coupon as the reference asset can normalize the price of the reference asset. The spread of the reference asset to a "risk-free" asset, such as an AAA Treasury security, is input into a bond pricing calculator. That way, as the reference asset approaches maturity, the price of the shorter maturity proxy bond can be used as the reference price to calculate the termination payment owed under the credit default agreement.

The following term sheet shows how this might work in practice. This can work for both dollar and nondollar assets, but let us look at a U.S. dollar–denominated asset and choose a U.S. Treasury security as a risk-free reference. This term sheet, although not as detailed as a confirmation, addresses the issues discussed earlier and summarizes them on one term sheet.

BRAZIL CREDIT DEFAULT SWAP
Indicative Term Sheet

Default Protection Buyer: Default protection buyer.

Default Protection Seller: Default protection seller.

Reference Obligation:

Issuer/Borrower: Federative Republic of Brazil (the Republic).

Rating: B1/BB–.

Type: Eurobond.

Currency Denomination: USD.

Coupon: 8.875% (payable annually 30/360).

Maturity: November 5, 2001.

Initial Reference Price: To be announced (approximately 104.125).

Initial Reference ISMA Yield: To be announced [ISMA is the International Securities Market Association].

Initial Risk-Free Bond: U.S. on-the-run Treasury with a maturity closest to that of the remaining maturity of the reference obligation.

Initial Risk-Free Bond Price: To be announced.

Initial Risk-Free Bond
ISMA Yield: To be announced.

Initial Reference Yield Spread: To be announced.

Trade Date: As soon as practical.

Effective Date: One week from trade date.

Termination Date: November 5, 2001.

Payments of the Default Protection Buyer:

Calculation Amount: USD 20 million.

Payment Amount and Dates: XXX basis points per annum calculated from the effective date to the earlier of

1. November 5, 2001, *or*

2. the termination payment date.

Day Count Convention:	Payments are made in USD based on an A/360 day count, where A is the actual number of days in the period.

Payments of the Default Protection Seller:

Calculation Amount:	USD 20 million.
Condition to Payment:	If the calculation agent receives notice of credit event prior to the termination date.
Calculation Date:	The date on which the termination payment is calculated.
Termination Payment Date:	Three business days following the valuation date.
Termination Payment:	The default protection seller pays to the default protection buyer the following amount:
	(Calculation Amount $\times$ Calculation Price) + Accrued but Unpaid Interest on the Reference Obligation
Calculation Price:	Equal to the price of a bond with the same coupon, coupon dates, and maturity as the reference obligation yielding the calculation yield.
Calculation Yield:	The yield according to the ISMA yield of the initial risk-free bond at the calculation date using the risk-free-bond settlement price plus the initial reference yield spread.
ISMA Yield:	Yield calculated on a 30E/360 basis following the method of the ISMA.
Risk-Free-Bond Settlement Price:	The default protection buyer and the default protection seller will agree on a midmarket price for the initial risk-free bond on the calculation date. If they cannot agree, then a dealer poll will be made to obtain the risk-free-bond settlement price.

(continued)

Obligation of the Default Protection Buyer:	The default protection buyer will deliver the aggregate principal amount of the reference obligation equal in value to the calculation amount. The bonds will be delivered versus payment on the termination payment date, if any.
Notification of Calculation Date:	Upon a credit condition, the default protection buyer shall have the right to designate the calculation date by delivering notice to the default protection seller.
Credit Event:	Occurs when the default protection buyer is aware of any credit conditions supported by publicly available information and at the same time materiality exists. Credit condition means an event of default as defined in the confirmation. The language of the agreed confirmation will supersede any deviations from that language in the following summary. In summary, a credit condition occurs if any of the following events occurs:

1. Default in any payment of principal or interest on any of the notes (reference obligations) and continuance of such default for a period of 30 days; *or*

2. Default that is materially prejudicial to the interests of the noteholders in the performance of any other obligation under the notes and the continuance of such default for a period of 30 days after written notice requiring the same to be remedied shall have been given to the principal paying agent by the holder of any note; *or*

3. Acceleration of in excess of USD 25 million (or its equivalent in any other currency) in aggregate principal amount of public external indebtedness of the Federative Republic of Brazil by reason of any default (how-

ever described) resulting from the failure of the issuer to make any payment of principal or interest thereunder when due; *or*

4. Failure to make any payment in respect of public external indebtedness of the Federative Republic of Brazil in an aggregate principal amount in excess of USD 25 million (or its equivalent in any other currency) when due (as such date may be extended by virtue of any applicable grace period or waiver) and the continuance of such failure for a period of 30 days after written notice requiring the same to be remedied shall have been given to the principal paying agent by the holder of any note; *or*

5. Declaration by the Federative Republic of Brazil of a moratorium with respect to the payment of principal or interest on public external indebtedness of the Federative Republic of Brazil that does not expressly exclude the notes and that is materially prejudicial to the interests of the noteholders; *or*

6. The Federative Republic of Brazil shall deny its obligations under the notes.

Materiality:	Occurs when the price of the reference obligation less price adjustment is 90 percent or less relative to the initial reference price. The default protection seller and the default protection buyer will agree on the price of the reference obligation at the calculation date. If they cannot agree, a dealer poll will be made to obtain the price of the reference obligation at the calculation date.
Publicly Available Information:	Information that has been published in any two or more internationally recognized published

(continued)

or electronically displayed financial news sources. Nonetheless, if either of the parties or any of their respective affiliates is cited as the sole source for such information, then such information will be deemed not to be publicly available information.

Price Adjustment:
The risk-free-bond settlement price less the initial risk-free-bond price.

Business Days:
Days on which commercial banks and foreign exchange markets settle payments in London, Frankfurt, and New York.

Business Day Convention:
Modified following.

Calculation Agent:
Default protection seller, whose determinations and calculations shall be made in good faith and in a commercially reasonable manner and which shall be binding in the absence of manifest error.

Documentation:
This transaction will be documented as a confirmation under the existing ISDA master agreement between the default protection seller and the default protection buyer.

Law:
Per the ISDA master agreement.

Suitability:
This transaction will be executed with a counterparty with such knowledge and experience in financial matters to be capable of evaluating the merits and risks of the prospective transaction.

Early Termination/Assignment:
An over-the-counter derivative transaction of this type may not be assigned, transferred, or terminated prior to its stated termination date by either party without the consent of the other party except as stipulated in the terms of the transaction.

Firm Unwind Prices:
The default protection seller may quote a firm price that the default protection seller would pay or charge to unwind the transaction prior

	to maturity. A firm unwind price for a transaction of this type will be affected by the then current level of the market, but it may also be affected by other factors. A firm unwind price for a transaction of this type can change significantly from day to day over the life of the transaction.
Periodic Pricing:	It is the current practice (but not a legal obligation) of the default protection seller to provide in a transaction of this type information in writing about the value of such transaction upon request of its counterparty. A routine periodic pricing may be different from a firm unwind price for the same transaction.

This term sheet gets us a lot closer to our ideal of the fair price in the market. Even this term sheet, however, ignores the term structure of the credit spreads of the reference asset. This term sheet creates a fictitious bond using the credit spread of the reference asset to the risk-free bond at the trade date, the beginning of the transaction. Most securities, however, have a term structure of credit spreads, and often the credit spread narrows as the bond approaches maturity. This effect is ignored. One way to adjust for this effect is to use the credit default offer spreads on the trade date to specify spreads to be used for years one through four. Spreads for intermediate time periods can be interpolated.

Market Value and Termination Payments

The time to negotiate the mechanism for determining the termination payment and market price of the reference asset is before the close of a transaction. This detail should not be left to lawyers drafting confirmation language after the transaction has closed. There is no standard language, so counterparties should be aware of the available choices. Reference asset market price determination is not always straightforward, and additional negotiated payments may be folded into termination payments if a credit event occurs.

The default protection seller may agree to pay accrued, but as yet unpaid, interest on the reference asset. This point must be negotiated up front. The payment or nonpayment of accrued interest is not "understood" between dealers, because there is no set rule. Therefore, if payment of accrued interest after the occurrence of a credit event has not been specifically mentioned, the default protection buyer cannot add it to the terms of a confirmation after the close of the transaction. If a default protection buyer requires this payment, the buyer must explicitly state that as one of the terms of the transaction and should insist on a term sheet that reflects this condition. If there is no term sheet and the transaction is a verbal agreement, save the recorded phone conversation until the final confirmation that reflects all of the required transaction terms has been signed by all parties. For any complex transaction, it is a good idea to insist on final term sheets because final confirmations may not arrive for a couple of weeks from understaffed legal departments. Furthermore, it is also a good idea to note the day and the time of a transaction in case you must refer to a tape recording of the transaction conversation. Human memories cause honest mistakes, and misunderstandings are quickly resolved in the face of good documentation.

Hedge costs are the wild card in credit default swaps. Often hedge costs are folded into termination payments. This is most common when a buyer of protection asks for credit default protection on a par asset swap package. The buyer will usually get a par–market value payment plus accrued interest plus hedge costs. The hedge costs are the costs of unwinding the swap in the asset swap package. Because the reference asset is often not priced at par, the price difference from par is reflected in the hedge cost. It is important to note that the seller of protection does not usually get a rebate if there is a net market gain in the hedge. If there is net market loss, however, the hedge cost will most likely reflect all costs to make sure the buyer is made completely whole. In credit-linked note structures (we will see an example later), issuers often incorporate the hedge costs of a swap from fixed to floating coupons as part of the termination payment. This is tricky for the seller because the theory is that the hedge costs make up for any price difference from par of the reference asset. This practice is even used in multicurrency structures in which an issuer may hedge a nondollar asset to dollars. This is fine if the intention of the default protection seller is to hedge all of the risks for the buyer on a dollar basis, but that cost should be factored into the seller's price of protection.

Market price determination can be tricky even for a TRORS. TRORS structures referencing liquid assets often use a cash settlement at the maturity of the TRORS with an option for physical delivery of the reference asset. The option to switch from cash to physical delivery may be the right of either the TRORS receiver or the TRORS payer. In the event of default of the reference asset in the TRORS, the mechanism for determination of market value is often a dealer poll. A calculation agent would typically call three to five dealers and take the average price. The calculation agent is very often one of the dealers offering a price.

Very illiquid assets may require measures other than a dealer poll. High-yield assets in the United States, for instance, can be very difficult to price. Many securities do not trade often, and dealers do not stand ready to help out competitors by providing pricing. For cases such as this, an auction method is preferable. The deal confirmation may call for an auction set at the maturity of a TRORS for a total rate of return transaction or after a credit event in the case of a credit default option. The receiver of the TRORS or the seller of credit default protection who is not happy with the results of the auction can retain the right to take physical delivery of the reference asset.

As we saw in the case of digital payments, a reference asset may not be available, or physical delivery may not be an option. Some structures may simply reference the "senior unsecured" obligation of a reference credit. There may be no stated reference asset at all; a protection buyer may simply wish to hedge general balance sheet exposure. In the event of default, the payout may be the Moody's standard recovery rate for senior unsecured debt—the recovery rate is 51 percent.

Buyers and sellers of credit default protection and counterparties in TRORS must be sensitive to the nuances of termination payments. If necessary, one can agree in principal to a transaction subject to a review of all of the conditions. That way, a buyer or a seller who is unsure or who needs to review information can take the time to do this and then go back and negotiate a final transaction. There is no need to rush into a transaction. Heading off a potential misunderstanding saves a lot of time in the long run.

PRICING AND APPLICATIONS

The Funding Cost Advantage

Credit default protection should logically trade at the spread of the reference security to a risk-free asset. For instance, if a 10-year maturity bond trades at a spread of 100 basis points to the 10-year U.S. Treasury, the amount of spread due to credit risk is about 100 basis points. Some of the 100 basis points may be due to liquidity. Credit default swaps, however, tend to trade at a level that is benchmarked to the asset swap market. This is because most banks benchmark their funding costs based on a spread to LIBOR and look at the net spread they can earn on a given credit relative to their funding costs.

Now that we have some familiarity with basic structures in the credit derivatives market, let us take another look at how a bank might put together a credit default swap while hedging the credit default risk by buying protection from another bank (see Figure 3.6). The commercial bank entering into this transaction has a funding cost of LIBOR – 15 bps per annum. The net spread earned by the commercial bank in this transaction is 90 bps minus the 50 bps the commercial bank pays for the credit default protection. That is a total of 40 basis points. But there is an additional benefit. Because the commercial bank borrows at a sub-LIBOR rate, LIBOR – 15 bps, the bank realizes an additional 15 basis points in spread. The commercial bank's advantage is actually 55 bps per annum.

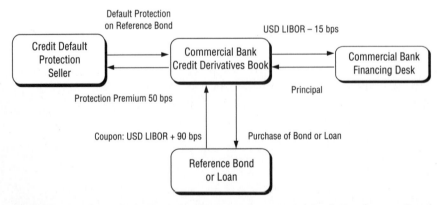

FIGURE 3.6   Credit Default Swap Application: Commercial Bank Purchases a Bond and Arranges a Hedge

Although it is always true that a lower funding cost is better, notice that if the commercial bank had a funding cost of 45 basis points per annum, this trade would not even be possible. The 40 bps per annum spread between the reference bond and the cost of the credit protection would have been inadequate. The high-cost borrower bank would have to pay LIBOR + 45 bps to raise the money to borrow the bond in the first place, leaving it with an all-in net spread of –5 basis points.

The high-cost borrower, however, is happy to receive the credit protection premium of 50 basis points to take the credit of the reference bond. That is a net spread of 50 basis points, which would have been unattainable for the bank if it had purchased the reference bond outright.

Often professionals new to the market ask why a bank would sell credit default protection when it could just buy the asset outright. The answer usually comes down to the funding cost of the bank. Other reasons include the opportunity to earn off–balance sheet income and the lack of need to use actual economic capital to earn income.

Pricing Credit Default Swaps

Although this book is not intended to provide a methodology for pricing credit derivatives, there are certain features of credit default protection that are worth pointing out before delving into new structures.

As one U.S. bank credit derivatives department head said, in talking about some of the more exotic credit default structures: "The spread is where it is because that's where the market says it is." What he was referring to is that the models for certain types of credit derivatives either don't exist or require assumptions about unknowable unknowns. Earlier we discussed unknowable unknowns, such as the U.S. homeowner's prepayment rate on mortgages when interest rates decline. Investment banking firms kept archives of historical data, researchers created sophisticated models to match the data, but the U.S. homeowner prepaid faster than the models expected. The U.S. homeowner didn't care about models, didn't care about data, but did care about favorable refinancing terms and shocked the market to its senses.

An illustration of how the unknowable unknowns in the credit derivatives market can lead to gross oversimplifications follows. One of the most common equations used in this example equates the probability of default (an unknowable unknown) to the credit swap spread divided by the expected loss rate, which is expressed as one minus the recovery rate of the obligor:

$$P_{(default)} = \frac{\text{Credit Spread}}{1 - R_{(obligor)}}$$

where

$$\text{Credit Spread} = \frac{\left[\Sigma_i \, D_{i+1} - \text{Cum}P(ND_{i+1})\right] \times \left[(1 - R_{obligor}) \times \text{Marg } P(\text{Def}_{i+1})\right]}{\Sigma_i \, D_{i+1} - \text{Cum}P(ND_i)}$$

and

$$\frac{\Sigma_i \, D_{i+1} - \text{Cum}P(ND_{i+1})}{\Sigma_i \, D_{i+1} - \text{Cum}P(ND_i)} = 1$$

Credit Spread   = Credit Swap Spread
$R_{(obligor)}$ = Obligor recovery rate in the event of default
Cum P (ND_i)   = Cumulative probability of no default at time i
Marg P (Def_{i+1}) = Marginal probability of default at time $i + 1$
D_{i+1} = Risk-free discount factor at time $i + 1$
Cum P (ND_{i+1})   = Cumulative probability of no default at time $i + 1$

This formula is often touted as a basic method for pricing credit swap spreads. It is neat, simple to grasp, and makes sense.

It is also a bright, shining lie. But it is a comforting lie. It makes my bosses feel much better.

The trouble with this neat formula lies in the input data. The cumulative probability of default in the future may not equal the cumulative probability of default today. The ratio of these two default probabilities almost certainly isn't one, except for very high investment-grade credits. But most of the transactions done with credit derivatives do not involve high investment-grade credits. In fact, as we can see from the Moody's and S&P tables, for long periods of time, the assumption of equal cumulative probabilities of default breaks down even for AAA credits. If that weren't bad enough, we sometimes see this expression boiled down to a simple formula:

$$\text{Credit Spread} = P(\text{default}) \times (1 - R_{(obligor)})$$

We are guessing at default probabilities, and we are guessing at recovery values for the issuer. There is a great degree of variance in both of these values. The lower the credit quality of the issuer, the more dramatic the variance.

This is why firms such as KMV and global banks invest computers, people power, and money to try to analyze financial data to come up with better estimates of default probabilities and recovery rates for companies. Right now, these data inputs are still unknowable unknowns, so we make our best-informed guesses given the economic resources, time, and intelligence available to us.

This is why the market relies so heavily on asset swap spreads. The theory is that if the market prices information efficiently—a big "if"—we will have the best information possible already imbedded in market levels. You know, just like the Dutch tulip bulb market.

There is much value in the market observation approach. We trade the market; we don't trade the models. Also, if we all suffer from the same hallucination about credit spreads, we can trade on the basis of this common hallucination. I can't trade uncertainty. I can trade certainty, however, even if the certainty is based on a common hallucination.

Lest market participants get too concerned about this ambiguity in the data, we need to remind ourselves that banks have always lent money on this basis, often using no data whatsoever. Often banks have lent money for even worse reasons.

Savings and loan associations in the United States nearly went under in the 1980s due to the losses suffered from real estate loans made on the basis of assurances by fast-talkers. The capital, the capacity, and the character of the borrower were brushed over in favor of whether the borrower was a "friend of the bank" or, worse, a contributor to the private pension funds of key officers of the financial institution. After the fact, due diligence sometimes revealed that there was no underlying building whatsoever. U.S. banks rushed to lend to Latin America in the 1970s to their regret in the early 1980s. Loan rates in Europe are ridiculously slim. Lending rates are often justified with the phrase: "That is how we have always lent money." The decision is whether to lend to the corporation, not what spread should we charge if we decide to lend the money. Generally, the level is based merely on what the bank feels the market will bear. The decision isn't based on a rigorous fundamental analysis of the balance sheet for well-known credits. The credit spigot is either open at broad-brush market levels, or the credit spigot is closed because the bank doesn't want any more of that type of credit. Global and European banks have billions of dollars worth of loans put on at levels that do not justify their current return on capital.

Taken in this context, credit derivative swap spread pricing starts to look like nuclear physics. I am not trying to make a case for complacency, however. We need to do better than we have done in the past, and we need to do better than we are currently doing in the pricing of credit derivatives.

Credit default protection has many features, which makes it difficult to model. For one thing, it is "sticky." This is primarily because human beings are "sticky." We tend to stick to one location. We have a need for stability. Most of us are homebodies. Although we claim we have efficient markets, electronic transfer of data, and instantaneous access to knowledge, this is somewhat of a myth.

Banks tend to lend money to people who are close to them. The credit concentration of a typical bank's portfolio tends to be concentrated among credits in their own country or neighboring countries. Often, bank credit concentrations will reflect the region of the country closest to them. That is natural. Banks tend to understand the credit risk of businesses that operate on their doorstep. We humans tend to feel we understand things that are familiar. We have only so much time and so much life in which to evaluate data and make our decisions. Although it is true that banks will buy foreign bank debt and foreign assets, the credit concentration buildup is most often to credits close to home.

Asset managers do their best to diversify risk. But over time they too see a buildup of well-known credits as they make the easy decision to concentrate in assets for which they have the most data and the most research. Although this is not universally true, it is often true. Investment banks provide research on the credits they sell, and the market—although professionals hate to admit it—has a herd mentality.

This is where credit derivatives can be helpful, because the main reason for the existence of credit derivatives is to diversify credit risk in a portfolio of assets. Purchasing credit default protection is one way to reduce exposure to a credit in a portfolio of assets. Many capital-rich entities, such as economic development corporations (EDCs), find themselves with a high degree of credit concentration in a few credits. These are the credits that borrow money to develop business, which supports the economy of the home country. The EDCs do not want to be seen selling off portions of their loan portfolio. At the same time, they need to diversify risk. A credit default swap is the ideal vehicle for removing this exposure from the EDC's balance sheet. An EDC can purchase credit default protection in the form of a credit default swap, or it can do a TRORS to remove this risk from its balance sheet. The EDC can then further diversify credit risk by purchasing other assets in the cash markets that meet the criteria of being related to the economic development of their home country.

The question is: How much should the credit default protection cost? There are inefficiencies in the credit derivatives market, which generate nonrational prices. Supply and demand drives this market. Nonetheless, it is useful to know when one is paying too much or when one is getting a better price than rational models will allow.

There are other factors that drive the market beyond supply and demand, that create nonrational pricing. Evaluation of credit default pricing requires several assumptions, as we shall see in a moment. It is a useful exercise to stress test these assumptions.

Most modelers of credit derivatives build models to predict the possible payoffs. If I were to buy credit default protection, I would build a model and make some assumptions. This model might be no more than looking up a few key variables and putting pen to paper, but I would still use an algorithm to come up with an answer that I find defensible and replicable.

Key inputs include the following:

- Credit quality of the issuer (or issuers, in the case of baskets) as defined by my internal credit committee.
- Correlation among the issuer(s) and the correlation of the issuer(s) with the credit protection seller.
- Credit quality of the default protection seller as defined by my credit committee.
- Probability of default of the issuer(s) and the credit default protection seller.
- Joint probabilities of default in the event that the issuer(s) and credit default protection seller are correlated.
- Assumed recovery rates in the event of default as defined by my exposure management group, and the leverage of the structure.
- Maturity of the deal and any provisions I have made regarding settlement.
- Supply and demand for the credit default protection.
- Economic research, which may change my view of the credit quality.
- Urgency of the need to reduce my credit exposure.
- Special documentation considerations.
- The BIS risk weighting of the default protection seller (this last one because I work for a bank).

Notice that most of the inputs to the model require some assumptions. The internal-credit-quality perception of the issuer is distinct from the probability of default and the recovery rate in the event of default. Although I may assess a low probability of default, my internal bank-credit people may have a view of an improving or a deteriorating credit based on fundamental analysis, which is not reflected in data tables for a given name. Supply-and-demand considerations are also based on market observations and assumptions.

Key variables, which also require assumptions, are probability of default, the recovery rate, and the correlation between the issuer(s) and the credit default protection seller. In the following discussion, I generally refer to the default risk of an issuer, but it should be understood that this also applies to the default risk of the default protection seller, the counterparty.

The probability of default and the recovery rate are based on historical data, and estimates are available from databases kept in the public market as well as from proprietary databases. The major rating agencies maintain tables that show the probability of default for bonds with given ratings. These data are based on historical data, which includes mainly U.S. and European credits. These data are often used to estimate default probabilities for any bond with the same rating.

KMV Corporation offers one of the best-known proprietary default risk models. Bank of America and Bank of Montreal as well as other large commercial banks use this model to manage their own portfolio risk. We discussed this model in Chapter 1, and these data are key components of that model.

The market as a whole is extrapolating these data to include Asian and sovereign bonds. There is limited information on sovereign default probabilities, however, and this tends to be both event- and credit-related. There is no way to refine the data, except to pay attention to global economic and political events.

Several characteristics of probability of default are worth noting. There is a low joint-default frequency among asset classes. Whereas credit spreads will be highly correlated for asset classes, default probability is not. Trading and hedging are much more difficult for default risk than for market risk. It is difficult to find a highly correlated—much less fungible—security in the same asset class to use as a hedge. All is not lost, however. It is the very absence of strong correlation that allows a portfolio manager to benefit from diversification.

Another characteristic is that default risk may vary over time. Rating agencies keep data that measure the cumulative risk of issuer default over the term of an obligation. For discrete time periods within the term of an obligation, rating agencies also measure the marginal risk of default, which shows the change in the default probability of the issuer over time. During the term of an obligation, it is wise to refresh these data to incorporate current data and revised predictions on the credit prospects of an issuer. Tables 3.1 through 3.4 show Moody's and S&P's cumulative and marginal default rates for a wide range of rated assets.

Recovery rates pose another problem. Credit officers at many institutions may do individual name analysis based on their experience and on the fundamentals of the company. A bank with a long lending relationship may have access to data that are difficult to obtain in the public market and may be the best source of a recovery value estimate. KMV keeps an extensive

TABLE 3.1 Moody's Marginal Default Rates (%), 1970–1994

	Years									
	1	2	3	4	5	6	7	8	9	10
Aaa	0.00	0.00	0.00	0.00	0.10	0.10	0.10	0.10	0.10	0.20
Aa	0.00	0.00	0.10	0.10	0.10	0.10	0.10	0.10	0.10	0.20
A	0.00	0.10	0.20	0.10	0.20	0.20	0.20	0.20	0.20	0.30
Baa	0.20	0.30	0.40	0.50	0.50	0.40	0.60	0.70	0.60	0.50
Ba	1.70	2.40	2.40	2.40	2.20	1.80	1.50	1.40	1.30	1.30
B	7.90	6.30	5.10	4.00	3.20	3.20	2.10	2.00	1.50	1.40

TABLE 3.2 Average Marginal Default Rates (%), S&P, 1981–1996

	Years									
	1	2	3	4	5	6	7	8	9	10
AAA	0.00	0.00	0.06	0.07	0.08	0.18	0.19	0.34	0.13	0.16
AA	0.00	0.02	0.09	0.11	0.16	0.21	0.18	0.15	0.09	0.16
A	0.05	0.09	0.10	0.16	0.20	0.19	0.23	0.29	0.30	0.31
BBB	0.17	0.25	0.26	0.54	0.50	0.56	0.53	0.46	0.37	0.33
BB	0.98	2.21	2.35	2.32	2.08	2.05	1.11	1.08	0.96	0.75
B	4.92	5.40	4.66	3.24	2.27	1.54	1.30	2.22	0.95	1.03
CCC	19.29	7.29	5.05	4.31	4.12	0.98	0.89	0.35	0.86	0.58

Source: Derived from *Ratings Performance* 1996, Standard & Poor's.

TABLE 3.3 Moody's Cumulative Default Rates (%), 1970–1994

	Years									
	1	2	3	4	5	6	7	8	9	10
Aaa	0.00	0.00	0.00	0.00	0.10	0.20	0.30	0.40	0.50	0.70
Aa	0.00	0.00	0.10	0.20	0.30	0.40	0.40	0.50	0.60	0.80
A	0.00	0.10	0.30	0.40	0.60	0.80	1.00	1.20	1.50	1.80
Baa	0.20	0.50	0.90	1.40	1.90	2.30	2.90	3.60	4.20	4.70
Ba	1.70	4.10	6.50	8.90	11.10	12.90	14.40	15.80	17.10	18.40
B	7.90	14.20	19.30	23.30	26.50	29.70	31.80	33.80	35.80	36.70

TABLE 3.4 Static Pools Average Cumulative Default Rates (%), S&P, 1981–1996

	Years									
	1	2	3	4	5	6	7	8	9	10
AAA	0.00	0.00	0.06	0.13	0.21	0.39	0.58	0.92	1.05	1.21
AA	0.00	0.02	0.11	0.22	0.38	0.59	0.78	0.93	1.02	1.18
A	0.05	0.14	0.24	0.40	0.60	0.79	1.02	1.31	1.61	1.92
BBB	0.17	0.42	0.68	1.22	1.72	2.28	2.81	3.27	3.64	3.97
BB	0.98	3.19	5.54	7.86	9.94	11.99	13.10	14.18	15.14	15.89
B	4.92	10.32	14.98	18.22	20.49	22.03	23.33	24.55	25.50	26.53
CCC	19.29	26.58	31.63	35.94	40.06	41.04	41.93	42.28	43.14	43.72

Source: Derived from *Ratings Performance* 1996, Standard & Poor's.

database on recovery rates for individual names, which can also be used in a credit default price analysis. The major rating agencies also compile data on public and rated securities and their recovery rates.

Although the rating of the security is important, it is only one component in determining recovery rates. Seniority of the obligation (see Table 3.5) and the capital structure of the issuer(s) are key factors in recovery rate estimates. Notice that senior secured debt has a much higher average recovery rate than even senior subordinated debt—53.8 percent with a standard deviation of 26.86 percent versus 38.52 percent with a standard deviation of 23.81 percent. The relatively high standard deviations indicate, however, that there is much overlap in the recovery values among the various classes of debt.

Among senior secured debt, there is a strong argument that loans may fare better than bonds. Moody's data show that for a limited time period,

TABLE 3.5 Moody's Recovery Rates (1% of Par)

Seniority Class	Mean (%)	Standard Deviation (%)
Senior secured	53.80	26.86
Senior unsecured	51.13	25.45
Senior subordinated	38.52	23.81
Subordinated	32.74	20.18
Junior subordinated	17.09	10.90

1991 to present, loans tend to have a higher recovery value than bonds. The average recovery value estimate was $71 for loans versus $57 for senior secured bonds, and loans have a much higher median value of $77. The caveat in pricing credit default remains, however. The 95 percent of the loan price observations fell in a band from $15 to $97 for loans; so although recoveries are skewed higher for loans than for senior secured debt, there is a great deal of overlap.

Even for the same classes of debt, average recovery rates vary dramatically. For senior secured debt, recovery rates in the 10th percentile are only 18.5 percent, versus 85.32 percent in the 90th percentile. There is a "binaryness" about recovery rates. This is the nature of default. One must make an assumption, and it is entirely fair to have an informed view that differs from the market consensus for a given credit or group of credits.

In general, loans tend to be more price robust than fixed rate bonds because loans have a floating rate coupon. If the coupon could adjust instantaneously and if credit spreads remained constant throughout the life of the loan agreement, the loan would always trade at par. As market rates moved, the loan's coupon would instantly readjust. In reality, there is some lag in the loan coupon adjustment, but this market price readjustment tends to be small compared to that for bonds. In a default situation, the price adjustment market coupon readjustment of defaulted bonds adds another element of confusion to the price of defaulted bonds.

The major advantage for the price robustness of loans is that loans are negotiated agreements between banks and borrowers. The bank may have a long-standing business relationship with the borrower and have access to extensive financial data. Often banks are advisers, and bank officers may be on the board of directors of the borrowing institution. Loans are often restructured with customized work-out periods.

The following table from the Moody's Investors Service November 1996 report, *Defaulted Bank Loan Recoveries*, compares data for defaulted loans and bonds.

Average Defaulted Bank Loan and Bond Prices
One Month after Default
(September 1989 to September 1996)

Bank loans	$71
Senior secured bonds	$57
Senior unsecured bonds	$46
Subordinated bonds	$34

Loan prices one month after default were on average 14 points, or nearly 25 percent, higher than prices for senior secured bond debt. The explanation seems to be related to the "inside" nature of loans. It should be noted, however, that even loans have a hierarchy. Loans secured by current assets have higher average recovery values than loans secured by plant and equipment.

Once the default probability and loss in the event of default, or the recovery value, has been determined or "guesstimated," the next step is to calculate the expected loss for the issuer. In its simplest form, expected loss is defined by the following formula:

$$\text{Expected Loss} = \text{Default Probability} \times (1 - \text{Recovery Rate}) \times \text{Loss Exposure}$$

It is important to stress that this is an average expected credit loss. If one wanted to examine a worst-case scenario, one could look at the worst-case default probability and worst-case recovery rate for a given loss exposure to calculate the expected loss.

If the security has been placed in a structure, the loss on the structure may have a different expected loss than that of the underlying issuer(s). The key expected loss variables remain the default probability and loss in the event of default for the issuer, however. The expected loss on the structure then follows from the cash flow characteristics of the structure.

Another note on structures is worth mentioning at this point. The expected loss on the structure can be compared with a senior unsecured bond that has the same expected annual loss rate as the structure. The implied rating on a structure will be the same as the rating of the senior unsecured bond. Rating agencies determine ratings on tranches of asset securitizations, collateralized loan obligations, and collateralized bond obligations in this fashion.

By now it should be easy to see that default risk has some unique characteristics that can cause pricing to vary significantly based on input assumptions. The following summary recaps the most important points:

1. Default risk is dynamic. Events and market conditions can cause risk to change suddenly and dramatically irrespective of historical data.
2. Correlation between default risks is low. Note, however, that although the *probability* of default for riskier credits can suggest that two risky credits simultaneously default, coincidence does not necessarily mean correlation.
3. Default probabilities in a portfolio have a very high variance. There is a large difference between the highest and the lowest default probabilities.
4. Recovery rates have a very high variance. There is a large difference between the highest and the lowest recovery rates.
5. Very little data exist to support correlation assumptions in the emerging market sector.
6. Diversification suggests that credit default losses will be lower than expected, but diversification cannot remove the probability of an infrequent catastrophic loss on an individual credit.
7. Portfolio loss distributions are skewed due to correlation effects.
8. There is no substitute for experienced active portfolio management.
9. Default protection prices are often distorted by tax, accounting, and regulatory considerations.

Several sophisticated pricing models have popped up in the marketplace. But most of the market trades credit default swaps off of asset swap levels. Traders look at the asset swap levels for a given credit and hypothesize that an investor should be happy to earn the same spread on a credit default as the investor would have earned had they invested cash in the asset itself. Traders take into account the funding cost of the institution.

The Funding Cost Arbitrage

Funding cost arbitrages drive much of the mainstream credit default business. Take the case of an AAA rated institution that funds itself at LIBOR

– 25 bps and an institution with a weak single A rating that funds itself at LIBOR + 20 bps. Further, assume that the AAA institution wants to lay off the credit risk of a BBB rated bond trading at LIBOR + 30 bps. Before laying off the credit risk, the position of the AAA bank is as shown in Figure 3.7.

The AAA institution must reduce its risk to this particular BBB asset on which the AAA institution earns 55 bps per annum. The AAA institution may be full on this particular credit, may be reducing risk to BBB institutions in general, or may need to expand credit lines to do more business with this particular BBB entity. Furthermore, the AAA institution may not want to be seen selling this risk in the public market. To accomplish this reduction in credit exposure, the AAA institution enters into an off–balance sheet agreement with a single A rated institution in which the single A rated institution agrees to accept a fee to take the credit default risk of the BBB rated institution.

If the single A rated institution were to purchase this bond outright, it would fund itself at LIBOR + 20 bps and earn LIBOR + 30 bps on the BBB asset. The A rated institution would have to put up the full cost of economic capital, and the asset would be booked on the A rated institution's balance sheet. The A rated institution would earn a net spread of 10 basis points per annum as shown in Figure 3.8.

In the case where an AAA rated institution pays the A rated institution 20 basis points per annum to take the credit risk of the BBB asset, however, the transaction would look as shown in Figure 3.9.

Both the AAA rated institution and the single A rated institution are better off. After the transaction, the single A institution earns a net spread

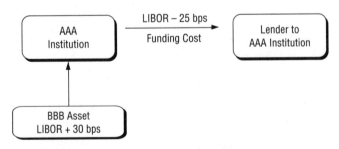

The AAA Rated Institution earns a net spread of 55 bps on the BBB Asset. The AAA Institution must lay off the risk of the BBB Asset.

FIGURE 3.7   AAA Institution Owns BBB Credit Risk

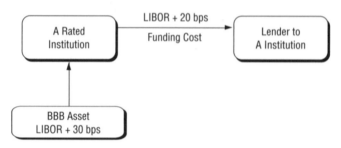

A Rated Institution purchases BBB Asset on balance sheet. A Institution puts up full economic capital.

A Institution earns a net spread of 10 bps per annum.

FIGURE 3.8   A Rated Institution Purchases BBB Asset

of 20 basis points per annum off–balance sheet. The AAA institution has a credit-risk-protected asset at a net spread of LIBOR + 10 bps. Assuming there is no correlation between the A institution and the BBB issuer credit, the synthetic asset created by the combination of the BBB asset and the credit default protection of the A rated institution would have an implied credit rating of AA–.

The major rating agencies publish their views of credit ratings of jointly supported obligations for various credits. Table 3.6 shows an excerpt from Standard and Poor's data. This S&P table (Table 3.6) assumes that the two credits are unaffiliated and uncorrelated, which is the condition specified earlier for this transaction. The AAA institution creates a synthetic AA asset

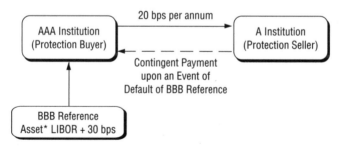

*A Institution receives a 20-basis-point fee in return for making a Contingent Payment if a predefined Credit Event occurs to the BBB Reference Asset.

FIGURE 3.9   Credit Default Swap to Offset BBB Risk

TABLE 3.6 Standard & Poor's Ratings for Jointly Supported Obligations, November 1995

	A+	A	A–	BBB+	BBB	BBB–
A+	AA+	AA+	AA+	AA	AA	AA
A	AA+	AA	AA	AA–	AA–	A+
A–	AA+	AA	AA–	A+	A+	A
BBB+	AA	AA–	A+	A	A	A–
BBB	AA	AA–	A+	A	A	BBB+
BBB–	AA–	A+	A	A–	BBB+	BBB

with a coupon of LIBOR + 10 bps, and the A rated institution takes on acceptable credit risk for a spread otherwise unattainable for the same credit risk in the market. Both the AAA rated institution and the A rated institution are better off. The net positions of the AAA rated institution and the A rated institution are shown in Figures 3.10 and 3.11, respectively.

The AAA rated institution does not necessarily need to own an underlying asset to purchase credit default protection. The AAA rated bank might be in a position of managing a credit line due to foreign exchange or interest rate swap exposures, for instance. In a public, well-traded market, both counterparties will look at the asset swap market as a benchmark price and begin negotiations from this point of reference.

A credit default protection buyer can have another reason for purchasing credit default protection independent of hedging an asset position or managing overall credit exposure. The credit default protection buyer can take a view on a given credit and inventory the protection or look for appreciation in the price of the protection. A buyer may view the premium as payment for cheap protection on a deteriorating credit. The credit default protection buyer can pay the default premium to create a short position in a credit.

Likewise, a credit default protection seller can receive the credit default premium and go long the credit exposure to fill in credit gaps in a diversified portfolio. Similarly, the credit default protection seller may be taking a long position in a given credit because of a positive view on the credit.

Credit default swaps can be used to create long or short positions in credit exposure to a given credit or credits just as total rate of return swaps can be used to create long and short positions in given assets.

The credit quality of the credit default protection seller is important for

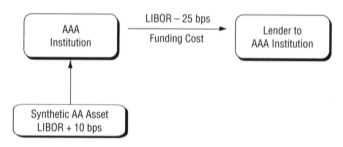

The AAA Rated Institution earns a net spread of 35 bps a Synthetic AA Asset.

FIGURE 3.10 AAA Institution Final Position

all of the reasons mentioned earlier: correlation, absolute credit risk, Bank of International Settlements (BIS) risk weight, and so forth. But there is another factor implied in the credit quality of the default protection seller. In order for the preceding credit arbitrage to work, *the funding cost of the default protection seller must be higher than the funding cost of the default protection buyer*. I believe this is the fundamental reason that many banks were keen to overlook possible high correlations of Korean banks, for instance, in order to do more credit derivatives business. Korean banks such as Hanil Bank and Shinhan Bank look on selling credit protection on Korean corporate names as "found money."

Of course, trades are done where the credit quality of the default protection seller is as high as or higher than that of the default protection buyer. When it is necessary to free up a credit line, supply-and-demand conditions may dictate paying up for credit protection. In the context of a larger business view, this can be a sensible transaction. This is particularly true among banks where buying credit protection on a 100 percent BIS risk-weighted

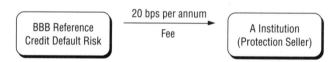

The A Institution earns 20-basis-point fee in return for making a Contingent Payment if a predefined Credit Event occurs to the BBB reference Asset.

A Rated Institution is 10 bps per annum better off than if it had purchased a BBB asset outright.

FIGURE 3.11 A Rated Institution Final Position

asset from a bank can lower regulatory capital from 100 percent to 20 percent, as we saw in Chapter 2 on total rate of return swaps.

From the funding cost arbitrage, we can see that key factors in pricing credit default swaps are the funding costs of the counterparties and the cost of capital for the credit default protection buyer. The likelihood of default and the likely recovery value for different counterparties and assets are also important; but in the given example, it was assumed that the market factored this information into the credit spread of the asset and the funding costs of the counterparties. Calculations were a matter of simple addition and subtraction.

The funding arbitrage transaction works well for public debt where there is a defined asset swap market and a general market consensus view on credit risk. Complications arise in nonpublic or controversial markets. If there is no asset in the desired maturity, or no public market, the task is more difficult. This is particularly true in emerging markets and in the Latin American markets.

In May 1997, I tried to purchase sovereign credit protection on Brazil for a five-year maturity. At the time, the Brazilian reference Eurobond was trading at a spread of 220 basis points to the five-year U.S. Treasury. That would have been an implied asset swap level of approximately 180 basis points. The range of quotes for the credit protection varied as follows:

Credit Default Protection Referencing a
Five-Year Brazilian Eurobond (May 1997)

Chase Manhattan Bank	240 basis points per annum
Broker Market	285 basis points per annum
JP Morgan	325 basis points per annum

It is possible that the broker reflected Chase's price plus the broker's markup. This range in price is typical of what one finds in the credit derivatives market. Supply and demand for this type of credit protection drives prices. It may be that Chase had just created a hedge whereby it was long credit default protection and did not want to inventory the protection but was willing to make a good offer.

Credit protection on Russian sovereign risk (Ba2/BB–) referencing a Eurodollar bond exhibited similar characteristics. It is extremely difficult to find sellers of protection in large size. This is partly because it is difficult to find bonds with which to hedge in large block sizes and because it is difficult to sell credit-linked notes, which create a hedge, in large block sizes. The Russian Eurobond, the 9.75 percent of 2001, asset swapped to a level of LIBOR + 252 bps per annum for a 4.5-year maturity. The following levels were offered as good indications of where three large commercial banks would sell credit default protection referencing this Eurobond. The offer size was for a principal amount of $50 million.

Credit Default Protection Referencing a 4.5 Year Russian Eurobond (July 1997)

1-year protection	230 basis points per annum
2-year protection	270 basis points per annum
4-year protection	320 basis points per annum

Notice that in each case, as one moves to a longer maturity, credit default protection is more expensive than owning the reference asset. There is no arbitrage possibility. An investor cannot purchase the underlying Brazilian debt or Russian debt and then purchase credit default protection and still earn a positive spread. It is also typical of emerging-market debt that the farther out an investor goes in maturity, the more expensive it is to purchase credit default protection. Much of the price structure has to do with the "specialness" or scarcity of the bonds as one moves farther out along the curve. This has to do with the fact that the supply of offers for large-size and longer maturities is limited.

There are a variety of reasons for this limitation. Among the most important is the exposure number. Bank of America estimated the following exposure numbers for a 1-year maturity credit default swap on Russia and for a 4.4-year maturity credit default swap referencing the Russian Eurobond (Ba2/BB–) just cited.

Bank of America's Exposure Estimates for Credit Default Swaps on Russian Debt

1-year maturity	4.86% × Notional Amount
	(4.86% × $50 million = $2.43 million)
4.4-year maturity	52% × Notional Amount
	(52% × $50 million = $26 million)

The Risk Management Analytics group at Bank of America makes the assumptions regarding recovery rates. For this BB credit, they assumed the exposure was huge. For a shorter maturity, the exposure number is not too onerous, but the exposure number jumps dramatically, *more than 10 times for an extension in the maturity of the credit default swap of 3.4 years.* This means that the credit risk of a credit default protection buyer to a credit default protection seller is also huge. Again we see that the counterparty matters, not just from a correlation point of view and not just from a regulatory capital point of view, but critically from a credit quality point of view. This means a large number of credit default protection sellers may be disqualified as credit lines are used for other business.

How does one create a model to deal with supply-and-demand conditions such as these? How does one reconcile a credit default protection pricing model with some of the intangibles we discussed earlier? Models are a good place to start, but they are not the complete answer. The fact of the matter is that no economic model can take into account all of the technical factors involved in credit default pricing.

The spread is where it is because that's where the market says it is.

CHAPTER 4

Exotic Structures

U p until now, we have looked at plain vanilla structures and the various features of plain vanilla credit protection. Although we saw a variety of term sheets and looked at a variety of ways to hedge risk, we did not look at structures that were exotic. The points of negotiation centered mainly on fairly straightforward structures. A series of complicated structures has appeared on the market. The market's ability to create structures has outstripped the market's ability to price these structures. That makes these structures less liquid than the plain vanilla structures we have discussed.

Credit spreads are very narrow versus historical levels, and investors who want to enhance return must either be willing to invest in lower-credit-quality assets or to take other risks. Other risks can include event risks and market-contingent risks. Market-contingent risks related to credit spreads or credit default events are becoming increasingly popular in the market. We will return to this theme again and again. Market-contingent risks appear to be credit risks that financial institutions understand and deal with daily. Banks, for instance, have often made credit decisions without rigorous models to support credit decisions. This was not unusual because relationships, future business prospects, and past lending rules of thumb dictated lending behavior. Often there were market-contingent components of the lending decision.

Although lenders were aware of these components of risk, not much was done to model or to quantify these risks. For a large commercial bank, it was important to be right more often than one was wrong. The risk most dreaded by commercial bankers and portfolio managers was not the "invisible" market-contingent risk, but rather the catastrophic loss of a default on a lending position.

New credit default and credit spread products have cropped up in the market that incorporate features of this invisible market-contingent credit risk. Often the price risk is not rigorously analyzed. But the market is paying more attention to these structures; and as the demand for better methods of pricing this risk increases, more attention in portfolios will be focused on market-contingent risk that is not transparent at first glance.

The following section discusses many of the new structures that have appeared in the market, but because this is an evolving market, new structures will continue to appear. A firm grasp of the fundamentals will guide anyone through the shoals of new structures. The three key components of value remain (1) the timing of the cash flows, (2) the magnitude of the cash flows, and (3) the probability of receipt of the cash flows.

ASSET SWAP SWITCHES

One way of increasing spread on an asset swap is to exchange a current on–balance sheet asset swap package for another asset swap package contingent upon a change in market conditions. In Europe, this is called a switch asset swap. In the United States, it is sometimes called an asset swap swap.

A brief word on terminology may be useful here. The U.S. bond market has historically used the word *swap* for the sale of one security and the purchase of another. These swaps are sometimes further described as credit swaps (exchanging lower-rated for higher-rated bonds), yield pick-up swaps (exchanging a lower-yielding for a higher-yielding bond), or maturity swaps (exchanging a shorter-dated for a longer-dated bond), and so on. In the United States market, *switching* is often used as a pejorative term for "bait-and-switch" sales techniques, in which a customer is baited by a tempting offer of an unavailable bond and switched to a less attractive but conveniently available bond.

The European market—and often the Asian market—has traditionally used the term *switch* to denote the sale of one security and the purchase of another security, the same way that the U.S. market uses the word *swap* to denote a bond swap.

Markets globally also use the word *swap* for interest-rate swaps, currency swaps, and credit default swaps. The exchange of one asset swap package for another asset swap package can correctly be called a swap of asset swaps or a switch of asset swaps, depending on where the market professionals learned their craft. To avoid confusion it is best to immediately reiterate the terms of the transaction. I know several seasoned market professionals who have run into difficulty as a result of not clarifying terminology.

Salomon Brothers has a long-standing anecdote, probably apocryphal, in its Corporate Finance Department. One of its U.S. investment bankers wanted to check the creditworthiness of an equity issuer and called a colleague in the London office. The British colleague told his U.S. counterpart that the equity issuer was "on his uppers." On the strength of this recommendation, the U.S. investment banker accepted the equity as collateral. After all, if the equity issuer was "on his uppers," then the equity issuer's credit quality was improving, the American thought. The only problem was that the equity collateral was nearly worthless. In England, the expression "on his uppers" means that someone is broke. The individual has no soles on his shoes because he is too poor to replace the shoes or to get them resoled and is literally left with only the upper part of the shoes.

I had a similar misunderstanding with a British colleague when I said that someone was "tap city." My British colleague took this to mean that the client was doing well. Fortunately, I headed off the misunderstanding. This is actually a typically American expression referring to Depression-era shantytowns in which unemployed men tap-danced for money.

These are classic misunderstandings illustrating the old joke that the United States and England are two nations divided by the same language. Unfortunately, that is often true in the global marketplace, where two counterparties can be divided by the same market jargon.

For the purposes of this section I use "asset swap switches" to refer to a transaction in which one counterparty exchanges a current on–balance sheet asset swap package for another asset swap package contingent on a change in market conditions. The asset swap switch can also apply to an exchange of floating rate notes.

In an asset swap switch, an investor purchases an asset and agrees to deliver the asset in exchange for another, usually uncorrelated asset, if the new asset's spread widens to a prespecified level. For instance, an investor purchases an Italian bank asset swap at the London interbank offering rate (LIBOR) plus 20 basis points (bps). A commercial bank offers to pay the investor an additional 20 basis points if the investor will agree to exchange the Italian bank asset swap for a Korean bank asset swap. The exchange is market contingent. The Korean bank asset swap is currently trading at LIBOR

+ 45 bps. If the spread widens to LIBOR + 65 bps, then the commercial bank has the right to deliver the Korean bank asset swap to the investor in exchange for the Italian bank asset swap. Diagrammatically, the transaction is as shown in Figure 4.1.

For both counterparties to feel better off in an asset swap switch transaction, the investor and the commercial bank must have slightly different points of view. In this example, the investor must have the view that Korean bank debt is a good investment even if the asset swap spread widens to LIBOR + 65 bps. The investor might feel, for example, that Korean debt is priced too rich at LIBOR + 45 bps for the credit risk under current market conditions. If the spread widens to LIBOR + 65 bps, however, the investor might feel that that is the credit spread at which he is willing to own an asset linked to the credit risk of a Korean bank. The investor must have the further view that the credit spread widening is due more to market levels coming in line with the true credit risk than to a credit spread widening that indicates that Korean bank debt will slip into default.

The commercial bank must have the view that Italian bank asset swap spreads will not widen in sympathy with or more than Korean bank spreads. In other words, this transaction works best when both counterparties feel that the asset swap spreads have a low correlation. Further, the commercial bank must have the view that it is unwilling to own the Korean bank asset swap at a spread wider than LIBOR + 65 bps. This may be either because the commercial bank cannot tolerate a further widening in this asset position or because it feels the asset swap spread widening is symptomatic of fundamental underlying credit problems. Notice that the commercial bank bears the risk of a credit spread widening of the Korean bank asset swap

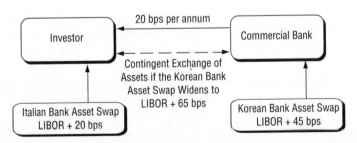

Investor earns an enhanced yield of LIBOR + 40 basis points on the Asset Swap Switch transaction.

FIGURE 4.1 Asset Swap Switch

package up to the point that the asset swap widens to LIBOR + 65 bps. The commercial bank is hedged for a credit default event, however.

Another variation on the asset swap switch is known as a credit exchange agreement or a credit risk switch. This looks similar to the asset swap switch transaction but has some important differences. The investor is generally paid a higher premium to compensate for the credit risk. The credit risk switch occurs only in the event of default of the reference credit. The transaction is as shown in Figure 4.2.

In this transaction, the investor purchases an Italian bank asset swap package at LIBOR + 20 bps. The investor also earns a premium of 55 basis points to take the credit default risk on a BBB asset. In the event of default on the BBB asset, the investor delivers the Italian bank bond to the counterparty and takes delivery of the defaulted BBB asset. Often the investor will be held responsible for potential adverse costs associated with unwinding the swap in the asset swap package. As we see later, the costs of unwinding this swap can be significant for longer maturities and especially for cross-currency swaps. The mark-to-market for these swaps does not necessarily have to be negative; the investor may have a gain in the swap. Nonetheless, the potential adverse cost is a real one, which is rarely factored into the premium earned by the investor.

KNOCK-IN OPTIONS, CREDIT SPREAD OPTIONS, AND FORWARDS

The asset swap switch in the previous section had an interesting feature. The exchange took place based on a change in market conditions, not based on

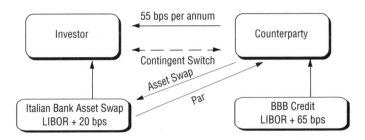

Investor earns an enhanced yield of LIBOR + 75 basis points on the Credit Switch transaction.

FIGURE 4.2   Credit Risk Switch

an actual default event. This market-contingent feature can be viewed as a knock-in structure. This is familiar to users of derivatives as a "barrier option." The option becomes active only when the preset barrier is reached. The credit spread of a reference asset must widen to a preset barrier level before the option becomes active. The commercial bank does not have the right to demand delivery of the Italian bank asset swap package in exchange for the Korean bank asset swap package until the Korean bank asset swap spread widens to LIBOR + 65 bps. Of course, the commercial bank also has a form of default protection on the Korean bank because it is unlikely that the Korean bank would be in default if its asset swap spreads were LIBOR + 65 bps or less.

Credit spread options are more conventionally used in one of two ways: (1) to hedge index-related basis risk and (2) to hedge credit default risk. An insurance company or a fund manager can purchase an option on the credit spread between a single-A corporate bond index and an index on similar duration and maturity U.S. Treasuries. As we saw earlier, the same kind of credit spread protection can be accomplished using the index swap market.

Credit spread options have been around for approximately 15 years in various forms. One of the classic spread options is the mortgage/Treasury spread option. This market started with a simple strategy in which investors sold calls on mortgage-backed securities (MBS) and bought calls on Treasuries. This protected mortgage investors against a widening in yield spreads between mortgages and Treasury securities. This strategy was unsatisfactory, however, because it did not provide spread protection in all interest-rate scenarios. When spreads widened as prices of both security classes fell, both options expired out of the money. This scenario was unhedged.

Salomon Brothers, Merrill Lynch, and others began selling mortgage/Treasury spread options to correct the flaw in the hedging strategy. The holder of the spread option has the right to buy MBS and sell Treasuries (or the opposite if the investor is hedging a spread-narrowing scenario) at prespecified prices and a prespecified ratio of face amounts. The hedge ratio accounted for spread changes due to price-level changes, and any residual spread change was due to a true widening or narrowing of MBS/Treasury spreads.

Investors can also simply purchase a call option on a spread. For example, an investor could purchase a call option on the spread between Mexican and U.S. Treasuries. If the spread widens, the investor receives a payment based on the new spread versus the initial strike spread. In this way, an investor long a portfolio of Mexican government bonds can protect the investment in the event that the credit of the Mexican government bonds weakens relative to U.S. Treasuries. These contracts are usually structured with a one-time exercise. For ongoing protection, an investor might want to structure the hedge as a credit spread forward (or credit spread swap).

If an investor wants to target a purchase of a security at a wider level than today's market spread, the investor can write a credit spread option. The investor can earn an up-front premium and must purchase the bonds if the spread widens to the preagreed level. The investor has written a credit spread put on a bond. This strategy is generally used in the emerging and the high-yield markets, but it is not limited to these markets. Several European banks are writing these options on investment-grade debt. Some European banks receive favorable capital treatment for selling credit spread put options versus selling credit default protection.

Credit spread forwards, also known as credit spread swaps, are similar to credit spread index swaps. Credit spread forwards are indexed to an identified security or an index of securities. The investor pays a per annum fee and receives the credit spread. The credit spread is calculated as the yield of the security minus the yield of a reference risk-free rate. An investor who wishes to have an ongoing hedge for a long position can receive a periodic payment based on the credit spread to a risk-free reference yield. The investor pays an ongoing premium. This can be structured as a swap, with a continuous exchange of net payments, or as an option for which the investor pays an up-front fee.

The second use of credit spread options incorporates elements of a credit default swap. The motives of the counterparties in a credit spread option agreement are necessarily very different. For instance, a bank may wish to sell credit spread protection for a fee because it feels the asset is undervalued at current market levels and further feels that a credit spread widening is not a leading indicator of a default event. The buyer of the protection is willing to take some risk of credit spread widening. At a certain trigger level, the buyer must either reduce credit exposure or hedge a potential default.

Notice that the buyer and the seller of a credit spread option never reference a default event, only a widening in credit spreads. If the reference for a credit spread option is a floating rate note or an asset swap, it is very easy to tell if the option is in the money or not. If the discount margin has increased, the credit spread has widened; if the discount margin has decreased, the credit spread has narrowed.

If the reference security is a fixed-income instrument, however, then we must use another methodology for determining whether the credit spread has widened or narrowed. The spread to a reference Treasury may not be enough. As a bond ages, it becomes shorter in maturity. We call this "rolling down the yield curve." The spread to the Treasury curve using a similar duration risk-free reference Treasury rate may narrow as the implied risk of the credit declines the closer the bond gets to maturity. In this case, one can use a risk-free reference Treasury (see also the Brazil credit default example in the section on the normalized price method in Chapter 3) combined with a credit spread curve for the reference asset. One can also use asset swap spreads and compare the spreads to a reference asset credit spread curve constructed at the time the credit spread option transaction was initiated.

Credit spread options can take the form of puts or calls. If credit spreads tighten, a call on credit spreads becomes more valuable. If credit spreads widen, credit spread puts become more valuable.

Just as with all options, volatility of the credit spreads is an important input into pricing. In addition, recovery rates and credit spread curves are important inputs. The pricing methodology difficulties incorporate all of the difficulties we discussed earlier.

Credit spread options can take on as many variations of form as interest-rate options, including knock-in structures, knock-out structures, levered structures, and so on. An example of a knock-out structure is one in which a credit spread put becomes null and void if credit spreads tighten to a certain level, say by 10 basis points. This would indicate that the credit quality of the reference asset improved, possibly even upgraded; and the perceived need for the credit put disappears. The resulting credit spread put would be cheaper than the conventional put. Current demand for this structure is low. Credit spread differentials between various rated credits are at historically low levels. It is possible that more applications will arise linked to highly leveraged transactions and to high-yield bonds.

A knock-in credit spread put does not become active until spreads widen to a certain level. When that happens, the investor will take delivery of an asset at a much wider credit-spread level. The counterparty essentially has credit default protection. One German bank enters into this transaction in the one-to-five-year maturity range. They reference assets trading around LIBOR + 20 bps and write the protection for a spread widening to LIBOR + 250 bps. If the spread widening occurs, the German bank has a commitment to purchase the assets at par. They carefully review the underlying credits and demand a premium equal to the full asset swap spread of the reference asset, the same premium demanded for credit default protection. The German bank gets unfavorable capital treatment for selling credit default protection. The German bank experiences favorable capital treatment, however, for selling credit spread puts because they never reference a credit default event.

BALANCE SHEET SWAPS AND EXPOSURE MANAGEMENT

Most of the calls I receive in the U.S. market are from counterparties wishing to buy and sell credit risk for the purposes of balance sheet management. Often a bank will call looking to sell credit default options for lower A rated credits, hoping to book acceptable credit risks. In most cases they are looking to reference a drawn term loan and to take delivery of the loan in the event of default. Unfortunately, these credits usually yield only 5 to 8 basis points for an undrawn back-up commercial-paper revolver. Often I will receive calls in which counterparties want to purchase a credit default option to lay off credit default risk. In this case, the counterparty agrees to pay a full commitment fee on a loan in order to deliver the loan in the event that it is drawn.

These are logical uses of bank balance sheet capacity and will eventually change the way banks do business globally. Figure 4.3 shows an example of a consolidated portfolio composition of a hypothetical U.S. bank with a

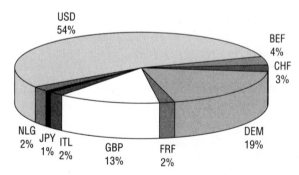

FIGURE 4.3 Portfolio Distribution of Bank Percentage Assets by Region—BEF: Belgian Francs; CHF: Swiss Francs; DEM: Deutsche Marks; FRF: French Francs; GBP: British Sterling; ITL: Italian Lira; JPY: Japanese Yen; NLG: Dutch Guilders; USD: U.S. Dollars

branch in the United Kingdom. The bank's assets are concentrated in U.S., British, and German assets, due to the bank's marketing reach. Although the bank has credit capacity for other-country risk, most risk concentration is low in areas where the bank has poor marketing reach.

It may not be cost-effective to add marketing staff to attempt to generate assets in a variety of underconcentrated countries. One solution might be to offer credit default protection to other banks that are overconcentrated in those countries. Approaching regional banks in desirable countries is one way to diversify risk. The bank could offer credit default protection to banks in Holland, Belgium, France, and Switzerland on local assets.

Banks buy and sell credit risk. Banks lend money. Banks provide financing and make assumptions about the credit risk of their customers. This is the nature of what banks do. The buying and selling of credit risk between global banks is a natural extension of the banking business.

Another area in which banks can enhance business is in providing credit protection for credit exposures between banks and customers of banks. Banks often have unused exposure lines, which can be bought and sold. For instance, trade lines or exposures in interest-rate swaps can be exchanged between banks. Exposures on interest-rate swaps can be very large. Table 4.1 shows potential exposures and potential interest-rate line usage for U.S. dollar interest-rate swaps for various maturities.

Using this chart, how does one look up the exposure for a $100 million notional interest-rate swap in which a bank will pay the fixed rate and the counterparty will pay LIBOR? Looking down the column labeled "5 years" in which the bank pays fixed in an interest-rate swap, one can see that the maximum exposure (14.44) occurs in 2.5 years. This maximum exposure is read as a percent of the total swap notional amount. For a $100 million notional interest-rate swap, the peak exposure would be approximately $14,440,000. For a swap with a longer maturity, a 15-year swap, for instance, one would look down the column labeled "15 years" and read down the column for which the bank pays fixed in an interest-rate swap. The peak exposure (46.05) is in 8.5 years, and the total exposure is $46,050,000. The longer the maturity of the swap, the greater the exposure.

The exposure numbers tell us that we have a great deal of exposure to a counterparty in a long-dated swap and that we also have it for a long time. In addition, if the bank does a great deal of business with a counterparty, the accumulation of exposure, even for short-dated swaps, can quickly add up. One way to lay off some of this risk is to buy a credit exposure option.

TABLE 4.1 Credit Exposure for U.S. Dollar Interest-Rate Swaps, as of July 1997

Maturity	1 Year		5 Years		10 Years		15 Years	
Time	Fixed	Floating	Fixed	Floating	Fixed	Floating	Fixed	Floating
0	0.00	0.00	0.00	0.00	0.00	0.00	0.00	0.00
2 weeks	0.32	0.30	1.85	1.79	2.95	2.92	3.89	3.92
1 month	0.47	0.43	2.74	2.62	4.35	4.29	5.70	5.77
2 months	0.68	0.59	3.99	3.72	6.28	6.13	8.17	8.29
3 months	0.84	0.71	4.99	4.57	7.79	7.56	10.08	10.24
4 months	0.96	0.79	5.83	5.27	9.07	8.74	11.67	11.85
5 months	1.08	0.87	6.63	5.90	10.27	9.82	13.15	13.34
6 months	1.18	0.93	7.37	6.46	11.35	10.77	14.48	14.66
9 months	1.30	0.84	9.52	7.39	14.57	12.65	18.44	17.36
1.0 year	1.33	0.85	11.24	8.51	17.16	14.73	21.55	20.28
1.5 years	—	—	13.22	9.18	20.82	16.92	26.22	23.77
2.0 years	—	—	14.23	9.24	23.47	18.29	29.79	26.26
2.5 years	—	—	14.44	8.88	25.39	19.16	32.60	28.14
3.0 years	—	—	14.20	8.23	26.98	19.66	35.12	29.62
3.5 years	—	—	13.15	7.19	28.09	19.80	37.21	30.68
4.0 years	—	—	11.11	5.77	28.73	19.62	38.88	31.36
4.5 years	—	—	8.04	4.06	29.04	19.20	40.30	31.76
5.0 years	—	—	4.27	2.05	29.07	18.40	41.57	31.76
5.5 years	—	—	—	—	28.94	17.47	42.83	31.63
6.0 years	—	—	—	—	28.29	16.36	43.76	31.30
6.5 years	—	—	—	—	27.32	15.15	44.54	30.89
7.0 years	—	—	—	—	26.01	13.80	45.21	30.36
7.5 years	—	—	—	—	24.11	12.26	45.57	29.63
8.0 years	—	—	—	—	22.24	10.69	45.98	28.75
8.5 years	—	—	—	—	19.46	8.87	46.05	27.71
9.0 years	—	—	—	—	15.97	6.86	46.00	26.54
9.5 years	—	—	—	—	11.53	4.69	45.75	25.24
10.0 years	—	—	—	—	6.03	2.34	45.42	23.79
11.0 years	—	—	—	—	—	—	43.34	20.76
12.0 years	—	—	—	—	—	—	35.44	17.29
13.0 years	—	—	—	—	—	—	26.85	12.97
14.0 years	—	—	—	—	—	—	18.75	7.92
15.0 years	—	—	—	—	—	—	7.24	2.67

Conversely, if another bank wants to use some of the excess line capacity of another bank, it can purchase a credit exposure option. The credit exposure option is an exchange of a fee for a guarantee on the swap line credit exposure for a given transaction. Because these exposures may vary over time as market conditions and yield curves change, the credit exposure option can be linked to a given transaction. More simply, however, the credit exposure option can also be sold as exposure coverage for a fixed amount for a fixed time period. The latter method will cover a number of swaps to a given counterparty to provide a broader hedge for the swap line. In this way, a bank can avoid assigning a swap to another bank, which could make a counterparty aware of what it is doing and possibly damage a business relationship.

How much will banks charge each other for these credit exposure options? The answer depends on each individual bank's appetite for more business with a given counterparty. For instance, if bank A needs to free up swap lines so that it can provide an interest-rate swap linked to a profitable bond underwriting, it may be willing to pay more than the net spread earned on the interest-rate swap itself. Bank B, as provider of the exposure protection, will look at its opportunity cost of selling part of its swap line capacity to bank A. If bank B only does interest-rate-swap business with the counterparty, it should be happy to earn the swap spread plus a small fee for the potential—however small—shrinkage in its ability to do business with the client counterparty.

Another instance is one in which a bank wants to do lucrative business with a counterparty but has no credit line to the counterparty. Recently, a U.S. bank asked for credit exposure protection for a French bank that was an equity derivatives client. If the U.S. bank could offset the credit exposure risk of the French bank, it would earn 150 basis points on an equity derivatives transaction with the French bank. The total calculated exposure was a maximum of $50 million for one year. Normally, one would expect to earn a level commensurate with a commitment fee on an unfunded loan, which would be only 6 to 8 basis points in the Euromarket—hardly worth the trouble, given the number of banks wanting to offset risk in their unprofitable European loan portfolios. Because the equity derivatives specialist was in great need of locating a hedge for the credit risk, however, the specialist paid 25 basis points for the credit hedge. The U.S. bank used a credit derivative to facilitate a profitable equity derivative transaction, and the provider of the credit protection earned a spread on its credit line that was unattainable in the conventional market.

As banks review their concentration of credit risk in portfolios, they may do swaps of credit risks in which banks offer an exchange of default protection. This is under discussion with several large commercial banks in the United States; and in the future, bank portfolio managers may routinely swap credit risks in a growing interbank market.

Figure 4.4 illustrates an example of a credit event exchange swap. Two banks, the U.S. branch of a European bank and a U.S. bank, wish to free up credit lines on their balance sheets. As in the previous example, the two banks may want to increase their capacity to lend money to these credits or to participate in loan syndications or revolvers. The two banks agree to exchange credit risks. The credit event can be defined as an undrawn revolver becoming drawn. In the case in which the U.S. bank holds the drawn revolver, one of two things can happen: (1) The U.S. bank can deliver the drawn revolver to the European bank and take delivery by assignment of the undrawn revolver owned by the European bank, as shown in Figure 4.5. (2) The U.S. bank can deliver the drawn revolver and begin receiving a credit protection fee for the as-yet-undrawn revolver held by the European bank, as shown in Figure 4.6.

The major challenge that banks face to the efficient management of exposures is bank managers. I once lost a deal when a AAA/AA+ rated U.S. bank gave me an exclusive to consider selling credit protection on a pool of letters of credit (LOCs) having underlying U.S. corporates with an average rating of single A. The average life of the pool of LOCs was 8.5 months. All of the final maturities were under one year. The pool's notional size was more than $1 billion. The proposed fee was 12 basis points per annum. At the same time, the bank for which I was working was trying to sell $30 million of loan risk on a single-A corporate name. The maturity was two

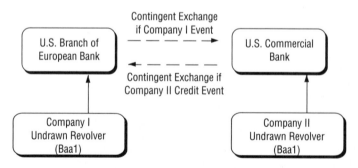

The U.S. Branch of the European Bank and the U.S. Bank swap credit risks with no up-front or ongoing exchange of payments. An exchange occurs only if there is a Credit Event.

FIGURE 4.4   Exchange of Credit Event Protection

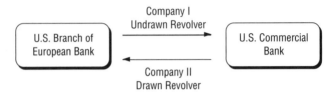

The U.S. Branch of the European Bank and the U.S. Bank swap the drawn and undrawn revolvers. The exchange occurs only if there is a Credit Event.

FIGURE 4.5 Exchange of Credit Event Protection Workout, Method One

years, and we proposed paying 12 basis points to purchase protection for our risk. Note that the maturity was more than a year longer than the risk we were being asked to take on board.

Because the bank did not wish to take on more category I (loan and LOC exposure) at the time, we turned down more than $850 thousand in fees on very short dated risk. Fee income was not the real issue here. We didn't object to the level; we didn't attempt to negotiate for a higher fee; we didn't even consider the fee. The fact of the matter was that we were a seller of risk, and we were a buyer of credit protection. We were not a buyer of risk; we were not a seller of credit protection. We did not even consider the alternative idea of identifying exposures we wanted to sell and swapping them for the exposures the U.S. bank wanted to sell.

This is typical of banks starting out in the credit derivatives market. The market is one way. Bank managers are quite happy to sell their exposure,

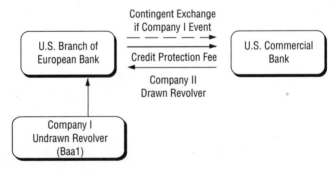

The U.S. Bank delivers the drawn revolver to the European Bank. The European Bank begins paying a credit protection fee on its undrawn revolver to the U.S. Bank.

FIGURE 4.6 Exchange of Credit Event Protection Workout, Method Two

but not to purchase exposure. The demand for credit protection outstrips the supply. Reasons cited include spread (but as I mentioned, that is not the key issue), the fact that we are not doing "relationship" business when earning fees off balance sheet, and the fact that multiple credit managers must be consulted when more than one credit is considered.

It is difficult for banks to make a decision, at least initially, to take on a large exposure, even when it makes good business sense. Mental kluge sets in.

The head of credit derivatives at a U.S. bank expressed a similar frustration to me. She said that the bank would readily book low-fee loans, citing relationship building, but wouldn't do more profitable credit derivatives business because it is off balance sheet. She put it this way: "We're in the business of taking on risk for the wrong fee for future business we're never going to get." She coined this amusing exaggeration to make a point. There is no reason to leave good money on the table when often the premise of lending is a false one. Often there is no future business garnered by the bank. But that isn't the main issue here, as the credit derivatives head also pointed out.

Banks are in the business of buying and selling risk. The management of balance sheet risk via the credit derivatives market cannot be a one-way market. Banks need to sell risk and banks need to buy risk. The petrified mind-set of having one-way market risk and failure to use corporate credit lines other than to make direct loans will necessarily change over time. A large part of the future flow business in the credit derivatives market will be driven by large credit line swaps in the credit derivatives market.

CALLABLE STEP-UPS

The callable step-up structure is a balance sheet transaction designed to reduce regulatory capital requirements. This credit derivative transaction opportunity was popular for large commercial banks in the late 1990s and may enjoy resurgence in popularity as more banks feel the pressures of regulatory capital constraints. Participants who sell credit protection usually book income in their credit derivatives trading books where returns on both regulatory and economic capital look attractive. The following example illustrates the motivation of both the buyer and the seller of credit default protection in a callable step-up structure:

Example: You are the risk manager for a Japanese bank. Your bank has accumulated a $3 billion position in loans to several investment-grade U.S. corporations. The per annum coupon on these loans averages LIBOR + 25 basis points. You wish to reduce the regulatory capital required for this position and thus report a higher return on capital for year-end reporting purposes. You feel that buying a credit default option from a bank would reduce your required regulatory capital from 100 percent to 20 percent and that your return on capital would increase fivefold. You wish to purchase the default protection for a short period of time, ideally just over your quarter-end, so that you can pay the smallest possible premium for this protection.

You are faced with a dilemma. Most of the loans have maturities of five or more years. Although there are no explicitly stated guidelines, you believe the Japanese Ministry of Finance (MOF) will not recognize a regulatory capital reduction unless the credit default protection is purchased for the maturity of the underlying asset. What do you do?

Suggestion: The Callable Step-Up structure was designed in response to this dilemma. It works as follows: The Japanese bank purchases protection for three months at an agreed premium for this initial time period. The premium for this initial period is in the neighborhood of the return on the underlying assets. The market usually commands a slight premium to the three-month implied yield of the underlying loans, chiefly due to supply and demand but also due to documentation and regulatory risk. After the initial period of three months, the premium steps up dramatically. This gives the Japanese bank a compelling economic incentive to call back the risk, thereby terminating the contract. In this way, the seller of the protection is reasonably certain that the Japanese bank will terminate the contract. If for some reason the Japanese bank does not terminate the contract, the protection stepped-up premium is large enough to satisfy the protection seller's internal approval board that they are getting a superior deal for the potential use of their credit lines. Based on the given pricing, a protection seller might pay approximately 5 to 6 bps flat (20 to 24 bps per annum) for the first 90-day period. Thereafter the premium would step up to 100 bps or 125 bps per annum unless the protection seller terminated the transaction at the end of the 90-day period.

Deals in the market place have been for time periods as short as a week. Initial premiums have been as low as 2 basis points with a step up to several hundred basis points if the deal isn't terminated at the end of the week. Although 2 basis points doesn't sound like much, on an annualized basis a protection seller with a funding cost of LIBOR flat is earning much more than the net 25 basis points on the underlying asset. Because these deals are usually done for $1 billion to $3 billion, the fee income is worth the trouble of the detailed documentation required for a successful deal.

Typically, underlying assets for these transactions have been U.S., investment-grade, corporate-unfunded commitments. Ratings are generally BBB or better, with an average rating of A to A–. The maturity of the reference obligations is usually approximately five years. Potential protection sellers usually are asked to sign a confidentiality agreement before they can examine the underlying reference credits.

The motive of the protection buyer is to reduce U.S., investment-grade, corporate credit exposure reported in their U.S. Federal Reserve Board (Fed) call reports over a quarter-end. This reduces regulatory capital requirements for the commitments.

The notional size varies but is typically $2 billion to $3 billion, with each reference credit approximately $25 million to $100 million in size. The deal should be structured so the protection buyer must pay all protection premiums at the beginning of each relevant protection period. Therefore, the protection seller has no credit risk to the protection buyer.

The protection seller assumes the credit default risk of the underlying unfunded commitments of the U.S., investment-grade, corporate obligors. The protection seller is not responsible for funding. The protection buyer assumes responsibility for funding of commitments, if any. Funding of an unfunded commitment would *not* be a credit-event trigger. A credit default event would occur only if a commitment funds *and* there is failure to pay.

There is no balance sheet impact for the protection seller. Exposure is usually footnoted. If the protection seller were a U.S. bank, regulatory capital as reported in the Fed call reports would increase by 4 percent times the notional amount of the transaction.

The protection seller usually increases credit exposure to the reference obligors by the full notional amount of the unfunded exposures. For the short time periods involved, this is usually not a problem. The legal lending limit of the protection seller is unaffected as long as the credit default option remains unexercised.

Many banks acting as protection sellers view this transaction as similar to a standby letter of credit. They would hold regulatory capital of 8 percent on the notional amount of both unfunded and funded (if any) assets in the transaction. For example, if the protection seller earns 5 bps for a 90-day period, the return on regulatory capital for the initial 90-day period would be approximately 0.625 percent for the 90-day period, or approximately 2.5 percent on a per annum basis.

There is no market consensus on how to calculate the rate of return on economic capital for these transactions. Ideally, one would calculate the credit exposure for the investment credits for a 90-day period (a very small number) and from that the required economic capital required and a return on economic capital.

One approach is to consider the return on capital without accounting for expenses or taxes based on internal-bank-developed economic capital factors. Internal capital charges vary widely from bank to bank, so it is difficult to generalize. For example, assume the economic capital factor required for an unfunded commitment is 0.29 percent, and the operating capital factor for a derivatives transaction is 0.486 applied directly to revenues. If the protection seller earns 5 bps for a 90-day period, the return on capital is 15.9 percent for the 90-day period, or approximately 63.63 percent on a pretax, preexpense annualized basis. This estimate is pretaxes and preexpenses. The protection seller could then factor in expenses for its credit derivatives operations and compare the result with its internal pretax, *post*expense hurdle rate on an annualized basis.

This transaction has further challenges. It is extremely difficult to determine a fair price on very short dated credit risk. Assume KMV shows a one-year probability of default of around 0.15 percent. A protection seller might translate this to an estimated probability of default (EDF). Assume a median EDF of 11 bps, or 0.11 percent. The premium for the first 90 days of the structure is 5 to 6 bps for 90 days, or about 20 to 24 bps per annum. Theoretically the premium more than covers the likely default risk as reflected by EDF.

But there is a problem. Assume that the five-year and one-year probabilities of default for the credits are on average 0.17 percent and 0.15 percent, respectively. The probability of default for the 90-day period is probably lower than the one-year rate of 0.15 percent, but it is difficult to exactly determine how much lower. Martha Seller at KMV commented on this. KMV points out they really do not know anything about 30-, 60-, or 90-day default probabilities; there just isn't enough default data. There are few observations of default (roughly 15 in 10,000 for a one-year time period). A reasonable approach might be to assume that it is a function of the square root of time, so one might expect that the 90-day probability of default is *higher* than one-quarter of 0.15 percent. On the other hand, there is no evidence that credit default probabilities vary with the square root of time. It is simply a convenient fiction. Although this might be allowed for investment-grade credits, for noninvestment-grade credits this is actually a dangerous and usually false assumption. To date, I don't know of any agreed method to estimate default probabilities for short discrete time periods.

Nonetheless, using a common sense approach, JP Morgan, Citibank, Deutsche Morgan Grenfell, Svenska Handelsbanken, Wachovia (to a more limited extent), Toronto Dominion, and CIBC, among others, have been participants in these transactions.

Participants in these transactions view the income as more than fair compensation for their assessment of the risk. These transactions are booked in credit derivatives trading books, and the regulatory and capital charges are much smaller when viewed from the perspective of the trading book as opposed to the bank book. Most of these competitors use a value-at-risk (VAR) model, or a modified VAR model. The corresponding return on capital for both regulatory and economic capital is much higher for the trading book than comparable calculations made for the bank book.

Protection sellers must decide whether they want to participate in transactions that are motivated by regulatory capital management to enhance reported performance over quarter-end or year-end reporting periods. Suitability is usually an internal bank decision.

SYNTHETIC LENDING FACILITIES

Synthetic lending facilities (SLFs) are often used to describe loan total rate of return swaps. More typically, SLFs refer to forward commitments to purchase revolvers and loans. Investors can gain exposure to credits that otherwise would be unavailable.

Maturity, fees, and sometimes credit enhancements can be customized. For example, an investor can synthetically create a participation in an unfunded revolving loan. As long as the loan remains unfunded, the investor receives a commitment fee. If the loan remains unfunded throughout the period of the SLF agreement, the investor's commitment terminates or converts into a term loan at the option of the borrower. If the unfunded commitment converts into a term loan, it converts at a predetermined credit spread agreed on at the start of the transaction.

Investors receive a fee for providing—via an asset swap transaction—a forward commitment to purchase a security. This is not the same transaction as a credit default swap. In this transaction, the trigger event is not a default. The trigger event is usually the funding of the revolver. The investor does not make a termination payment if a funding event occurs. The investor allows the borrower to convert to a term loan at a predetermined credit spread.

The synthetic credit facility (SCF) is the sister product to the synthetic lending facility. SCFs are sometimes used for general debt obligations. For instance, a German bank currently participates in an SCF linked to the debt obligations of the Republic of Ireland, rated AA. The German bank earns 4 basis points per annum. In exchange, the German bank's counterparty has the right to put Irish debt obligations to the German bank for a period of three years. This is an American-style put, exercisable at any time over the three-year period. The debt obligations can have a final maturity no longer than 2007, and the level at which the counterparty can put the obligations is LIBOR + 8 bps. The German bank feels that LIBOR + 8 bps for the zero percent, Bank for International Settlements (BIS), risk-weighted obligations of Ireland is a fair level. Meanwhile, the German bank earns 4 basis points just for standing by to purchase something it is happy to own at a price at which it is happy to own it. The counterparty has an outlet for its Irish government risk at a price of 4 basis points per annum.

GEARED DEFAULT OPTIONS

Many banks, reaching for more fee income, will accept a geared, or leveraged, credit default structure. This structure has enjoyed popularity in the

United Kingdom and Asia in particular. These structures are sometimes confused with basket structures, which we discuss later. Geared structures are linked to only one name credit risk. If credit default occurs, however, the seller of the default protection pays a multiple of the loss.

One AA rated bank provided a geared credit default swap for a five-year maturity on an unfunded Philip Morris loan. Instead of earning the expected fee of 25 basis points for a five-year maturity credit default swap, the AA bank earned a fee of 40 basis points. The loss severity would be twice the default loss exposure. The bank that hedged its Philip Morris position reduced the Philip Morris exposure by $20 million and took exposure to the AA rated bank for only $10 million, the notional amount of the geared credit default swap, albeit leveraged to hedge the loss of $20 million worth of the Philip Morris loan. The AA bank had the view that the Philip Morris credit would improve rather than decline. Both banks felt they were better off in this transaction.

We look at credit-linked notes in more detail in Chapter 6, but at least one structure is worth mentioning now. The following term sheet shows a three-year maturity credit-linked note linked to Mexican sovereign credit risk. Note the boldface type, which highlights some key points.

MEXICO CREDIT-LINKED NOTE
Indicative Term Sheet

Issuer:	AA rated European bank, Indonesian branch.
Investment Amount:	USD 5 million.
Calculation Amount:	USD 5 million.
Trade Date:	To be determined.
Issue Date:	Trade date plus three weeks.
Maturity Date:	The earlier of:
	1. issue date + three years, *or*
	2. early termination date, if any.
Interest Payments:	**Six-month USD LIBOR + 215%** paid semiannually on an Act/360 basis modified following with no adjustment for period end dates.

(continued)

Interest Payment Dates:

Semiannually. If a credit event occurs, accrued interest will not be paid.

Redemption Amount:

The note will be redeemed at 100 percent of the investment amount on the scheduled maturity date provided that a credit event with respect to the reference credit has not occurred on or prior to such date; provided, however, that if a credit event with respect to the reference credit has occurred on or prior to such date, the note will be redeemed on the early termination date by **delivery of a portfolio of securities selected from the list of reference obligations. The amount of securities will be such that the current market value is equal to the cash redemption amount. The calculation agent will determine the composition of such portfolio.** The issuer or any of its affiliates will make the delivery of such portfolio.

Cash Redemption Amount =
Face Amount of Reference Security
× MV − Hedge Costs

where MV equals the market value of the relevant reference security on the notification date.

Hedge costs are the sum of the mark-to-market value of the swap that swaps fixed-rate cash flows to floating-rate cash flows that are paid on the note *plus* the product of 30 percent and the calculation amount.

Early Termination Date:

In the event that a credit event occurs during the term of the transaction, the issuer shall have the right to designate an early termination date that is not less than 10 business days from the delivery of notice to the investor of the occurrence of the credit event.

Credit Event:

The occurrence of any of the following events with respect to the reference credit:

1. The reference credit fails to make when due any payment under any financial obligation, and such failure continues for more than 10 days.

2. A default, event of default, or other similar condition or event occurs in respect of such reference credit under any financial obligation that has resulted in such financial obligation becoming, or being capable at such time of being declared, due and payable before it otherwise would have become due and payable.

3. A waiver, deferral, restructuring, rescheduling, exchange, or other adjustment occurs in respect of any financial obligation, and the effect of such adjustment is overall materially less favorable from a credit and risk perspective to the relevant creditor.

Reference Credit:	United Mexican States (UMS).
Reference Security:	United Mexican States, global bond.
	Maturity: February 6, 2001.
	Currency Denomination: USD.
	Coupon: 9.75%.
	Face Amount: USD 6.5 million (Calculation Amount × 1.3).
Financial Obligation:	With respect to the reference credit, *any financial obligation in an aggregate amount of not less than the threshold amount incurred by the reference credit in any capacity.*
Threshold Amount:	**USD 3 million.**
Market Value:	On any day, with respect to the relevant reference security, the percentage equal to the unweighted arithmetic mean of the bid prices

(continued)

	(expressed as a percentage of principal amount and exclusive of any accrued but unpaid interest) for such reference security provided to the calculation agent on such day by at least two but not more than five dealers in the market for such reference security; **provided, however, that if only one or if no such bid prices are so provided, the market value shall mean the market value as determined by the calculation agent.**
Reference Obligations:	UMS 9.75% of February 6, 2001.
	UMS FRN of February 6, 2001.
	UMS 9.875% of July 15, 2007.
	UMS 11.375% of September 15, 2016.
	UMS 11.5% of May 15, 2026.
	In addition, if in the future the reference credit issues obligations that rank equal in priority of payment with the above list of reference obligations, then those obligations will be included in the list of reference obligations.
Business Days:	**Days on which commercial banks and foreign exchange markets settle payments in Tokyo, London, New York, Labuan, and Mexico City.**
Calculation Agent:	**AA or better rated European bank, Indonesian branch (the issuer).**

At first this appears to be very similar to the other term sheets we have seen. The issuer, a AA rated bank, would otherwise have paid about 200 basis points per annum for protection. The investor is purchasing a note issued by a AA European bank branch—one that has the same credit standing as the main bank. The bank would normally fund at around LIBOR – 25 bps—but the investor should disregard this. The credit risk is Mexican sovereign credit risk, not the credit risk of the AA rated issuer. The bank should not get a discount for its Mexican protection just because it lends its name, and only its name, to the issuance of a credit-linked note with underlying Mexican sovereign risk. But it appears this has been taken into account. The issuer is not getting a discount. In fact, at first glance it appears the bank may be paying the full offer side of the market, perhaps even a bit more. The bank is paying a coupon of LIBOR + 215 bps.

Caveat emptor: Let the buyer beware.

BASIS RISK: DELIVERY, HEDGE COSTS, AND CALCULATIONS

This brings us back to the sections in boldface type. Eight key points create value for the issuer of the credit-linked note but are potentially to the advantage of the issuer and not the investor:

1. The calculation agent is the issuer of the note.
2. The issuer has the right to deliver any one of several securities with various maturities in the event of default. The calculation agent, the issuer, determines the composition of the portfolio.
3. The issuer has the right to add more securities to the list of deliverable securities if Mexico issues more obligations in equal rank to the reference obligations.
4. The value of the delivered securities must be equal to the cash redemption amount. The issuer has the final say in the determination of the value of the delivered securities. If only one or if no bid prices are available with which to determine market value, the calculation agent, the issuer, determines the market value of the securities in the issuer-designated portfolio.
5. Default means default on *any financial obligation of Mexico incurred in any capacity* not less than the threshold amount.
6. The threshold amount is only $3 million.
7. The materiality clause is absent.
8. The usual cash redemption amount is reduced by *hedge costs*. The calculation agent, the issuer, determines the value of the hedge costs.

By now it is easy to see that there are several new key issues we have not seen before. In fact, only the first key issue, the issuer as calculation agent, is one we have seen before. Using the issuer as calculation agent is quite usual. This is fine as long as the investor has some objective recourse for the note calculations and as long as the investor has some remedies if the investor feels the calculations are arbitrarily disadvantageous. But that is not the case here. Let us examine this in more detail.

The calculation redemption amount is calculated using the defaulted market value of the United Mexican States 9.75 percent of 2001. This is not what the investor will necessarily receive in the event of default, however. The calculation agent, the issuer, can deliver securities ranging in maturity from the year 2001 to the year 2026. In a default situation, prices on several securities may not be readily available, especially for longer-dated securities. Further, the pricing may be more volatile for longer-dated maturities. A number of factors contribute to this. One is the uncertainty of what may happen in a workout situation with longer-dated paper. There may be restructuring of longer-dated securities, whereas shorter-dated paper may be paid down at least partially. Longer-dated paper with the loss of a long coupon stream may trade at deeper discounts and experience price volatility for a small change in rates, similar to a zero-coupon bond, while speculation rages over whether the sovereign will resume payments or restructure its debt.

The investor should not be indifferent to the composition of the portfolio of securities. Furthermore, as more Mexican debt is issued with the same credit standing as the reference pool of securities, the issuer can add these securities to the list. The investor, however, has no choice. Worse, the investor has no recourse other than an expensive and difficult-to-win after-the-fact litigation if the investor is unhappy with the final result.

Not only does the investor not have the right to choose or to veto deliverable securities, the investor does not have the right to designate a disinterested third party to oversee the process. The same is true of pricing. In the event of default, it would not be surprising if one or more of the reference pool securities had no bid. This leaves the investor at the mercy of the issuer to determine the price of the reference pool securities. In that instance, the market value would be whatever the issuer says it is. In this way, the issuer can potentially manipulate the cash redemption amount owed the investor. From the investor's point of view, this is a potentially dangerous situation.

Of course, neither the investor nor the issuer believes that Mexico will default within three years on its sovereign debt obligations. I don't believe that will happen, either. The investor certainly would not enter into this transaction if the investor thought Mexico would default on one of its sovereign obligations.

But wait just a minute! The reference credit is the United Mexican States. The reference security for purposes of calculation of the cash redemption amount is the UMS 9.75 percent of 2001. The reference credit for purposes of defining the default event, however, is *any financial obligation of Mexico with a value no lower than $3 million.* Notice that this is the lowest threshold value we have seen so far. This means any obligation that ranks in seniority with the UMS global debt, even over-the-counter transactions, could potentially be cited for a default event. The conveniently low threshold makes it even easier for the issuer to declare a default event. Easier still is the complete absence of any materiality clause. The materiality clause is meant to avoid spurious declarations of default events when there may be merely a legitimate dispute over a payment. For a sovereign, a dispute amounting to only $3 million leaves room for a declaration of a default event even when the principal and interest payments on global debt are not in jeopardy.

We saw some potential problems in the calculation of the cash redemption amount owed to the investor in the form of the determination of the market value and the determination of the market value of the reference securities that can be delivered in satisfaction of the cash redemption amount. Looking back, we see the following:

$$\text{Cash Redemption Amount} = \text{Face Amount of Reference Security} \times \text{MV} - \textit{Hedge Costs}$$

There is more to this formula than the previous formulas we have examined. There are other problems as well, from the point of view of the investor. For example, there is the little matter of subtracting off the hedge costs.

Hedge costs? This is the first time we have seen hedge costs thrown into a redemption amount calculation. There are two components to the hedge cost calculation, as previously discussed. The hedge costs is the sum of (1) the mark-to-market value of the swap that swaps fixed-rate cash flows to floating-rate cash flows that are paid on the note and (2) 30 percent of the calculation amount.

In the first component of the hedge cost calculation, the issuer is asking the investor to bear the brunt of the mark-to-market value of an interest-rate swap in which fixed-rate cash flows are swapped to a floating-rate coupon. That doesn't sound unreasonable. The swap is a fixed-dollar for a floating-dollar swap. After all, a swap can have a gain as well as a loss in the event of default, depending on prevailing market conditions in the U.S.

interest-rate market unrelated to a Mexican default. This is possible, but in
the case of this particular swap, not probable. The reason is that the reference bond is originally trading above par, and the coupon on the bond is
higher than the prevailing fixed-rate market. The fixed payment owed on
the interest-rate swap is well above market. Therefore, it is very likely, even
if there has been a substantial rise in U.S. interest rates, that the mark-to-
market value of the swap will be against the investor. According to the payoff
structures discussed earlier, the investor is essentially giving the issuer a payoff
based on the initial price, an above par price, instead of a par minus market
value structure. The hedge costs compensate the issuer for the initial price
risk of the reference security plus swap package. This is fine, provided the
investor realizes that the implied payoff formula is essentially a payoff based
on a premium price for the reference asset, as the premium price of the
reference asset is imbedded in the swap payments. In addition, the investor
is also hedging for market risk on the swap. Nowhere is this clarified in the
term sheet, so the investor must be clear on the initial cash flows of the
transaction. How many investors actually look at this and are capable of
pricing the value?

The second component of the hedge cost calculation is more subtle. The
issuer subtracts 30 percent of $5 million from the cash redemption amount.
At first this seems reasonable, given that the cash redemption amount calculation includes the face amount of the reference security. The face amount
of the reference security, we recall, is as follows:

$$\text{Calculation Amount} \times 1.3 = \$5,000,000 \times 1.3 = \$6,500,000$$

The 30 percent differences should offset one another—or do they? A
closer look shows us they do not. Whether by omission or by design, the
only reference to the calculation amount in the term sheet is in the definition
of the face amount, which leaves us to imply a value of $5 million for the
calculation amount. In the cash redemption amount, we must first multiply
this number by the market value of the reference security (either the UMS
9.75 percent of 2001 or an appropriate substitute) and then subtract off the
hedge costs.

Notice that no matter what the market value of the UMS reference
security is, we are always subtracting off a fixed value of:

$$\$5,000,000 \times 30\% = \$1,500,000$$

The investor should insist that instead of subtracting off a fixed amount, the face amount of the reference security should equal $5 million, the calculation amount, in the cash redemption amount calculation.

How much can this potentially hurt the investor? Let us take a look at some sample calculations assuming market values of 40, 60, and 80 for the UMS reference security, and let us ignore the mark-to-market on the swap, setting this to zero for now. If we compare the cash redemption amount calculation as it now stands in the term sheet with the suggested revisions, we see the following results:

Cash Redemption Amount Difference Using Term Sheet Formula versus Revised Formula (Setting swap mark-to-market to zero)

	Market Value of Reference Security		
	40	60	80
Term Sheet Amount	$1,100,000	$2,400,000	$3,700,000
Suggested Revision Amount	$2,000,000	$3,000,000	$4,000,000
Difference	($900,000)	($600,000)	($300,000)
Percentage of Initial Investment	(18%)	(12%)	(6%)

The difference in cash redemption amount is significant. If after a default event the market value of the UMS global bond drops to 40, the investor's cash redemption amount is $900,000 lower than by using the suggested revised formula. That is a difference of 18 percent of the initial investment amount. Even at a price of 60, the difference between the two formulas is 12 percent of the initial investment amount. The lower the market values, the greater the difference in the calculated amounts. This kicks the investor when he or she is down. It may not even have been the intention of the issuer to create this anomalous result, but under the term sheet conditions, the formula works to the advantage of the issuer and not the investor. So it is up to potential investors to ask for clarification and modifications to the term sheet if there is any doubt.

If that weren't bad enough, there is also the matter of the swap mark-to-market, which we temporarily set to zero for purposes of the preceding calculations. This can also be a significant number. Because the swap coupon payment is an off-market coupon payment, the mark-to-market value could be over 10 percent of the $5 million notional amount, or an additional $500,000. Let us plug in this number and see how much that changes the difference:

Cash Redemption Amount Difference Using Term Sheet Formula versus Revised Formula (Setting swap mark-to-market to $500,000)

	Market Value of Reference Security		
	40	60	80
Term Sheet Amount	$600,000	$1,900,000	$3,200,000
Suggested Revision Amount	$2,000,000	$3,000,000	$4,000,000
Difference	($1,400,000)	($1,100,000)	($800,000)
Percentage of Initial Investment	(28%)	(22%)	(16%)

The swap mark-to-market can be lower than $500,000, of course, depending on the time remaining to the maturity of the swap and on the prevailing market conditions. I am using this number as an illustration without calculating sensitivities. The point is, however, that investors need not suffer the swap mark-to-market at all unless they are getting compensated for the risk. At the levels offered in this particular credit-linked note, however, that additional risk does not seem to be factored in to the spread offered to the investor.

This particular credit-linked note looks as if it is a geared structure offering a slightly above-market spread. If fact, the coupon offered is just about at the market. The term sheet is rife with hidden risks to the investor. The term sheet seems unclear on terms such as calculation amount, and the term sheet interpretation does not work in favor of the investor. Investors must carefully examine terms and conditions and ask for modifications to term sheet language. If necessary, investors may wish to restate calculations and to ask for different pricing if they find they are taking more imbedded risk than they realized at first glance. Further, investors must carefully scrutinize confirmation language to make sure it agrees with the terms and conditions as they understand them.

Unfortunately, the credit derivatives market is flooded with this kind of paper, and most of it is offered in the Asian markets, where there seems to be less regulatory scrutiny of structured product. It is this kind of structure that gives derivatives market professionals a bad name. I don't think it is an accident that this particular note was offered to a Japanese leasing company.

Japanese leasing companies are looking for securities with high spreads because their funding costs are high, in the area of LIBOR + 100 bps. The AAA issuer credit makes it appear, for booking purposes, as if the creditworthiness of the offered security is also high. Unfortunately, this investor base is also new to the credit derivatives market and less sensitive to the subtleties of structures. My intention is not to characterize Japanese leasing companies as victims, but rather to point out that any investor lured by high yield should take a hard look at a deal that appears to be too good to be true. As the saying goes, it usually is.

BASKET CREDIT DEFAULT SWAPS

Just as a portfolio manager can purchase protection on a single credit, a portfolio manager can purchase protection on a basket of credits. If a portfolio manager chooses four credits with an asset value of $100 million each, the portfolio manager can purchase credit protection in a first-to-default structure. For example, if one of the credits experiences default on any of its debt, which remains uncured for five business days, the credit default swap terminates. The default protection seller will pay $100 million to the portfolio manager, who will deliver to the default protection seller the asset of the credit that has experienced the credit default event.

One can think of the first-to-default basket structure as similar to a senior/subordinated collateralized bond obligation (CBO) or as a senior/subordinated collateralized loan obligation (CLO). The credit default protection seller is like an investor in the subordinated tranche of a CBO or a CLO. The default protection seller takes the risk of the first loss in the structure. The remaining credits in the basket are similar to the senior tranche of a CBO or a CLO. The holder of these remaining credits, the senior position, has been protected from the first loss by the default protection seller, the holder of the subordinate position.

Although this comparison is often made in the marketplace, there are very important differences between first-to-default baskets and senior or subordinated CBOs and CLOs. The risk of the default protection seller is an off–balance sheet risk as opposed to an on–balance sheet risk for the buyer of a subordinated tranche of a CBO or a CLO. Furthermore, the default protection seller does not invest capital but earns a fee. It is also important to note that the assets that compose a first-to-default basket are generally small in number and not necessarily well diversified. The construction of a first-to-default basket does not meet the same rigorous tests that rated CBOs and CLOs must meet in determining the composition of assets, which make up the collateral for these instruments.

The following abbreviated term sheet has simplified terms for a basket credit default swap referencing three credits.

BASKET CREDIT DEFAULT SWAP
Indicative Term Sheet

Default Protection Buyer:	Portfolio manager.
Default Protection Seller:	Default protection seller.
Reference Credits:	Issuer Maturity.
	Merita Bank (A2) June 2004.
	Philip Morris (Moody's A2) September 2004.
	IcelandAir (NR) February 2005.
Calculation Amounts:	Merita Bank USD 25 million.
	Philip Morris USD 25 million.
	IcelandAir USD 25 million.
Trade Date:	To be determined.
Effective Date:	One week after the trade date.
Maturity Dates:	Five years after the effective date.
Notional Amount:	USD 25 million.
Adjusted Notional Amount:	If any of the issuers prepays an underlying loan, another loan of a maturity not longer than seven years from the effective date may be substituted for the relevant credit. If none is available, the notional principal will be reduced on the next payment date to reflect the lowest outstanding value of the remaining loans.
Credit Default Fee:	Portfolio manager will pay to the default protection seller a fee of 30 basis points per an-

	num on an actual/360-day basis on a notional amount of USD 25 million.
Termination Payment:	If there is a credit event, the credit default protection seller will pay the notional amount to the portfolio manager. The portfolio manager will deliver the underlying credit asset for the credit that experienced the credit event with a face value equal to the notional amount. If there is no credit event up to and including the maturity of the basket credit default swap, the credit default protection seller makes no payments.
Credit Event:	A filing for bankruptcy protection by any one of the underlying credit issuers or a payment default on any debt that remains uncured for five business days.

There is something different and unique about basket credit default swaps, which we have not seen before. Figure 4.7 shows the exchange of

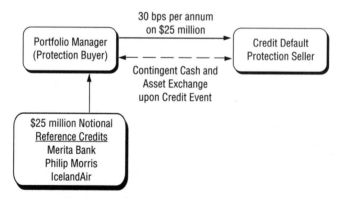

An Institution receives a 20-basis-point fee in return for making a Contingent Payment if a predefined Credit Event occurs to one of the credits.

FIGURE 4.7   Basket Credit Default Swap

contingent and actual flows in such a swap. If there is a credit event on one of the reference credits, for instance, Philip Morris, the portfolio manager delivers the underlying Philip Morris asset and receives the notional amount of $25 million (if there have been no notional amount adjustments) from the default protection seller. The swap then terminates, and the portfolio manager remains unhedged on the remaining credits, Merita Bank and IcelandAir. The termination payment is then as shown in Figure 4.8. The portfolio manager either can purchase default protection separately on the remaining assets or can reform a new basket, possibly adding more uncorrelated credits.

Because of this contingency, in which a portfolio manager is left with unhedged assets, the strategy of the composition of the basket is very important. Basket structures are generally best suited for investment-grade credits with low correlations and low covariance. It is generally best to use credit risks with similar credit ratings as well. Otherwise, a very weak credit risk would dominate the basket pricing, and one would have to question the value of the hedge on the stronger credits. Low correlation between the basket credits and the default protection seller is obviously another important constraint. If the default protection seller were highly correlated with the credits in the basket, the value of the "protection" would be open to ques-

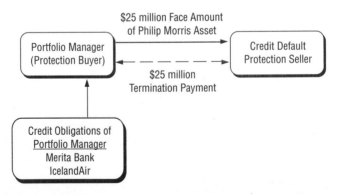

If the Notional Amount has not been reduced and Philip Morris defaults on any of its obligations, the Credit Default Protection Seller accepts delivery of the Philip Morris Reference Credit versus delivery of $25 million to the Portfolio Manager. The Basket Swap terminates with no further obligation by either party.

FIGURE 4.8 Basket Credit Default Swap Termination if Philip Morris Defaults

tion. If the creator of the basket follows these guidelines, the likelihood of multiple defaults declines.

Why not use uncorrelated high-yield, or "junk," bonds? There is nothing wrong with this strategy, if one can tolerate potential problems. If a portfolio manager uses high-yield debt, even uncorrelated names might result in a basket in which two names default within a short time of each other. This is because the probability of default matters. The probability of default of high-yield bonds is generally higher than that for investment-grade debt, and two uncorrelated credits may experience a coincident (or nearby time frame) default. Even if high-yield bonds don't experience actual coincident default, a couple of credits may have deteriorated to the point where they are unsuitable for another basket and the individual cost of a hedge is prohibitive.

The probability of default of investment-grade credits is generally much lower than for high-yield bonds, as we saw earlier. If one investment-grade credit defaults, it is very likely a portfolio manager can repurchase protection on the remaining viable names at a cost-effective level. The remaining credits are very likely to be suitable as components of a new basket or as an individual credit default swap.

The credit event on a basket of loans can be defined as bankruptcy, restructuring, default on an obligation in excess of a threshold level, failure to meet financial covenants, adverse change in a credit spread greater than a preagreed amount, or a ratings downgrade below a prespecified rating. These events are included in the criteria discussed earlier.

Default payments are generally structured as payment versus delivery of the defaulted credit asset (as we saw earlier) or as cash settlement. Cash settlement is usually the notional amount (or original price minus default price times the notional amount) minus the market value of the asset whose credit is in default as determined by a dealer poll, or cash settlement based on a preagreed fixed percentage of the notional amount.

PRICING BASKET CREDIT DEFAULT SWAPS

How does one price a basket credit default swap? Basket credit default pricing is subject to the same challenges we discussed earlier. We can, however, get an intuitive feel of the boundary conditions that occur in a public well-traded market.

Let us take a general cash settlement example of three uncorrelated investment-grade credits, W, X, and Y, each with a $25 million notional amount. In the basket first-to-default structure, if one of the credits defaults, the protection seller's cash payment is $25 million × (Original Price – Recovery Value) on the defaulted credit. After that, the protection seller has no obligation whatsoever.

Let us assume that of the three credits, W, X, and Y, we intuitively know that the upper bound would be the sum of the premiums of credit default protection on W, X, and Y. We also know this is too much. The protection buyer is not getting default protection on all three credits, only on the first one to default.

Suppose we also know that W is the weakest among "equals" and most likely to default. The price of the basket protection at the lower bound should be the price of credit default protection on W's $25 million notional amount. Intuitively, we know this is not enough. The credit default protection seller must be compensated something beyond this. The probability of exercise of the option is greater than just the probability of W's default. The probability of exercise is equal to the probability of W *or* X *or* Y defaulting.

It is a common misunderstanding of probability theory to say that the probability of W *or* X *or* Y is the product of each of the individual probabilities. That is simply incorrect. Assume for a moment that the transaction is a two-year transaction and that the marginal default rates for W, X, and Y are as follows:

Marginal and Cumulative Default Rates for W, X, and Y

Default Rates for W, X, and Y	Year 1 Marginal Default Rate	Year 2 Marginal Default Rate	Cumulative Default Rate in Year 2
W's Rates	0.28%	0.42%	0.70%
X's Rates	0.20%	0.30%	0.50%
Y's Rates	0.24%	0.36%	0.60%

Given these default rates, what is the likelihood of W *or* X *or* Y defaulting in either year one or year two? It is easier to consider the probability of no default for the three credits, W, X, and Y, that is, to find the probability of none of the credits defaulting. First, look at the probability of W and X and Y not defaulting in year one and then the cumulative rate in year two. The probability that a default has not occurred for each of the individual credits is as follows:

Default Rates	No Default Year 1	No Default for 2 Years
W's Probability	99.72%	99.30%
X's Probability	99.80%	99.50%
Y's Probability	99.76%	99.40%

Notice that the probability of no default is very high. This is because we are using investment-grade credits. I made the assumption that these are all BBB credits as rated by Standard & Poor's (S&P) and at least investment grade as rated by Moody's. The probability that none of the credits will default in year one is the product of the probability of no default. The probability of no default for the entire two-year period is the product of the cumulative probabilities of no default for two years.

For year 1, the probability of no default is $(0.9972 \times 0.9980 \times 0.9976)$ = 0.9928, or 99.28 percent. The probability of at least one default during this period is simply $(1 - 0.9928) = 0.007182$, or 0.7182 percent. For a trade lasting two years, the probability of no default is $(0.993 \times 0.995 \times 0.994)$ = 0.9821, or 98.21 percent. The probability of at least one default during this period is simply $(1 - 0.9821) = 0.0179$, or 1.79 percent. Notice that this is 2.55 times as likely as the cumulative probability of default of the three credits in year one.

We can see, however, that the probability of default of any one of the credits is very low individually, or as an agglomeration of credits, or as a first-to-default basket structure. Default rates for the individual credits and the basket first-to-default structure for W, X, and Y are as follows:

Comparison of Individual and Basket Default Rates

Default Rates	Individual Year 1	Basket Year 1	Cumulative Individual Year 2	Basket Year 2 Cumulative
W's Rate	0.28%	0.72%	0.70%	1.79%
X's Rate	0.20%	0.72%	0.50%	1.79%
Y's Rate	0.24%	0.72%	0.60%	1.79%

The default rate of the basket is higher than any individual default rate. In year one, the basket default rate is 257 percent higher than W's default rate, the highest in the group, and almost exactly the same as the sum of the individual default rates. However, on an absolute level, the basket default rate is still a very low rate—less than 1.00 percent. The basket cumulative rate for year two is 1.79 percent, 255 percent higher than W's rate of 0.70 percent and just slightly below the sum of the individual default rates.

How much, then, do we add on to the fee over and above what one would pay for credit default protection on W alone? One reasonable method is to add the sum of the commitment fees for unfunded loans on the remaining credits, X and Y. This theoretically compensates the protection seller for the increased probability of default. This method also implies that differences in recovery value have been factored in via different commitment fee levels.

Often a market professional might say that the protection buyer should pay the sum of the credit default protection fees because the basket probability of default is almost the same as the sum of the individual credits. This is an error in logic. The default protection seller will make a payment on only one of the credits, not on all three; so the protection seller is compensated for only one default plus the increased likelihood of a default occurring. When that increased likelihood is still low, the probability of payout is still low.

Of course, one could also look at the individual credit default price of each of W, X, and Y and the relative likelihood of default. In this way, a proportional amount of each individual fee could be used. The weakness of this method is that it requires a fudge number to compensate the seller of protection for the increased likelihood of exercise. This pricing methodology is more difficult to defend, and the results are not reproducible across baskets. Consistency in methodology breaks down. The pricing ultimately comes down to what the buyer and the seller of the basket credit default protection agree is fair.

A note at this point on the importance of using investment-grade credits might be helpful. If I use, instead, noninvestment-grade credits with a higher probability of default, how much does this affect the increased likelihood of default? The answer is quite a bit. A look at the following table for default rates on assets rated single B by S&P illustrates this point. The lower-rated credits here are W*, X*, and Y*.

Marginal and Cumulative Default Rates for W*, X*, and Y*

Default Rates for W*, X*, and Y*	Year 1 Marginal Default Rate	Year 2 Marginal Default Rate	Cumulative Default Rate In Year 2
W*'s Rates	5.70%	6.01%	11.71%
X*'s Rates	7.90%	6.30%	14.20%
Y*'s Rates	6.50%	7.00%	13.50%

Notice the dramatically higher default rates for each of the credits compared to W, X, and Y. Let us look at the reduction relative to the investment-grade credits in the probability of no default for each of the credits.

	No Default Year 1	No Default for 2 Years
W*'s Probability	94.30%	88.29%
X*'s Probability	92.10%	85.80%
Y*'s Probability	93.50%	86.50%

Performing the same analysis as we did for the investment-grade credits, we can examine the probability of at least one default in year one and also for the entire two-year period. For year one, the probability of no default is $(0.9430 \times 0.9210 \times 0.9350) = 0.8121$, or 81.21 percent. The probability of at least one default during this period is simply $(1 - 0.8121) = 0.1879$, or 18.79 percent. For a trade lasting two years, the probability of no default is $(0.8829 \times 0.8580 \times 0.8650) = 0.6553$, or 65.53 percent. The probability of at least one default during this period is simply $(1 - 0.6553) = 0.3447$, or 34.47 percent.

Comparison of Individual and Basket Default Rates

Rates	Individual Year 1	Basket Year 1	Cumulative Individual Year 2	Basket Year 2 Cumulative
W*'s Rate	5.70%	18.79%	11.71%	34.47%
X*'s Rate	7.90%	18.79%	14.20%	34.47%
Y*'s Rate	6.50%	18.79%	13.50%	34.47%

The default rate for the first-to-default basket in year one is 18.79 percent versus 20.1 percent for the sum of the three credits in the basket. In year two, the first-to-default basket probability is 34.47 percent versus 39.41 percent for the sum of the individual credits. The difficulty here is that although there should be some theoretical savings for the difference in the default rates, the probability that at least one of the credits in the basket will default is very high. It is 242 percent higher than in the case of X*'s rate of 14.2 percent for the two-year cumulative rate. Unlike the investment-grade case, however, the absolute probability of default is high. The protection seller should demand a much higher premium for this protection because of the dramatically increased likelihood of exercise.

The first-to-default basket default rate is 34.47 percent for only three credits, and that is assuming zero correlation among the three credits. If I add another credit with a two-year cumulative default rate of 13 percent, the probability of at least one default during the two-year period jumps to 43 percent! This, again, assumes no correlation between the credits in the basket. The probability of no default increases with increasing correlation between the credits in the basket. Stated more simply: The probability of at least one default decreases with increasing correlation between the credits in the basket.

The problem with correlation between assets has to do with concentration risk. The following example illustrates this concept. Let's use a simple two-asset basket, and let's assume that the correlation between the assets in the basket and the counterparty is equal to zero. Let's assume that the probability of default for asset i is 0.2 and the probability of default for asset j is 0.3. The basket is comprised 50 percent of asset i and 50 percent of asset j. The correlation between the assets is 0.4. The equation for credit exposure due to event risk is as follows:

$$UL_{(u,\,c)} = \sqrt{\sum \rho_{ij} n_i n_j \sqrt{\frac{(P_{(ui|c)})(1 - P_{(ui,\,c)})(P_{(uj|c)})(1 - P_{(uj,\,c)})}{(1 - P_{(c)})}}}$$

where UL = Unexpected Loss due to credit event risk
$P_{(ui|c)}$ = 0.2 = Probability of default of asset i
$P_{(uj|c)}$ = 0.3 = Probability of default of asset j = 0.3
$P_{(ui,\,c)}$ = 0 = Joint probability default of asset i and counterparty

$$P_{(uj,\ c)} = 0 \quad = \text{Joint probability default of asset } j \text{ and counterparty}$$
$$P_{(c)} \quad = 0.05 = \text{Probability of counterparty default}$$
$$\rho_{(i,\ j)} \quad = 0.4 \quad = \text{Correlation of default between asset } i \text{ and asset } j$$
$$n_i \quad = 0.5 \quad = \text{Asset } i\text{'s weight in the portfolio}$$
$$n_j \quad = 0.5 \quad = \text{Asset } j\text{'s weight in the portfolio}$$

Plugging into the formula, the credit exposure due to event risk is 0.15852. If the assumed correlation between the assets is 0.6, the credit exposure due to event risk increases to 0.19415.

Because we are not protecting market risk or the risk of credit downgrade but only the risk of the probability of default, we can multiply the notional amount of the transaction by our result to get the credit exposure.

As long as investors stick to investment-grade credits with very low default rates, the basket trade does not pose much of a problem. Investors and structurers alike should avoid using this structure for noninvestment-grade-rated securities.

The reasons for doing this transaction include the fact that the buyer of the credit default protection gets default protection at a lower cost than hedging each of the credits in the basket individually. Basket default structures can aid management of concentration risk within a credit portfolio, where the portfolio is overconcentrated in certain investment-grade credits but does not want to sell holdings to reduce concentration.

REGULATORY VIEWPOINTS

The challenge for the buyer and the seller of basket protection is in viewing the results of the trade. The Bank of England suggests that in the banking community the protection seller adopt a "worst-case" approach. The seller should consider the exposure of the highest possible payoff amount under the contract. This highest possible payoff amount is applied to the issuer in the basket with the highest risk weighting. The buyer of protection would have protection against the issuer in the basket, which attracts the lowest risk weighting. The protection amount is limited to the lowest possible payoff amount under the contract.

Let us see how this would work in practice using three hypothetical credits, two corporates and one bank, each with a notional of $100 million.

Payoff Profiles for Credits with $100 Million Notional

Credit Type	BIS Capital Ratio	Recovery Value	Payoff
Bank	20%	75%	$25,000,000
Corporate 1	100%	80%	$20,000,000
Corporate 2	100%	65%	$35,000,000

The seller of protection must apply the $35 million payoff amount against one of the 100 percent risk-weighted corporate credit risks for purposes of calculating its return on capital for this transaction. Its risk capital is 8% × 100% × $35,000,000, or $2,800,000.

The buyer of protection can reduce its risk capital by only $20 million applied to the lowest risk-weighted asset, in this case, the bank at 20 percent. The buyer of protection can reduce risk capital by 8% × 20% × $20,000,000, or $320,000.

No one ever said life is fair in the land of bank regulations. The adoption of this worst-case approach from the perspective of both the buyer and the seller of the credit default protection is meant to protect banks from overstating protection (when buying protection) or understating risk (when selling protection). This seemingly arbitrary approach is the best the Bank of England could come up with in the absence of defensible models. This does not mean regulators won't entertain a different treatment if they see a thoroughly reasoned approach. The burden is on the market to provide the approach.

The U.S. Federal Reserve had yet a different view on basket first-to-default swaps when I checked with them in the fall of 2000. The protection buyer gets a break on one of the exposures, but not on all four. For instance, if there are four reference obligors each with a notional exposure of $20 million and each rated A, the protection buyer can assign protection to only one of the obligors. In this instance, the Fed doesn't care which of the obligors gets the capital relief.

But the Fed stance becomes really interesting when the basket is not homogenous. If the basket is composed of three single-A rated obligors and one BBB rated obligor and if the notional amounts are each $20 million, the Fed does not address the credit quality at all. The Fed doesn't care which of the obligors gets the capital relief. If the notional amounts are asymmetrical—the notional amounts for the four obligors are $5 million, $10 million, $15 million, and $20 million—only the smallest exposure will get capital relief.

Of course, the "worst-case" approach affects only banks. But the bulk of loans used in basket default swaps are on the balance sheet of banks, so what affects banks is likely to affect the rest of the market.

Booking of fees and reduction of credit exposure might follow the example of regulatory capital, but not necessarily. Although the banking authorities can dictate regulatory capital, they do not dictate how banks view their risk-adjusted rate of return on capital (RAROC). They also do not dictate how banks should reduce their line exposure.

Banks and nonbanks could just model the above approach and take a worst-case approach for determining credit exposure and fee booking. The seller could view that they have sold protection on the worst credit (not necessarily the highest BIS risk weighting). Fees could be booked against this credit only and switched if this is not the first credit to actually default. The buyer could reduce the credit exposure to the best credit in the basket and view the cost of protection as being paid out against this protection. But we have already said this is arbitrary, and the recognition of the fee in this manner goes against our intuitive boundary conditions set out earlier.

Unfortunately, there are no completely satisfactory alternatives. One alternative has the virtue of being fairly straightforward and consistent for both the buyer and the seller of protection. Both the buyer and the seller estimate the likelihood of being the first to default for each of the names in the basket and for the protection seller. They then take into account any correlation of the basket names and the protection seller and then allocate the fees and line usage to each name proportionally.

There is as yet no set guidance for banks on the regulatory capital issues, although the Federal Reserve and the Bank of England are leaning in the direction mentioned earlier. For internal accounting and exposure management and for rate of return on economic capital, banks have a great deal of discretion in how to handle basket credit default swaps. Insurance companies closely watch what the banking community is doing to determine how they are going to view credit derivatives. Corporations and fund managers are subject to fewer regulatory constraints in these matters and have yet to come to a consensus on how to handle these issues. We discuss this in more detail in Chapter 7.

KNOCK-IN BASKET OPTIONS

The cost of credit default basket options and of stand-alone credit default options cannot be significantly reduced using a knock-in structure. Knock-in default swaps are more accurately called credit event trigger swaps, or options. The reference asset does not have to default; in fact, the reference asset may be a performing asset. Nonetheless, the protection buyer has the right to put the asset to the credit event protection seller at a preagreed price or at a preagreed spread, which corresponds to a market price. Knock-in credit default options are usually priced deeply out of the money. They are, in fact, deep out-of-the-money puts.

The protection seller feels that the likelihood of default is low and is happy to own the asset at a wider level. The protection buyer feels that if credit spreads widen, the reference asset is either headed to default or to a credit rating and credit risk that is no longer acceptable to the protection buyer. The protection buyer may have another motive, however. The protection buyer may be looking for a cheap source of credit default protection. This is the same as buying an out-of-the-money put. The protection buyer will tolerate a credit spread widening. The market does not as yet efficiently price the difference in these products.

For the most part, the market does not see a real difference between these products reflected in price. One German bank offers this product in the two-to-five-year maturity range for corporate names. The German bank gets favorable capital treatment for selling a deep out-of-the-money put. Credit default options, however, attract a 100 percent BIS regulatory capital charge. Because of this favorable capital treatment, there may be a regulatory capital charge arbitrage. It may be more advantageous to buy credit default protection in this form from a bank that gets favorable capital treatment than from a bank that does not get favorable capital treatment. We will look at economic and regulatory capital treatment in more detail in Chapter 7.

REDUCED LOSS CREDIT DEFAULT OPTIONS

One way to reduce the cost of credit default protection is for the default protection buyer to offer to take a fixed percentage of the loss in the event of default. One large European export finance company approached me about reducing the credit risk in their portfolio to corporate names in their home country. Their lines were full to corporates, including a gas company, an auto manufacturer, an engineering construction company, and a telecommunications company. All of the corporations were investment grade and theoretically should have had low correlation credit risks with each other.

The export finance company wanted to know how much they could reduce the cost of credit default protection on a first-to-default structure if they agreed to absorb the first 30 percent of the decline in market value. There is no absolute model for determining this.

One way to evaluate this is to look at the weakest credit in the portfolio. This means that the expected recovery rate for the weakest credit in the portfolio would be 30 percent higher than expected. This is as if there were a senior or a subordinated structure created from this credit. The subordinated piece would absorb the first 30 percent of loss in the event of default (LIED), and the senior piece would not lose any principal until this buffer had been exhausted.

In earlier discussions, we saw that the expected loss and LIED are related according to the following formula:

Expected Loss = Probability of Default × Loss in the Event of Default

The structure is different from the usual senior/subordinated structure, however. In a typical senior/subordinated structure, we examine a pool of assets. The lower-credit-quality assets in the pool have a higher probability of default than the higher-credit-quality assets in the pool. This lower probability of default is assigned to calculations for the subordinated piece. For a single reference asset, however, the probability of default for the senior and the subordinated tranches is exactly the same. We can rewrite the equation as follows:

Expected Loss Senior Piece = Constant × LIED of Senior Tranche

Expected Loss Subordinated Piece = Constant × LIED Subordinated Tranche

We can ignore the probability of default and concentrate on the LIED or on the recovery rate, which is simply equal to 1 − LIED. One very quick method to determine how much the credit default swap price can be reduced for a company that will absorb the first 30 percent of the expected loss is to look at the Moody's table for recovery rates. Senior unsecured debt has a mean recovery rate of 51.13 percent, with a standard deviation of 25.45

percent. Subordinated debt has a mean recovery rate of 32.74 percent, with a standard deviation of 20.18 percent. Junior subordinated debt has a mean recovery rate of 17.09 percent, with a standard deviation of 10.9 percent. If the first 30 percent of the loss is absorbed by the export finance company, that is similar to upgrading junior subordinated debt to a recovery rate of 47.09 percent or upgrading subordinated debt to a recovery rate of 62.74 percent. Notice that the standard deviations still indicate a lot of overlap across debt classes in recovery rate. The point is, however, that the absorption of 30 percent of the LIED upgrades the implied debt rating by a full notch and possibly by two notches for single-A reference assets. This single-notch upgrade in credit quality is worth something.

In a basket credit default structure, the cost of the basket option can be reduced by the credit spread differential between a strong AA asset and a single-A asset. If that credit spread differential is 10 basis points, the basket option cost is reduced by at least that amount. The add-on for the remaining assets in the basket can also be slightly reduced, by approximately 2 basis points each for the difference in unfunded commitment fees between a strong AA and single-A asset. The total cost reduction would be approximately 16 basis points.

This is a quick estimate, but as we discussed earlier, there is general market dissatisfaction with basket option pricing models. Rule-of-thumb pricing as a supplement to unsatisfactory models is an essential part of any toolkit. In most cases, the market will negotiate around these rules of thumb as opposed to having "dueling models" when credit derivatives specialists negotiate prices.

PRO RATA DEFAULT STRUCTURES

Pro rata default structures are often incorrectly called basket structures. This is a mistake and can lead to pricing confusion. The market standard currently understands a basket structure to mean a first-to-default basket structure, as discussed earlier. The pro rata structure is commonly called a pooled structure.

The purpose of the pro rata default structure is simply documentation convenience. Several separate credit default swap transactions are documented under the same letter confirmation. Each transaction relates to one reference obligation issued by one reference credit.

Transactions may have different maturity dates. The credit default protection seller offers performance protection on each specified reference obligation. The credit default protection buyer pays a pro rata premium representing the sum of the protection premiums on each of the individual reference credits.

If a reference credit experiences a defined credit event during the term of the transaction, the default protection seller pays the default protection buyer the calculation amount. In exchange, the default protection seller receives delivery of the relevant reference obligation with a face value subject to the transaction. Neither the default protection seller nor the default protection buyer has any further obligations with respect to this particular reference credit. The pro rata premium paid on the remainder of the transaction is reduced by the premium on the reference credit that experienced the credit event.

A credit event with respect to one reference credit does not constitute a credit event with respect to any other reference credit. If the other reference credits do not experience a credit event during the term of the transaction, the credit default protection seller will make no payment on any other reference obligation. If any of the other reference credits experiences a credit event, the credit default protection seller will make a payment versus delivery only on the occurrence of one or more additional credit events. Obligations for both the credit default protection seller and the buyer terminate for each individual reference credit upon a credit event and satisfaction of required payments or upon maturity of each individual reference credit.

CHAPTER 5

Sovereign Risk and Emerging Markets

T he emerging-markets credit derivatives market is much more driven by supply and demand than is publicly traded investment-grade European or U.S. debt. Although it is true that these markets are supply-and-demand driven, spreads commanded for credit default protection tend not to get seriously out of line with asset swap spread levels. This is because the market is well known, management at financial institutions is more familiar with the history of the market, and more institutions have an appetite for these risks.

The emerging markets are a different matter, however, for the following reasons:

- The emerging markets experience more price volatility.
- There are fewer traders and fewer reliable pricing sources for these assets.
- Fewer institutions have the authority to invest in these securities.
- Size constraints tend to be more stringent for the institutions, which have investment authorities.
- These markets have fewer instruments and less trading history.
- Fewer pricing sources, such as Telerate, Bloomberg, and Reuters, offer reliable prices on the spectrum of countries. Some prices exist only in the off-screen markets.
- These markets are more subject to event risk.

■ When a severe credit event occurs in one emerging market region, spreads tend to widen globally. Credit spreads exhibit correlation.

Emerging markets is the term usually reserved for developing economies. The liquidity and depth of the debt markets is relatively undeveloped. The emerging markets are often classified as Latin America, including Mexico, Eastern Europe, and most Asian countries. There is debate about this definition. Several market professionals claim that Latin American countries such as Brazil, Argentina, and Mexico should not be included in the list. Further, Korea and Thailand are often excluded, although most professionals agree the Philippines and Vietnam are emerging markets.

For the purposes of this book, all of the above markets are included. One of the reasons for this is that Asian event risks and Latin American event risks tend to affect spreads across the board. In the late 1990s, currency events in Indonesia and Thailand suggested the classically defined emerging markets rather than developed debt and currency markets. Further, these instruments are usually traded in the emerging-markets groups of most financial institutions. Therefore, I classify them as emerging markets for credit derivatives as well.

In the fall of 1997, the correlation between emerging markets in Asia, Latin America, and Eastern Europe was clear, at least in terms of credit spreads and, in some instances, perception of ability to repay debt. Even the superpower economies felt repercussions. On July 2, 1997, Thailand's decisions to allow the baht to float sparked a series of currency devaluations in Asia. The Malaysian ringgit, Philippine peso, Indonesian rupiah, and South Korean won plunged in value versus the U.S. dollar. This in turn sparked an Asian debt and stock market crisis. The effects were felt globally as spreads dramatically widened in Latin America and Eastern Europe in sympathy with Asia. By the end of 1997, the South Korean banking and corporate debt system was in severe crisis, and the International Monetary Fund (IMF) constructed a $57 billion bailout for the South Korean economy. Other measures were under consideration for Malaysia, Indonesia, and Thailand. Russia was in the process of refinancing its debt. Japan's economy and banking system suffered partly because of the Asian crisis and partly because of internal tax increases. Japan's fourth-largest securities firm and Japan's tenth-largest bank declared bankruptcy. Although Japan is the world's second-largest economy with enormous foreign currency reserves and huge trade surpluses, funding costs for all Japanese banks soared. Spreads of Latin American debt widened several hundred basis points in the fall of 1997, recovering steadily toward the end of 1997. Even the United States felt the effects. By the end of 1997, economists were predicting slower growth for the U.S. economy, partly due to turmoil in the Asian markets.

THE GUESSTIMATERS' MARKET

The debt markets of emerging-markets countries are complicated by past debt restructuring, particularly in Latin America. Brady bonds are named after former U.S. Secretary of the Treasury James Brady. They were created in the early 1980s in response to the overconcentration of Latin American loans held by U.S. banks. The Latin American economies produced commodities whose prices were declining. Interest rates were on the rise, and Latin American countries were unable to buy raw materials as U.S. banks began refusing additional loans.

Secretary Brady averted a banking crisis in the United States by restructuring the bank loans and coaxing U.S. banks to forgive part of the debt. The U.S. banks actually had little choice. At first, U.S. banks balked and took the view that debtor nations should worry about their unpaid debt and the reputations of their countries. Unfortunately, a U.S. bank does not have as much clout over a Latin sovereign nation as it does over a U.S. consumer behind in his or her home mortgage or automobile payments. The U.S. banks eventually realized that if a sovereign debtor doesn't pay its bills, an overexposed lender has much more to worry about than the borrower.

Brady bonds are the result of this restructuring. The principal is often backed by long-dated U.S. Treasury zero-coupon bonds. Interest-due-and-unpaid bonds (IDUs) have no collateral except in the case of Costa Rica. Debt conversion bonds (DCBs) also have no collateral for principal or interest. Front-loaded interest-reduction bonds (FLIRBs) have no principal collateral, but they do have a rolling interest guarantee (RIG), which with a AA backing covers 12 months of interest payments for the first five years of the life of the bond. Zero-coupon U.S. Treasury bonds collateralize the principal of collateralized floating-rate discount bonds (discount bonds). They also have an RIG, which covers 12 to 18 months of interest payments. Collateralized fixed-rate par bonds (par bonds) have principal collateralized by U.S. Treasury bonds and an RIG covering 12 to 18 months of interest payments. This discussion of Brady bonds does not exhaust the peculiarities of emerging-market debt, but it does highlight some of the idiosyncrasies. A credit derivative structurer must examine the terms of emerging-market debt obligations to determine the risk profile of the debt.

Bradys are usually quoted in terms of the *stripped yield*—the yield on the non–U.S. dollar exposure of the bond. The sovereign spread is quoted after normalizing for the U.S. Treasury collateral. There is no standard method, and the various methods often result in different values of sovereign spread.

Credit spread options allow investors to buy options of the credit spread of Brady bonds over U.S. Treasuries. Call options on the Brady spread over U.S. Treasuries increase in value when credit spreads tighten, and puts increase in value when the credit spreads widen (the market for Bradys weakens). Not all banks will offer this product. The ambiguity in the method for calculating residual sovereign spread from Bradys means that hedges will be imperfect and banks must manage and take risk on resulting hedge management exposure. Not all banks and investment banks are willing to manage this risk.

Most banks are willing to sell credit default protection, however. Reference pricing is based on the prices of liquid and semiliquid bonds and hedge instruments. Table 5.1 (see pages 193–194) shows prices for selected hard currency–denominated Eurobonds for emerging market countries. Table 5.2 (see page 195) then shows broker prices for emerging-market debt credit default swaps on the same day. The prices for long-dated credit default protection represent what I usually refer to as a "Guesstimaters'" market. As one moves farther along the maturity curve, credit default premiums decouple from asset swap spreads.

One cannot purchase a long-dated emerging-markets asset and purchase credit default protection and still earn a positive spread. Five-year Mexico trades at the London interbank offering rate (LIBOR) plus 126 basis points (bps), whereas the credit protection trades at Treasuries plus 195 (midmarket), or around LIBOR + 165 bps. Purchasers of long-dated credit default protection are often hedging lucrative transactions, freeing up credit lines for very profitable transactions, or are the beneficiaries of a tax advantage.

Most offers for credit default protection are for smaller sizes, blocks of $5 million to $10 million. There are no offers for blocks of $50 million. The broker market indications are often thrown up on a screen without a real counterparty behind them, merely an indication of where someone might do a transaction if a deal is brought to them. Often brokers have no details on exact structure or language requirements. Early on in the credit derivatives

TABLE 5.1 Eurobond Prices for Selected Emerging-Market Countries

Country	Coupon	Currency	Final Maturity	Issue Spread	Issue Size	Bid Price	Offer Price	Bid Yield	Offer Yield	Rating Moody's	Rating S&P
Argentina											
Argentina	10.950	USD	1-Nov-99	350	500 thou.	108.70	108.88	T + 82	74	B1	BB
Argentina	9.250	USD	23-Feb-01	410	1 bil.	105.20	105.38	T + 151	147	B1	BB
Argentina	8.375	USD	20-Dec-03	280	1 bil.	102.90	103.00	T + 157	156	B1	BB
Argentina	11.000	USD	9-Oct-06	445	1 bil.	114.50	115.00	T + 246	239	B1	BB
Argentina	11.375	USD	10-Jan-17	462.5	2 bil.	114.90	115.00	T + 307	306	B1	BB
Brazil											
Brazil Republic	8.875	USD	5-Nov-01	265	750 thou.	104.125	104.38	T + 161	154	B1	BB–
Brazil Republic	10.125	USD	15-Mar-27	395	3 bil.	99.00	99.15	T + 366	365	B1	BB–
Mexico											
BNCE	7.250	USD	2-Feb-04	163	1 bil.	94.50	94.55	T + 214	213	Ba2	NA
UMS	9.750	USD	6-Feb-01	445	1 bil.	106.50	107.00	T + 158	143		
UMS	3 mn L + 125	USD	27-Jun-02	138	1 bil.	99.98	100.08	L + 126	123	Baa3	BBB–
UMS	9.875	USD	15-Jan-07	335	1 bil.	107.2	107.40	T + 252	249	Ba2	BB
UMS	11.375	USD	15-Sep-16	445	1 bil.	115.90	116.00	T + 298	296	Ba2	BB
UMS	11.500	USD	15-May-26	552	1.75 bil.	118.10	118.25	T + 305	304	Ba2	BB
Russia											
Russian Republic	9.250	USD	27-Nov-01	345	1bil.	101.85	102.15	T + 260	252	Ba2	BB–
Russian Republic	9.000	DEM	25-Mar-04	370	2 bil.	103.75	104.00	T + 317	312	NA	BB–
Russian Republic	10.000	USD	26-Jun-07	375	2 bil.	101.52	101.72	T + 352	349	Ba2	BB–

TABLE 5.1 *(continued)*

Country	Coupon	Currency	Final Maturity	Issue Spread	Issue Size	Bid Price	Offer Price	Bid Yield	Offer Yield	Rating Moody's	Rating S&P
Turkey											
Republic of Turkey	8.250	USD	11-Jun-99	222	250 mil.	100.35	100.70	T + 215	195	B1	B
Republic of Turkey	10.0	USD	23-May-02	348	500 mil.	104.45	104.85	T + 272	262	B1	B
					Specials						
Russia											
City of Moscow	9.5	USD	31-May-00				102.375		L + 222	Ba2	BB–
City of St. Petersburg	9.5	USD	18-Jun-02		300 mil.		101.60		L + 260		BB–
SBS-Agro Bank	10.25	USD	21-Jul-00		200 mil.		99.65		L + 382		B+
Turkey											
City of Ankara	6.8	yen	10-Nov-97		50 bil.				L + 280		B
Republic of Turkey	6.0	yen	10-Jun-98		100 bil.				L + 235	B1	B
Republic of Turkey	4.0	yen	14-Dec-98						L + 260	B1	B
Republic of Turkey	6.8	yen	24-Sep-99		50 bil.				L + 320	B1	B

Notes: "3mn L": 3-month LIBOR; "T": Treasuries; "L": LIBOR; "B": rating grade; "USD": U.S. dollars; "DEM": Deutsche marks; S&P: Standard & Poor's.

Source: Marc Phillips, Bank of America London Branch, July 14, 1997.

TABLE 5.2 Sovereign Default Protection for Selected Emerging-Market Countries, Bid/Ask Broker Indications (basis points per annum)

	6 months	1 year	2 years	3 years	4 years	4.4 years	5 years	5.5 years
Argentina								
Cantor								
Prebon		74/90	115/145	140/175	165/195		175/210	
Tullett		70/NA						
Brazil								
Prebon	65/85	NA/90	115/145	130/NA	150/NA		215/240	
Tullett		70/95						
Bulgaria								
Cantor								
EXCO	NA/350	NA/600						
Intercapital		250/NA						
Prebon	215/NA						400/NA	
Tullett	270/350							
Mexico								
Cantor		NA/65						
Prebon	NA/95	65/75	100/125	140/175	165/195		180/210	
Tullett		70/105						
Russia								
Cantor		195/215						
EXCO	NA/195	190/210						
Intercapital		NA/210				240/350		
Prebon	170/NA	190/NA				210/NA		
Tullett		190/215						NA/460
Turkey								
Cantor		250/NA	275/NA	300/NA				
EXCO		245/NA	275/NA	295/NA				
Intercapital				330/NA				
Prebon		250/NA	275/NA	300/NA			320/390	
Tullett		245/315	270/NA	295/NA				

Note: NA indicates bid or offer was not available.
Sources: Cantor Fitzgerald; EXCO; Intercapital Credit Derivatives, Inc.; Prebon Yanmane; Tullett Capital Markets.

business, many brokers had no idea which reference asset was used. Large transactions are almost exclusively private, nonbroker-negotiated transactions between financial institutions. As size and maturity of a credit default swap increase, so does the ability to negotiate a price between counterparties.

TAX ARBITRAGE

Many emerging-markets transactions are dominated by tax considerations. For instance, many European countries have double tax treaties with emerging-market countries, which they would like to exploit. In most instances, although European investors are ready to take on tax-law-interpretation risk, they are not as keen to take sovereign credit risk of emerging-market countries. Often these European investors will pay an off-market price for credit default protection because the number of credit default protection sellers is limited and the rewards of the tax advantage allow the investor to earn an above-market spread on the securities.

Austrian investors, for instance, took advantage of a double tax treaty with Brazil to purchase Brazilian Brady bonds with a put back to the bank that sold them the securities. The following term sheet shows the transaction.

BRAZILIAN BRADY BONDS WITH PUT/CALL
INDICATIONS AS OF AUGUST 4, 1995
Term Sheet

Underlying Bond:

Issuer:	Federative Republic of Brazil, DCB.
Notional Amount:	USD 50 million.
Maturity Date:	April 15, 2012.
Coupon:	7.3125% (six-month USD LIBOR + 87.5 bps) (on a semiannual A/360-day basis, where A is the actual number of days in the period). (Next coupon date: October 16, 1995).
Sale Price:	51.692% (50.25% + Accrual of 1.442%).
Settlement Date:	June 28, 1995.
Put/Call Expiry Date:	October 11, 1995.

Put/Call Settlement Date:	October 13, 1995.
Strike Price of Put:	51.862% (48.246% + Accrual of 3.616%).
Strike Price of Call:	51.862% (48.246% + Accrual of 3.616%).

Credit Protection:

While the client is the owner of Brazilian Brady bonds for the length of the transaction, a bank provides credit protection on the principal amount in the form of a put option. Bank protection provider is rated AA3/AA–.

Put/Call:

The investor has the right to put the bond at the strike price of the put option to the bank. The investor agrees to sell a call to the bank on the trade date through a side letter agreement. Under the terms of the side letter agreement, the bank is obligated to enter into the call option agreement three weeks from the trade date. The strike and the exercise date of the call option are the same as that of the put option.

Assumed Relevant Customer Tax Rate:	34.00%.
Net Interest Income (Coupon Interest – Accrued):	USD 1,086,718.
Call Option Premium (Income):	0.
Put Option Premium (Payment):	0.
Tax Deductible Capital Loss:	USD –1,001,762.
Tax Offset (Tax Rate × Capital Loss):	USD 340,599.
Cash Benefit to Investor:	USD 425,555.
Yield on Tax-Adjusted Cash Flow ($A/360$):	5.54%.
Equivalent Pretax Yield ($A/360$):	8.39%.

The equivalent pretax yield at the time was equal to LIBOR + 200 bps for the investor in a transaction, which lasted three and one-half months. The tax benefit in Austrian schilling (ATS) terms was even greater. The yield curve in Austria had lower interest rates than in the United States, and the investor was able to take advantage of a tax benefit for loss on forward sale of foreign currency in converting USD to ATS.

The investor had the right to put the securities to the bank. In a side letter agreement, the investor gives the right to the bank to call the securities at the end of the transaction. Either way, the bank will get the securities back at the end of the transaction. This is similar to a buy/sell back or to a repurchase agreement. The structure has some subtle differences, however. In the event of default of the Brazilian reference securities, the investor can put the bonds back to the bank at the end of the transaction period at the original agreed-on price. If the securities default, there is no margin call as there might be in the case of a repurchase agreement. The investor has what appears to be a credit put to the bank. The investor's credit risk is no longer the Republic of Brazil but the bank.

This transaction works only because the investor has capital gains against which it can deduct the capital loss generated in this transaction to get an effective pretax equivalent yield of LIBOR + 200 bps on an essentially AA rated transaction.

Another key element of the transaction is the double tax treaty between Brazil and Austria. Austrian corporations pay no tax on the coupon interest income from Brazil. For a period of nearly two years, Austrian investors purchased Brazilian government bonds via this method at levels where the pretax cash flow was negative. The premium paid to get the credit protection was worth it to the Austrian investors. After tax, the returns were well above market levels. As more competitors figured out the driving forces of these transactions, Austrian investors were able to earn a slightly positive pretax cash flow and even higher pretax equivalent yields.

CREDIT PLAYS—THE HOME CURRENCY ADVANTAGE

Standard & Poor's (S&P) often rates sovereign debt higher in the home currency than in a foreign currency. It is more likely for a sovereign to increase revenues via taxes and duties in their home country and thus meet debt obligations. Often market professionals will claim that the government can always "print more money" to meet debt obligations. Although this is theoretically true in the short run, it leads to economic chaos, which could overthrow even the strongest dictatorship. Therefore the S&P ratings are based on claims paying ability through conventional governmental revenue sources.

The local currency debt ratings are generally stronger than those for foreign currencies, although the ability to pay is not viewed as unlimited. Table 5.3 shows the ratings in foreign and local currency for most emerging-

TABLE 5.3 Comparison of Emerging-Markets Sovereign Foreign and Local Currency Debt Ratings in 1998

Obligor	Foreign Currency Debt Ratings			Local Currency Debt Ratings		
	Moody's	S&P	IBCA	Moody's	S&P	IBCA
Argentina	B1	BB	BB	B1	BBB–	NR
Barbados	Ba1	NR	NR	NR	NR	NR
Bermuda	Aa1	AA	AA	NR	NR	AAA
Brazil	B1	BB–	B+	NR	BB+	NR
Bulgaria	B3	NR	NR	NR	NR	NR
Chile	Baa1	A–	A–	NR	AA	AAA
China	A3	BBB+	NR	NR	NR	NR
Colombia	Baa3	BBB–	NR	NR	A+	NR
Costa Rica	Ba1	NR	NR	NR	NR	NR
Cyprus	A2	AA–	NR	NR	AA+	NR
Czech Republic	Baa1	A	A–	NR	NR	NR
El Salvador	Baa3	BB	NR	NR	BBB+	NR
Hungary	Baa3	BBB–	BBB	NR	A–	A–
India	Baa3	BB+	NR	NR	BBB+	NR
Indonesia	Baa3	BBB	BBB–	NR	A+	NR
Korea	A1	AA–	AA–	NR	NR	AAA
Latvia	NR	BBB	NR	NR	A–	NR
Lithuania	B1	BB–	BB	NR	BBB+	BBB+
Lebanon	Ba2	BBB–	BB+	NR	BB	BBB–
Malaysia	A1	A+	NR	NR	AA+	NR
Malta	A2	A+	A	NR	AA+	NR
Mexico	Ba2	BB	BB	Baa3	BBB+	NR
Moldova	Ba2	NR	NR	NR	NR	NR
Pakistan	B2	B+	NR	NR	NR	NR
Paraguay	NR	BB–	NR	NR	BBB–	NR
Philippines	Ba1	BB+	NR	NR	A–	NR
Poland	Baa3	BBB–	BBB	NR	A–	A–
Romania	BA3	BB–	BB–	NR	BBB–	NR
Russia	BA2	BB–	BB+	NR	NR	NR
Singapore	AA1	AAA	NR	Aa1	AAA	NR
Slovakia	Baa3	BBB–	BBB–	NR	A	A–
South Africa	Baa3	BB+	BB	Baa1	BBB+	BBB
Taiwan	Aa3	AA+	NR	NR	NR	NE
Thailand	A3	A	NR	NR	AA	NR
Trinidad & Tobago	Ba1	BB+	NR	NR	BBB+	NR
Tunisia	Baa3	BBB–	BBB–	NR	A	NR
Turkey	B1	B	B+	NR	NR	NR
Uruguay	Baa3	BBB–	BBB–	NR	BBB+	NR
Venezuela	BA2	B+	NR	NR	NR	NR

Note: NR means not rated.
Sources: Moody's Investor Service, Standard & Poor's, Fitch IBCA.

market countries. S&P rates Indonesia's foreign currency obligations as BBB but its local currency obligations A+. Lithuania's foreign debt gets a below-investment-grade rating of BB–, whereas its local debt gets an investment-grade rating of BBB+. This difference in foreign currency and local currency debt rating suggests some market opportunities.

Commercial banks and investment banks created special purpose corporations (SPCs) incorporated in Luxembourg or the Netherlands. Both of these countries have tax treaties with Italy. The SPCs claimed back the withholding tax on the coupons of Italian government bonds. This transaction was created for funds in countries that did not have a double tax treaty with Italy. At the time when these transactions were most popular, Italy was rated single A (Italy is now rated AA). The SPCs, however, were rated AAA. The actual transaction is diagrammed in Figure 5.1 for Deutsche mark investment for a German fund.

The reason that the SPC managed to get a AAA rating is that the Italian government debt was denominated in lira. If the Italian government debt had been denominated in Deutsche marks or U.S. dollars, the rating would have been lower. Because there is a swap from Italian lira to Deutsche marks, the swap counterparty must either have a AAA rating or be guaranteed by a AAA guarantor.

Many of these structures were sold as "black box" structures: Investors were told they were buying AAA Organization for Economic Cooperation and Development (OECD) sovereign collateral. A list of OECD countries was provided in the offering circulars. Most of these countries were rated AAA or had strong AA ratings in their local currency. Often investors had the impression that what they were buying was sovereign debt, which had

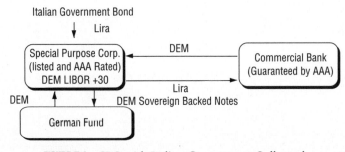

FIGURE 5.1   SPC with Italian Government Collateral

a AAA rating in the home currency. What investors actually purchased, however, was the structure shown in Figure 5.1, which was Italian government debt.

Today in most markets S&P rates local currency debt for many countries higher than the foreign currency debt. The credit derivatives market has not yet exploited these opportunities, but I anticipate we will see various structures using this theme.

THE CURRENCY QUESTION IN SOVEREIGN DEFAULT PROTECTION

Inconvertibility and Nontransferability

The Italian government bond structure shown in Figure 5.1 required the guarantee of a AAA entity. Dresdner Bank guaranteed one of these swaps for the now-defunct Kidder Peabody and had several questions related to the Italian lira. One question was whether the lira was domestic lira or Euro lira.

What is the difference? After all, the value should be the same. The difference is in where the lira is delivered. Would the lira be delivered to Dresdner Bank inside of Italy, or would the lira be available to Dresdner Bank in a European bank account? This mattered to Dresdner. Although Dresdner Bank was willing to guarantee the lira payment Italy would make, it was not willing to risk owing a lira payment in Europe if Dresdner Bank's only access to lira was within Italy itself.

The issue of currency, unrelated to the actual exchange rate for the currency itself, has fallen into the category of credit derivatives. The currency question is different from the credit derivative question, however, and in many ways more complicated. The sovereignty of a government itself is closely tied up with the issue of currency.

It doesn't matter whether we are talking about gold, salt, cowry shells, silver, cacao, or tulip bulbs; currency is nothing more than a store of value. It helps if the standard store of value is measurable in a reliable manner and abundant. It wasn't until nation states arose that "money" in the form of coins and paper replaced commodities. Central banks still use gold as a store of value and go to great lengths to stockpile physical gold. The gold standard in an official or unofficial form existed in Europe for approximately nine hundred years prior to the dissolution of the gold standard in 1971. Nonetheless, gold is still viewed as a benchmark, although the "hard currencies," such as the dollar, the Deutsche mark, and the yen, are used as world standards, with the dollar in the forefront.

There are three basic kinds of money. Any child who has swapped toys with another child understands the first kind of money—*commodity money*, now represented by gold or silver or oil, and formerly represented by cowry shells, beads to purchase Manhattan, wheat, salt, or any other usable commodities humans valued.

The second kind of money is *credit*. Most of us understand this in the form of checking accounts. Earlier, money flows were understood in the form of trade receivables, credit against a shipment of salable goods. In fact, international banking arose around the need to trade goods between various countries.

The international Jewish community was instrumental in the formation of early banking practices such as banker's acceptances, trade receivables, and letters of credit. The Jewish community was educated; they could read and write and cipher. More than that, they could read, write, cipher, and communicate in a common language. Even more important than the former, they had a close-knit community, a common code of ethics bound in religious law. The Jewish people had a means of censuring members of their community who broke the law through social and commercial ostracism. These were the reasons that the first world bankers were Jewish. A merchant in one country could rely on the standards of banking in his home country to agree with the standards of banking in another country, whose common thread was not a fickle sovereign edict but rather the standards of a community of people with common goals. Indeed, that is the definition of a sovereign state, and the Jewish people had their first international "sovereign" state visible outside of their community in the form of the first standards for international banking.

The third kind of money is *fiat money*. (This isn't money used to buy Fiats, a commodity, as one investment banker once tried to explain.) Fiat money is a government-issued currency note. Fiat money isn't backed by a commodity, as is commodity money. Fiat money isn't backed by an asset, as is a checking deposit or trade receivable. Fiat money is backed by the faith and the credit of a government.

We use sovereign debt as money, as collateral, and as an exchange for goods and services. This works only because we agree that it has value and that the government would pay us back. We have a common hallucination of what this "money" is worth.

This seems arbitrary, but the other two forms of money are also arbitrary. Commodity money is less arbitrary than the other two, especially when the commodity has a use. In times of war, I can eat wheat, but I can't eat gold. When I am hungry with no hope for quick replenishment of supplies, I'd prefer to stockpile wheat rather than gold. This is how the concept of money began—as a practical means of enhancing the conditions of survival for a community. Nonetheless, gold would have more value to me than credit in these circumstances. The reason is that I would have a strong demand for a reliable means of exchange. The physical commodity seems less arbitrary in a distress situation.

Credit money has assets to back it and a definable benchmark for value. Although inflation can cause fluctuations in the value, there is generally a common standard of value. Fiat money is backed not by bank assets or commodities but by the wealth of a society, and not the wealth of an individual (or individual entity such as a corporation).

Special Event Risks

A variety of events can happen to a sovereign currency. A government that does not choose to participate in a currency area, such as the European Monetary Union (EMU), values monetary policy autonomy and tries to control capital mobility and exchange-rate stability. The harder a government, such as a dictatorship, tries to maintain monetary policy autonomy, the more it must either limit the movement of capital into and outside of the country or compromise exchange-rate stability.

I lived in Iran when the shah was overthrown in 1978; shortly after, Khomeini returned in 1979. The new government wanted to prevent flight capital from leaving the country. It also wanted to prevent sympathizers to the shah's regime from getting out of the country alive. It further wanted to preserve a sense of economic normalcy to the outside world.

There was nothing normal about it. Citizens thought to be beneficiaries of the shah's largess were dragged out of their homes in the middle of the night. Often their accuser was a jealous neighbor. Kangaroo courts called "komites" condemned citizens to death. Their assets were confiscated.

In the panic to leave the country with some of their wealth, citizens found that although there was an official exchange rate of 7 toman (10 rials) to the U.S. dollar, there was no means to convert money. Banks were closed much of the time. The government put a further restriction on conversion of currency: Citizens could take only $1,000 in U.S. currency out of the country and could take only a suitcase of clothing. The idea was to prevent citizens from taking valuable carpets, now labeled "national protected works of art," out of the country.

Individuals found ways around these restrictions, proving once again that "governments rise and fall, but the economy goes on." A black market for hard currency quickly sprouted up. There were severe penalties if one were caught exchanging money. Nonetheless, people just became more clever about the exchange.

Merchants were given dispensations to do business. Importers would fake invoices to reflect that they had increased orders by 100 percent. In reality, they hadn't doubled their orders with merchants in Europe. They created this fiction so that they could exchange currency for Deutsche marks or dollars. In this way, they accumulated hard currency deposits in Europe. Land and housing values went to almost zero in the wake of the upheaval. This was the time to pick up bargains on the back of someone else's crisis. If you wanted land or a nice house and you had hard currency deposits, you could strike a hard bargain. People purchased diamonds and gemstones, which were portable currency when they were fleeing the country. People bartered land, Persian carpets, and homes for portable, concealable wealth.

Importers didn't have a problem faking their invoices. This raised no suspicion. The population eagerly purchased freezer chests to keep their meat frozen during the frequent electrical "brownouts" with the new inefficient government. They purchased televisions, stereos, and refrigerators as the only hard goods of value. Money was almost meaningless, so why not have conveniences? Sales skyrocketed.

In a situation like this, the ability to convert currency, either legally or in a way that was not transparent to a punitive government, would have been very valuable. Unfortunately, an easy way didn't exist. This is one of the reasons for the growth of currency convertibility protection in the credit derivatives market.

Revolutions upset currency flows. During the Russian civil war in 1919, most Russian currencies devalued, except for the North Russia ruble. The National Emmission Caisse, formed in November 1918, issued notes denominated in rubles pegged at a fixed rate of 40 rubles per pound British sterling. The notes were backed by a reserve equal to 75 percent of the issue, an interest-bearing deposit in the Bank of England. North Russian government bonds backed the remainder. When North Russia fell in February 1920, the North Russian bonds were worthless. This scheme to keep convertibility at a fixed exchange rate in this currency nearly worked. If the Caisse bonds hadn't been partially backed by bonds, which became worthless after the Bolshevik Revolution, it would have worked. As it was, this currency was convertible until April 1920, when the Caisse stopped redeeming its notes.

That is the key to evaluating currency risks: What backs the currency? In times of political upheaval, having additional backing by a bank willing to convert currency is an alternative.

In this decade, trade finance has become a key area of focus for convertibility. Trading companies cite Venezuela as typical of the problems they encounter. In the early 1990s, foreign exporters received payment in Venezuelan currency that they could not easily convert to their home currency or another hard currency. The government never declared an inconvertibility event or a change in exchange rates. Instead, the government forced foreign exporters to get permits to exchange currency. Once and if the permits were obtained, the window of opportunity for conversion was only a few hours every week. It was physically impossible for conversion demand to be met. There was not enough banking time allocated to fulfill the business demand.

One large, Japanese, London-based securities firm, a subsidiary of a large Japanese bank, routinely takes on enormous amounts of convertibility risk. So far, this convertibility risk has not caused any major problems. Nonetheless, the risks are considerable. Recently, the Japanese securities firm provided Mexican-government default protection to investors in Mexican-government foreign currency debt. The Japanese securities firm then bought default protection from a Mexican local entity. That protection was denominated in pesos. The first potential problem is the correlation of the local guarantor with the government of Mexico. A second potential problem is that in the event of a default by the government of Mexico, there may be a convertibility event, which makes it impossible to convert a large amount of pesos to a hard currency. How valuable is the protection? The Japanese security firm's auditors did not think it was very valuable. They refused to sign off on the strategy after the fact.

From the foregoing discussion, it is easy to see that different events can trigger an inability to exchange money. The event could be a revolution and a change in limits of convertibility, it could be the inability to transfer local currency out of the country, it could be lack of reserves, or it could be a new type of government barrier to conversion.

Solutions to Currency Risk

Convertibility protection language is often very broad. Trigger events are often defined as war, hostilities, confiscation of nonlocal bank assets, a moratorium, and a broad definition of any event that restricts conversion.

The following is typical of language for the definition of a credit event found in a term sheet or confirmation.

Sovereign risk means:

1. Failure by the Central Bank generally to approve or permit the exchange of Brazilian reals for USD, or any other action by the Central Bank party of the government that has the effect of prohibiting such exchange, or the transfer of any funds outside the Republic of Brazil, or the transfer of Brazilian reals within the Republic of Brazil, or USD are unavailable in any legal exchange market in the Republic of Brazil in accordance with normal commercial practice;
2. The existence of any prohibition on the receipt within the Republic of Brazil or the repatriation outside the Republic of Brazil of all or any portion of the principal, interest, capital gains, or other proceeds of assets owned by foreign persons or entities in the Republic of Brazil, including but not limited to any prohibitions imposed by the government;
3. A declaration of a general banking moratorium or any general suspension of payments by banks in the Republic of Brazil;
4. Any war (whether declared or not declared), revolution, insurrection, or hostile act that prevents the convertibility of Brazilian reals into USD; or
5. A general expropriation, confiscation, requisition, nationalization, or other action by the government that deprives OECD-domiciled banks of all or substantially all of their assets in the Republic of Brazil.

The last clause is usually inserted only when dealing with non-OECD countries. As Mexico is a recent entrant, however, it is often put in confirmations for Mexico.

Contrast the preceding definition of credit event with the following language:

> "Convertibility event" means, in the determination of the calculation agent, the enactment, promulgation, execution, or ratification of, or any change in or amendment to, any law, rule, or regulation (or in the application or official interpretation of any law, rule, or regulation), or any other act, by any governmental authority that (other than due to the failure by the counterparty to comply with such law, rule, regulation, or act) in a transaction conducted through any customary legal channels, (1) makes the conversion in all legal methods of Brazilian reals into United States dollars impossible, (2) makes the payment in all legal methods of Brazilian reals from accounts inside the Republic of Brazil to accounts outside the Republic of Brazil impossible, and/or (3) makes United States dollars unavailable in all legal methods at a spot rate of exchange from Brazilian reals. As used herein, "governmental authority" means any de facto or de jure government (or any agency or subdivision thereof), court, tribunal, administrative or other governmental authority, or any other entity (private or public) charged with the regulation of the financial markets (including the Central Bank) of the Republic of Brazil.

This definition is an attempt to cover every contingency. The language doesn't matter so long as both parties agree and are aware of what the protection will and will not do for them if a convertibility event occurs.

Naturally, settlement must be physical settlement. All payments are on a payment-versus-payment basis. But where does settlement take place? What if you can't get local currency out of the country?

Provisions are usually made for this. Physical settlement can be made to an escrow agent. This means that the protection buyer can deliver local currency to a local bank and receive U.S. dollars in an account in the United States. This satisfies the requirement that in the event of local restrictions on transferability and convertibility, the protection buyer can deposit currency locally and receive hard currency outside of the country. Exchange rates are decided by an average of a dealer poll.

Let us take a look at a typical term sheet for Argentine peso convertibility risk.

REPUBLIC OF ARGENTINA CONVERTIBILITY RISK PROTECTION
Indicative Term Sheet

Protection Buyer:	Protection buyer.
Protection Seller:	Commercial bank.
Protection Type:	Currency convertibility.
Notional:	USD 50 million.
Trade Date:	As soon as practical.
Effective Date:	One week from trade date.
Termination Date:	One year from effective date.
Protection Premium:	140 basis points per annum on the notional amount payable on an actual/360 basis paid semiannually at the beginning of the period.
Payment Terms:	On the occurrence of the defined convertibility event, the protection buyer has the right to exercise the option. Two business days after the exercise of the option (the settlement date), the seller of protection will pay the protection buyer the notional amount by wire transfer of funds immediately available in New York City. The protection buyer will pay to the protection seller the convertibility amount.
Convertibility Event:	As determined by the calculation agent, the occurrence of any of the following:

1. failure of the government of the Republic of Argentina to exchange or to approve or to permit the exchange of Argentine pesos (ARP) for U.S. dollars (USD); *or*

2. the general unavailability of USD at a spot rate of exchange (applicable to the purchase of USD for ARP) in any legal exchange market transfer officially recognized as such

by the government of the Republic of Argentina and in accordance with the normal commercial practice; *or*

3. the issuance of any order or decree by any regulatory authority in the Republic of Argentina, which has the effect of imposing any material exchange controls, limitations, or restrictions on the convertibility of ARP to USD or limiting or restricting the transfer of ARP or USD in any fashion outside the Republic of Argentina; *or*

4. the general unavailability of USD at a spot rate of exchange (applicable to the purchase of USD for ARP) in any legal exchange market transfer officially recognized as such by the government of the Republic of Argentina and in accordance with the normal commercial practice; *or*

5. any suspension of payments by banks in Argentina due to imposition by the government of the Republic of Argentina of any moratorium on the payment of indebtedness; *or*

6. war (declared or undeclared), civil strife, hostilities, or similar events in which Argentina is involved; *or*

7. the expropriation, confiscation, requisition, nationalization, or any action by the government of the Republic of Argentina that deprives Argentine or foreign entities of all or a significant portions of their assets without the assumption of liabilities of these assets in connection with the aforementioned government actions, having the effect of prohibiting these entities from paying amounts owed in USD; *or*

(continued)

8. any action taken by the Central Bank (or any successor thereto) that has the effect described in (1) or (2) in this paragraph.

Convertibility:
The convertibility amount is the notional amount multiplied by the Argentine peso exchange rate. The protection buyer will pay this amount to the protection seller either in ARP in immediately available or same-day funds by wire transfer to the account maintained by the protection seller with a bank or other financial institution in the Republic of Argentina, or in any other form then legal and continuing for settlement of ARP obligations.

Argentine Peso Exchange Rate:
The Argentine peso exchange rate will be computed based on the exchange rate determined by the calculation agent equal to the spot ARP/USD foreign exchange rate fixed by the Central Bank of the Republic of Argentina or any entity succeeding to its functions as the Central Bank and monetary authority of the Republic of Argentina (the "Central Bank of the Republic of Argentina") two business days prior to the settlement date, as such exchange rate is published. If no such quote is available on that date, the calculation agent will determine the Argentine peso exchange rate based on the foreign exchange rate then quoted by a major ARP/USD dealer in the Republic of Argentina for buying pesos for U.S. dollars in commercial or financial transactions or, if no such quote is available, the Argentine peso exchange rate will be based on the foreign exchange rate then quoted by a major ARP/USD dealer in New York for buying pesos for U.S. dollars in commercial or financial transactions. In the event that no such rate can be obtained, the calculation agent will determine the ARP/USD exchange rate in a commercially reasonable manner.

Calculation Agent:	Protection seller.
Business Days:	Days on which commercial banks and foreign exchange markets settle payments in New York, London, and Buenos Aires.
Law:	New York law shall govern this note.
Documentation:	The issuance of the protection will be documented under an International Swaps and Derivatives Association, Inc. (ISDA) master agreement.

This document simply says that the protection buyer must deliver Argentine pesos to an account in Argentina equal to the U.S. dollar notional amount at the exchange rate at the time of the convertibility event. The protection buyer has two business days to get the money to the account. If the protection buyer does this, the protection buyer will get the notional amount in U.S. dollars delivered to a New York City bank account.

Generally, the foreign exchange (FX) spot rate is the rate prior to the day of the event announcement. Most agreements allow for first looking for the Central Bank published rate for that day for the previous day. If the Central Bank hasn't published a rate, the counterparties look to four leading Brazilian banks for an average rate. If that isn't possible, the counterparties look for an average offshore rate from credible offshore dealers.

As we saw before, most of the details are negotiable, but the basic transaction is as outlined in the previous paragraph. Dealer polls, adjustments to business days, and so on are negotiable.

Physical settlement days are often adjusted so that in the event that a payment cannot be made, a grace period to make the remainder of the payments may be allowed. The period is usually three days. This is a negotiable feature between counterparties in this transaction.

The convertibility option is a solution to the currency issue. Export credit agencies and trade finance contracts can also provide protection for currency convertibility in the form of insurance guarantees. These can be expensive, however, and are not accessible in all cases to people wishing to do business in a particular country.

It is possible to purchase risk protection from a variety of sources, such as some export credit agencies, private insurers, and the trade finance market. Private insurers are rare and tend to be expensive. The trade finance market is currently looking for more convertibility protection. The market viewed recent conventional protection as inadequate (as in the case of Venezuela, mentioned previously).

Export credit agencies include, but are not limited to, the Overseas Private Investment Corporation (OPIC) in the United States or the Multilateral Investment Guarantee Agency (MIGA). OPIC will cover political risks, such as currency inconvertibility, expropriation, and political violence, with up to 20 years of protection. OPIC will insure 90 percent of the investment, but investors must bear the remaining 10 percent of risk. MIGA will cover up to 15 or even 20 years of protection, which is noncancelable by MIGA but cancelable by the insured on any anniversary date. MIGA will assume up to $50 million of liability per project.

Although insurance from export agencies is generally cheaper than convertibility protection, it is not always available. Japan's Ministry of International Trade and Industry (MITI) recently suspended its foreign exchange risk insurance. Further, export agencies may not cover the full amount of the risk. OPIC leaves an investor with a need to hedge a residual risk of 10 percent. MIGA will insure only the first $50 million of exposure. If the project creates more exposure than that, the investor must look elsewhere for protection. Many project finance groups are up to their limit on certain country risks and require more sources of longer-dated protection for both sovereign default and convertibility events.

A further difficulty arises with export agency protection. Investors often encounter delays in realizing the value of their protection. Investors are often instructed to "see what you can negotiate, then come back." The delay can be intolerable to an investor who is temporarily short of liquidity. An investor caught in a situation like this finds that the "cheaper" protection offered by an export agency can end up costing him more in business problems.

Pricing Convertibility Protection

Most investment banks and corporations are looking to the banking community for convertibility protection. Given the ambiguities surrounding this protection, should banks be involved in providing convertibility protection? Banks actually already have this risk. That is what international commercial banks do, whether that is their intention or not. Having local currency deposits forces them into the position of having convertibility risk.

It seems a natural fit for banks to offer convertibility protection, provided they can put a price on the cost of this protection and mark it to market on their books. Another consideration is regulatory risk capital. How should banks account for it?

I called the Federal Reserve Bank of New York in July 1997 to ask them what the board of governors of the Federal Reserve System says about accounting for risk capital when a bank buys and sells currency convertibility protection. They had not examined this issue. They had to ask me for whatever materials I had on the subject because they were unfamiliar with the product. In the end, they decided to lump convertibility protection in with a number of foreign exchange issues and said they would get back to me on the capital treatment.

Although banks have always had this risk, it is only recently that banks have looked at buying and selling this protection. With this focus comes a need to agree on a pricing methodology for this difficult-to-define risk.

Table 5.4 shows a comparison of convertibility option premiums with credit default risk premiums in the broker market. Notice that convertibility premiums seem to trade wider than the premiums for credit default protection.

Disinformation and misinformation plague the credit derivatives market. When asked, the broker showing indications for one-year Argentine peso convertibility protection said that although he shows a bid of 100 basis points and an offer of 140 basis points, there is no actual bid or offer. This broker thinks that convertibility protection would "trade" at 120 basis points, the midmarket of the indications.

In other words, levels are thrown up on broker screens without substance behind them. This market trades between real counterparties. These

TABLE 5.4 Sovereign Credit Default Protection versus Convertibility Protection Prices, Bid/Ask Broker Indications (basis points per annum)

	6-Month Default	6-Month Convertibility	1-Year Default	1-Year Convertibility
Argentina			70/NA	NA/140
Brazil	60/80	110/NA	70/95	120/170
Mexico			65/75	NA/110
Russia	NA/195	150/185		

Note: NA indicates bid or offer was not available.
Sources: Prebon Yanmane, Tullett Capital Markets, July 14, 1997.

are negotiated transactions. Price, terms and conditions, and size are all negotiated directly between counterparties. As there are so few real counterparties for this type of protection, the broker market is nearly useless. It is much better to call the well-known names in the credit derivatives market and negotiate and get market levels directly. This market is driven by supply and demand, and prices vary from counterparty to counterparty.

One emerging-markets credit derivatives head trader describes this protection as a knock-in spot trade in which the knock-in is independent of currency levels but dependent on the whims of sovereigns. He feels one must look for the "pocket" in the market, the "pocket" of opportunity. This is not a dealers' market. One cannot go into the market to find a "fair market." When he goes to the broker market, he finds the levels are not there; the screen prices are fiction. In his view, one must find out where one can actually trade. Credit spreads don't matter; models don't matter; intuition doesn't count. The market tells you where the spread is.

There is no exact mathematical model for convertibility protection. Most banks have not sold any convertibility protection on a stand-alone basis. They have only traded this combined with default risk. When convertibility is lumped with default protection language, a bank can purchase the hedge imbedded in macro country default protection risk. It is difficult to determine whether the buyer or the seller got a fair price for convertibility protection if there was indeed a premium at all over the regular default protection market. This is especially confusing when a convertibility event is used as a credit default trigger event. We discuss this in more detail in the section on hidden costs in default language in Chapter 8.

Dr. Hei Wai Chan of JP Morgan's New York office has researched the issue of convertibility pricing. Chan feels the likelihood of convertibility default is greater than default of a sovereign on its debt obligations. The fact that most convertibility premiums trade above default options is intuitively correct. But Chan also says: "There is not an easy way to model the convertibility risk. It's quite a challenge. KMV can model default. In principal, I can create a balance sheet for a country, with data limitations, and come up with a default price. With convertibility, there are other issues involved. It's almost like trying to build an economic model and come up with a forecast."

One of my colleagues once said that convertibility protection should be priced like a foreign exchange knock-in option. Actually it is nothing like a foreign exchange knock-in option. Knock-in options have an exchange rate trigger. That is not the case for convertibility options. The convertibility option gives the protection buyer only the right to convert at the then-current exchange spot rate. It is similar to a contingent option to exchange at the spot rate in which the trigger is a government or Central Bank action.

Other market professionals sometimes describe convertibility options as a "sovereign-linked currency 'swaption.'" Chan maintains that this doesn't describe the risk at all; this false analogy actually confuses people. This isn't a swaption—it is more like, but different from, a default option.

There are important differences between default options and convertibility options. These differences are currently reflected in the fact that convertibility options trade at a premium to default options. But that need not always be the case. The spread between a default option and a convertibility option may contract as a default event approaches, if there is certainty that both events will occur simultaneously. If a default on sovereign debt seems imminent, but convertibility of currency exists and seems continuing—albeit at a probable depreciated value—the convertibility option will trade well below the default option.

A further complication is the lack of understanding of convertibility issues, which keeps many potential market makers out of this market. Supply-and-demand factors seem to dominate the pricing of convertibility protection. Some banks are booking convertibility premiums in the banking book. They do not mark it to market. They view the sale of convertibility protection as the functional equivalent of a loan.

Other banks are not prepared to do this and must grapple with a difficult mark-to-market decision. There is no economic measure other than what the dealers quote, and it is usually a one-way market. One can poll dealers for a mark-to-market. One can also develop a model. As of this writing, I am not aware of anyone who has developed a model for marking convertibility protection to market, a model that reflects market levels.

Nonetheless, there are some methods to find out what the market might be. For instance, one might look at local-currency, domestically traded sovereign debt swapped to U.S. dollars and compare it with Euro dollar debt for the same sovereign. For Mexico, one might look at Cetes, which are rated AAA. Swap the Cetes to U.S. dollars and compare the differential between this AAA and an actual dollar-denominated AAA; the differential in spread should be the convertibility risk. That sounds easy, but there may not be a well-developed swap market in the currency in which one is most interested. A further difficulty is that many countries do not have depth and breadth to their debt markets to enable such a comparison.

The Bank of Boston is a buyer of Brazilian convertibility protection. The bank is comfortable with Brazilian risk, but on their overall balance sheet, Brazilian risk is a high percentage relative to other banks. Their Brazilian risk rivals that of Citibank. As we saw before, the key to good portfolio management is diversification, and for that reason, Bank of Boston attempts to reduce this risk. One professional bemoans the premiums he pays for convertibility protection: "To be honest with you, if you ask me, it's free money."

In 1998, Bank of Boston issued U.S. dollar–denominated one-year maturity certificates of deposit (CDs) in Brazil, which traded at LIBOR + 80 basis points to LIBOR + 100 basis points. The CDs had convertibility risk. If Bank of Boston were unable to pay in dollars because of convertibility restrictions, the CDs would pay off in Brazilian reals. Meanwhile, Bank of Boston's U.S.-issued dollar-denominated CDs trade at LIBOR flat. This would imply that convertibility should trade at 80 to 100 basis points. But Bank of Boston paid 115 basis points for this protection. The price reflected the fact that it was difficult for Bank of Boston to find counterparties.

Most countries do not have convenient issues available, as does Brazil, for short-term exposures. It is even difficult to find references in the Brazilian market as one goes longer than one year in maturity. For Russia, it is possible to try to come up with approximate pricing. One can look to the dollar-hedged Gosudarstvenii Kratkrasochnii Obligatsii (GKOs), Russian Ministry of Finance zero-coupon bills. Some period before the maturity date, the investor is required to hedge the currency risk with a Russian bank with an FX forward. If one can assess the credit risk, this can be accounted for and the rest is convertibility. But the Russian banks are state owned. The spread contains elements of convertibility and default combined. One could also account for Russian state default risk for GKOs, because if there is a default, there is default risk on the FX contract. Another alternative is to find non-Russian GKO dealers who will quote the FX market. Ideally an FX hedge with a non-Russian counterparty would make it easier to back out the convertibility premium.

There are other ways to find out where the market clears for convertibility, and these involve convertibility-linked notes. Even AAA rated banks such as Rabobank offer notes with their own issue with a convertibility event tied to principal redemption. That is one way of creating the hedge and determining where the market prices this risk. The market prices the risk where it will purchase the note linked to a convertibility event.

A classic example of how this works, which incorporates stripping the convertibility risk out of a sovereign issue, is the Tesobono trade. Tesobonos were one-year instruments issued by the Republic of Mexico. They had an unusual feature. When an investor purchased a Tesobono, the investor paid the principal amount in U.S. dollars and immediately converted the dollars to pesos. The coupon on the Tesobonos was paid in U.S. dollars. At maturity, the investor received pesos at the then-current exchange rate and had to convert the pesos to dollars.

Although many Japanese investors were willing to accept Mexican sovereign risk, they were unwilling to accept the convertibility risk. Many Japanese investors remembered the early 1980s when Mexico declared a convertibility event and it was impossible to convert pesos to dollars. Investors felt that if this happened, the exchange rate would deteriorate while they held onto pesos waiting for the next opportunity to convert.

One bank-owned Japanese securities firm developed a clever solution. They put the Tesobonos into a special purpose vehicle (SPV). Japanese investors purchased these notes. The investors paid dollars for the notes, received dollar coupons, and received dollars at maturity. Although the collateral was Tesobonos, they were guaranteed dollars. The guarantor was a AAA rated Japanese insurance company affiliated with the Japanese bank.

The Japanese securities firm then created a hedge. They persuaded the Japanese bank to issue dollar-denominated CDs in the United States with the payoff at maturity linked to Mexican peso/U.S. dollar convertibility. If there were an inconvertibility event, the investors received pesos instead of dollars.

At the time of the transaction, before the "tequila effect" of December 1994, the Tesobonos were trading at about LIBOR + 120 bps. The Japanese investors purchased the SPV notes at LIBOR + 25 bps. The U.S. investors purchased the Mexican peso/U.S. dollar convertibility-linked notes at LIBOR + 40 bps, about 50 basis points higher than the Japanese bank's funding cost in the United States at that time. U.S. investors purchased the CDs at a level around 40 basis points cheaper than where they could have purchased secondary market paper for this Japanese bank. This meant that the price the U.S. investor put on this convertibility risk was 40 basis points. The net profit to the Japanese securities firm in the transaction was 45 basis points (120 basis points on the original Tesobono minus 50 basis points on the bank new-issue CD minus 25 basis points to the SPC for the Japanese investors). The transaction was as shown in Figure 5.2 for the sovereign risk and in Figure 5.3 for the convertibility risk.

Although Mexican bonds widened dramatically after December 1994,

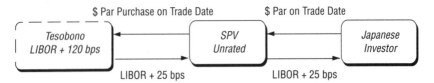

At maturity, the Tesobonos pay a Peso amount equal to the Dollar Par amount reflected at the then-current exchange rate.

The Japanese investor takes Mexico default risk, but is assured a USD payment if there is an inconvertibility event.

FIGURE 5.2   Bifurcated Tesobono Risk—Sovereign Risk

all of the investors who held their positions in a transaction that had less than a year to maturity got their money back in dollars. The inconvertibility event never occurred, and Mexico did not default on its obligations.

The method just described for finding a market clearing price for convertibility protection actually works and is defensible because it relies on true market levels. It is extremely difficult, however. We have now examined several different methods to try to get a feel for convertibility option market levels. Each has its strengths, weaknesses, and challenges. The following summary lists ways one might mark-to-market convertibility options.

- Observe market levels—the market defines the price, of course. The difficulty is that this is a one-sided market, and you may not be able to get accurate marks at all times. Broker levels are wholly unreliable for this product.
- Arbitrarily say that convertibility trades at some percentage spread above credit default protection, say 150 percent. This has the appeal of being easy as well as being currently observable for some currencies. Greater illiquidity, supply-and-demand factors, and higher probability of event risk seem to dictate that convertibility will trade wider; but there are scenarios in which it can trade inside the credit default spread. This would be when a default exists, but deeply devalued currency can still be converted. Even currently, this formula method is not true across maturities.
- Access domestically traded securities in the local currency and look at a Eurodollar sovereign issue in U.S. dollars. Swap the domestically traded security to dollars and compare the spread difference

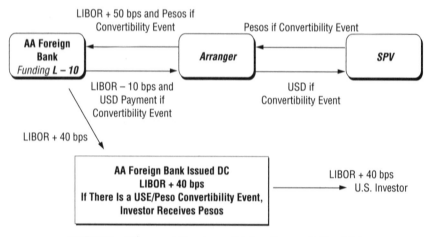

FIGURE 5.3 Bifurcated Tesobono Risk—Convertibility Risk

between the two. This spread difference should reflect the convertibility premium for the currency. This also means that there must be priceable local instruments as well as a Eurodollar issue that can be priced and referenced in the maturity of interest. At the very least, one must be able to build a convertibility curve. For many countries, there is a dearth of local currency and Eurodollar debt, which makes this method virtually impossible to implement.

■ Find a USD issue of a foreign bank that collects local deposits. This bank must convert local currency to USD. Compare that with where they issue in the U.S. market. The difference is convertibility risk premium. For example, a USD-denominated CD issued by a U.S. Brazilian bank branch that collects local deposits is Bank of Boston (A2/A). If this trades at LIBOR + 125 bps and Bank of Boston trades at about LIBOR + 20 bps for one year, the implied convertibility premium is about 105 basis points.

■ Find a convertibility-linked note and back out the convertibility premium. This method works, but you may not be able to find such a convenient issue in the market.

■ Find a sovereign with convertibility risk and strip out the convertibility risk (as shown earlier with the Tesobono transaction). The hard-dollar sovereign level in the market reflects the sovereign risk premium. The remaining spread is what the market implies is the convertibility premium. For instance, Tesobonos were trading at

LIBOR + 120 bps. The Mexico dollar SPV traded at LIBOR + 25 bps, and the convertibility-linked CD traded 65 basis points above the funding cost of the issuing bank. Therefore, the convertibility premium was 65 basis points at that time. The remaining difference was 120 – 65 – 25, or 30, basis points profit, and expenses. The challenge with this method is the unavailability of suitable debt instruments for many emerging-market countries.

If one must mark convertibility options to market, the best solution may be to adopt a policy based on a pragmatic combination of a few of the preceding reasonable methodologies. The key is to continue to observe market levels, however, because supply-and-demand factors dominate this market. "Reality checks" are essential.

I would rather be a seller of this protection than a buyer in almost all cases, with a few exceptions as noted in the next section. Banks, trading companies, leasing companies, and multinational corporations already take on convertibility risk, even if they don't currently attempt to quantify the risk on their balance sheets. At the high premiums achievable in many of these markets, banks should sell this protection.

Cross-Border Issues

With emerging-market debt, convertibility issues vary by country. There is no substitute for economic research on specific country risk. For instance, when one is trying to evaluate risks in an Asian country, one wouldn't view all Asian countries as the same. In the late 1990s, short-term interest rates in Thailand reached quadruple-digit levels, as high as 1,500 percent. There is a two-tiered foreign exchange system in Thailand, however, which means that there will not be an obstacle to delivery of the Thai baht currency, and convertibility risk was greatly diminished. Further, Thailand country cash flow was robust. Contrast that situation with Indonesia: There was a high degree of political risk in Indonesia. The largest currency issue in Indonesia was a *yen* issue. A bigger slice of Indonesia's foreign debt obligation was yen-denominated than anywhere else. This was mainly due to Japanese investment in the Indonesian local manufacturing markets and investment in debt markets.

Economists look at foreign exchange reserves as a cover against imports. Vietnam's foreign exchange reserves, for instance, were low, and trade increased. The import cover as of summer 1997 was only six to seven weeks.

Vietnam was (and still is) watched carefully for a possible default in ability to convert the local currency to hard global currencies. One of the key issues is the country cash flow with respect to foreign exchange reserves. *Country cash flow is measured as the change in foreign exchange reserves minus the change in the trading account.*

The Czech Republic ratio looked sick in summer 1997. Cash flow was rapidly draining out of the Czech Republic. Most of this money was flight capital. This looked like a situation ripe for convertibility restrictions.

In March 1995, Argentina looked close to default. In February 1997, Bulgaria looked close to default.

South Africa had only about five weeks of foreign exchange reserves. Nonetheless, South Africa relaxed convertibility laws. Despite the low reserves, lack of convertibility was strangling foreign trade. South Africa realized there was a trade-off and made the decision that trade was more important.

Brazil put a transaction tax on financial import and export of capital. There was a 7 percent transaction tax to repatriate capital. Once capital was out, it was costly to get it back in. In 1997, Brazil eliminated the tax or in some cases cut the tax to 1 percent, depending on the instrument. This means that Brazil may see more volatility in its country cash flows, although in general Brazil is a good short-term bet for sellers of convertibility protection.

Not every bank would agree with me that selling convertibility protection is a good idea. The head of credit derivatives in New York for a Japanese bank capital-markets subsidiary feels that the ability to transfer local currency can be a problem. Even if the convertibility agreement calls for a local currency deposit in the home country and a U.S. dollar deposit outside the home country, there may be a problem. He feels that central banks may try to buttress the spirit of the regulatory environment. They could limit the ability to increase local currency deposits so that the buyer of the convertibility protection cannot meet the requirements of the convertibility contract because the buyer will not be able to deliver local currency to a domestic account. The Japanese subsidiary credit derivatives head may be right. As already stated, I would risk this and sell the convertibility protection. Nothing is certain when dealing with government intervention, however.

CHAPTER 6

Credit-Linked Notes

REASONS FOR THE EXISTENCE OF CREDIT-LINKED NOTES

Credit default swaps can be imbedded in notes, which are generally referred to as credit-linked notes (CLNs). Earlier, we saw some examples of credit-linked notes. All of the types of credit derivatives we have reviewed up to now can be imbedded in note form. If credit derivatives and their off–balance sheet nature have so many benefits, why would anyone ever want to buy credit derivatives in note form?

There are five reasons to do so. The first two reasons apply to transactions in which an investor is buying either a credit-enhanced note or a note that has additional imbedded credit risk. The last three reasons apply to transactions in which an investor buys a note with additional imbedded credit risk.

1. There is no need for an International Swaps and Derivatives Association, Inc. (ISDA) master agreement or confirmation. Documentation is as simple as that for a medium-term note.
2. Investors who are not authorized to do derivatives or off–balance sheet transactions can participate in the credit derivative market through credit-linked notes.
3. Credit lines to the investor, the hedge provider, are not used. This is particularly valuable for very long dated or leveraged transactions. Unused credit lines remain open for future business.

4. If the investor is providing a hedge and is highly correlated with the reference credit, it doesn't matter. If an investor buys a note with principal risk linked to a default by the Mexican government, this creates a hedge on the Mexican government for the issuer. The issuer gets par up front. If Mexico defaults, either the issuer pays par minus the defaulted bond value, or the issuer delivers the defaulted bonds to the investor. The issuer therefore has the hedge money up front. The issuer has no credit risk to the investor. The issuer therefore does not care if the investor is another Mexican counterparty, for instance, because credit correlation between the reference credit and the investor is irrelevant.

5. For the same reason that correlation between the investor providing a hedge and the reference credit is irrelevant, the credit quality of the investor is irrelevant. A credit-linked note issuer can create a long-dated hedge with a massive payoff in the event of default with absolutely no concern about the credit quality of the investor.

The following sections discuss some typical examples that can serve as prototypes for imbedding other credit derivatives or credit risks in notes. Structured product often includes credit derivatives as a method of providing off–balance sheet transactions with trust vehicles or as means of providing credit enhancement or credit risk in structured products.

CREDIT DEFAULT–LINKED NOTES

As we saw in Chapters 3 and 5, credit default language can include many events, including convertibility events, but the events included are negotiable. There are as many variations in the definition of credit event for CLNs as there are for credit default swaps and options. Credit default–linked notes (limited recourse notes) are of four major structure types:

1. Principal-protected notes, which generally receive the credit rating of the issuer, but the investor risks loss of coupon income in the event of default of a different reference credit.

2. Boosted coupon notes, which generally receive the credit rating of the issuer, but the principal payment is linked to the default event and default value of a different reference credit, with underlying credit risk of a lower-rated credit.

3. Boosted coupon notes, which generally receive the credit rating of the issuer, in which the principal payment is linked to a default event of a different reference credit or credits and the principal payment may have levered risk or even risk of loss of the entire principal amount in the event of a default of the reference credit or reference credits.

4. Reduced coupon notes, which generally receive the credit rating of the issuer, in which the principal repayment is the face amount, and if there is a reference credit event, the termination payment is enhanced by the loss in the event of default of a reference asset.

Principal-protected notes are very popular with European investors. The investor receives a boosted coupon if there is no default on the part of a reference credit. If there is a default, however, the investor receives no further coupons and may not receive the original investment until the maturity of the note. The forgone interest income on the note mitigates the loss in the event of default for the issuer of the principal-protected note, but it may not cover all of the loss in the event of default. The value of this note is that the implied recovery value of the reference credit can be enhanced by the present value of the forgone interest on the note. This enhancement to the recovery value, particularly in the early years, can provide credit enhancement for a risky credit in a portfolio. Although this does not provide complete default protection, the asset quality of a portfolio, which benefits from this partial protection, can be enhanced. This partial protection may be enough to increase the implied rating of the reference credit from noninvestment grade to investment grade in certain instances.

The following term sheet gives an example of a boosted coupon note that receives the credit rating of a European bank, but the principal payment is linked to a default event for the Hellenic Republic. The principal repayment is also linked to the default value of a specific Hellenic Republic reference bond. These notes are also called limited recourse notes because the noteholder has no right to the issuer's general assets.

CREDIT-LINKED NOTE—LINKED TO DEFAULT BY THE HELLENIC REPUBLIC
Indicative Term Sheet

Issuer:	AA rated European bank.
Face Amount:	USD 100 million.
Currency Denomination:	USD.
Trade Date:	Today.
Settlement Date:	Five business days after trade date.
Maturity Date:	The earlier of:
	1. the early termination date, if any, *or*
	2. seven years from the settlement date.
Issue Price:	Par.
Coupon:	Six-month USD LIBOR + 125 basis points (Act/ 360, semiannual).
Redemption Amount:	If there is no credit event, par in U.S. dollars.
	If a credit event on the part of the reference credit has occurred prior to the maturity of the note, the obligation of the issuer to pay the USD redemption amount shall be discharged, and the note shall be redeemed with the early termination amount on the early termination date.
Early Termination Payment:	If a reference credit event has occurred, the issuer shall take a dealer poll of five dealers acting in good faith to obtain a market value for the reference asset. This value shall be converted to USD at the then-prevailing spot exchange rate. This amount shall be distributed to the noteholders on a pro rata basis, subject to a maximum of 100 percent.
	If the issuer is unable to obtain a market value for the securities prior to the termination date, the issuer shall deliver the reference asset to the noteholders on a pro rata basis.
Early Termination Date:	The 15th business day after a credit event.

Credit Event:

Occurs when the calculation agent is aware of publicly available information as to the existence of a credit condition.

Credit condition means either a payment default or a bankruptcy event in respect of the issuer.

Payment default means, subject to a dispute in good faith by the issuer, either the issuer fails to pay any amount due of the reference asset, or any other present or future indebtedness of the issuer for or in respect of moneys borrowed or raised or guaranteed.

Bankruptcy event means the declaration by the issuer of a general moratorium in or rescheduling of payments on any external indebtedness.

Publicly available information means information that has been published in any two or more internationally recognized published or electronically displayed financial news sources.

Reference Credit:

Hellenic Republic.

Reference Asset:

Hellenic Republic bonds.

Currency:

Greek drachma (GDR).

Amount:

To be determined (based on the USD/GDR exchange rate at settlement).

Coupon:

11.75%.

Maturity:

Seven years.

Nonrecourse Clause:

The noteholders have no right to the issuer's general assets. The principal of the note is repayable based only on the performance of the reference asset at the early termination date or at maturity, whichever is sooner.

Noncollateral Clause:

The reference asset does not serve as collat-

(continued)

	eral for the noteholders. If a credit event occurs, the noteholders have no priority claim to the reference asset.
Denomination:	USD 1 million.
Business Days:	Days on which commercial banks and foreign exchange markets settle payments in London, New York, and Athens.
Listing:	London Stock Exchange.
Lead Manager:	Issuer.

Although the note is USD denominated, in the event of default, the noteholder may take delivery of Greek drachma-denominated bonds. The investor then has not only the risk of default on the part of the government of Greece, the Hellenic Republic, but also the potential risk of convertibility from Greek drachma to USD.

The preceding is a term sheet and is not meant to be a legal document on which clients can rely in the event of a dispute. As such, the default events are rather loosely defined, and investors must examine final documentation drafts as well as final documentation for actual default language. For examples of possibilities of events that may be included in default language, refer to the section in Chapter 8 on hidden costs in default language.

Although it is not the final document and is not meant to be as complete in language, this term sheet includes important caveats as to the nonrecourse status of the note and clarifies that the reference asset is not deemed to serve in any way as collateral for the noteholder. Although term sheets are not necessarily meant to be drafted by lawyers, they should not be misleading and are often held in deal files. It is good practice that if key conditions of a term sheet are renegotiated, a final term sheet should complement the final legal documentation so that all parties to the transaction have up-to-date representations of the trade that replace outdated material.

Credit default notes referencing emerging-market debt and pools of emerging-market debt are becoming more popular. In June 1997, Dresdner Kleinwort Benson and JP Morgan brought a deal to market. The DEM 100 million note had a seven-year maturity. The credit event is based on a credit default event of any one of a pool of reference credits: Brazil, Argentina,

Venezuela, Ecuador, Mexico, Turkey, or Russia. If a credit event occurs, the investor gets a reduced principal amount.

In Chapter 4, we saw an example of a geared default option imbedded in a credit-linked note, linked to a default by the government of Mexico. The principal payment had levered downside risk in the event of a default of the reference credit. These notes are even riskier than the notes with one-for-one payoff amounts linked to potential credit events of a reference asset.

A rarer form of credit default note gives the investor an *enhanced* payoff in the event of a default of a reference credit. In this instance, the coupon on the note can be thought of as an option premium payment. Part or all of the coupon is reduced by the per annum option premium that would be paid for the credit protection purchased by the note investor. The investor receives a minimum of par or par plus the loss in the event of default of a reference asset. The following term sheet shows an example of a credit default–linked note in which the investor receives an enhanced payment in the event of default by the United Mexican States (UMS). The principal payment is enhanced by the decline in the value of the reference asset.

CREDIT-LINKED NOTE—LINKED TO UMS CREDIT EVENT
Indicative Term Sheet

Issuer:	AA rated European bank.
Face Amount:	USD 10 million.
Currency Denomination:	USD.
Trade Date:	Today.
Settlement Date:	Five business days after trade date.
Maturity Date:	
	The earlier of:
	1. the nonscheduled termination date, if any, *or*
	2. February 1, 2001.
Issue Price:	Par.

(continued)

Coupon: 3.00% payable semiannually on a 30/360 basis.

Redemption Amount: If there is no credit event, par in U.S. dollars.

                                           If there is a credit event, the investor shall receive the termination payment on the non-scheduled termination date, and all obligations of the issuer shall be discharged.

Nonscheduled Termination Date: With five business days notice (even if this date is after the maturity date) following a credit event with a termination payment being made.

Termination Payment: Investor receives the U.S. dollar amount calculated as follows *only* upon a credit event:

                                           [(Face Amount Par) + (Face Amount × (Par − Market Value)] + Accrued Coupon Interest, if any

                                           where Market Value means the USD-denominated market value of the reference security on the notification date determined by the calculation agent with reference to a dealer panel.

                                           Note: The issuer pays accrued coupon interest up to the earlier of the nonscheduled termination date *or* the maturity date.

Dispute: If there is a dispute between the parties as to the occurrence of a credit event unresolved on the maturity date, a credit event will be deemed to occur on that date.

Notification Date: If a credit event occurs during the term of the transaction, the investor shall have the right to designate a nonscheduled termination date by delivering notice (on the notification date) to the issuer of the occurrence of such credit event. Such notice must contain a description in reasonable detail of the facts giving rise to the credit event.

Credit Event: Occurs when the issuer is aware of publicly available information as to the existence of a credit condition and at the same time materiality exists.

Credit condition means either a payment default or a bankruptcy event in respect of the issuer; any war, revolution, insurrection, or hostile act that interferes with foreign exchange transactions; or the expropriation, confiscation, requisition, or nationalization of nonlocal banks, the declaration of a banking moratorium, or suspension of payments by local banks.

Payment default means, subject to a dispute in good faith by the issuer, either the issuer fails to pay any amount due of the reference asset, or any other present or future indebtedness of the issuer for or in respect of moneys borrowed or raised or guaranteed, in an amount in aggregate of not less than USD 100 million (or its equivalent in other currencies) becomes due and payable prior to its stated maturity otherwise than at the option of the issuer or any such amount of indebtedness is not paid when due or, as the case may be, within any applicable grace period.

Bankruptcy event means the declaration by the issuer of a moratorium in or rescheduling of payments on any external indebtedness.

Materiality means that the price of the reference asset less price adjustment is 90 percent or less relative to the initial price as reasonably determined by the calculation agent.

Publicly available information means information that has been published in any two or more internationally recognized published or electronically displayed financial news sources.

(continued)

Nonetheless, if either of the parties or any of their respective affiliates is cited as the sole source for such information, then such information will be deemed not to be public information.

Price adjustment means the price of a reference U.S. Treasury security on the valuation date less the price on the effective date. The reference U.S. Treasury security will be selected by the calculation agent to match, as far as possible, the maturity and other features of the reference asset.

Market value means on any day, with respect to the relevant reference security, the percentage equal to the unweighted arithmetic mean of the firm USD-denominated bid prices (exclusive of any accrued but unpaid interest and expressed as a percentage of principal amount) for such reference security provided to the calculation agent on such day by at least two but not more than five referenced dealers.

Reference Credit:	United Mexican States (Ba2).
Reference Security:	United Mexican States, global bond.
	Maturity: February 2001.
	Currency Denomination: USD.
	Coupon: 9.75%.
Business Days:	Days on which commercial banks and foreign exchange markets settle payments in London and New York.
Calculation Agent:	Issuer.
Denomination:	USD 1 million.
Listing:	London Stock Exchange.
Lead Manager:	Issuer.

CREDIT-SENSITIVE NOTES

Credit-sensitive notes provide for an increase in the coupon paid to an investor in the event of a downgrade. If the credit downgrade is severe enough, the investor may have the right to put the note back to the issuer.

IFC Thailand (IFCT) issued a credit-sensitive note in August 1997. The maturity of the note is 10 years, and the investor has the right to put the note to the issuer for any reason at the end of five years (European-style put). At the time of issue, IFCT rating was A3/A−. The coupon adjusts if the note is downgraded. If the note rating slips two notches to BBB, the coupon increases by 50 basis points (bps). If the note slips to BBB−, the coupon increases 75 basis points. If the note slips below BBB−, the investor can put the bond to the issuer any time over the life of the bond. This credit put is unrelated to the European put at the end of year five. Shortly after this bond came to market, five-year credit default put for IFCT traded at 50 basis points per annum.

INDEX-LINKED NOTES

Index-linked notes have been in the market for several years. The payoff at maturity, or sometimes the coupon of the securities, is subject to the performance of a basket of reference credits. This is very similar to the concept of an index-linked bond. Notes can be structured to give an enhanced payment if a basket of securities increases in value. Similarly, the note may give an enhanced payment if the basket of securities declines in value. This allows investors to take either a bullish or a bearish view on a basket of emerging-market countries or on a selected set of countries. The investor may earn a reduced coupon. The coupon is reduced by the amount of premium necessary to purchase an option on the upside or downside of the selected reference credits. These notes can also be structured as discount notes. If investors are willing to take principal risk, highly leveraged structures can be created.

For instance, an investor may accept a zero-coupon for the upside of a basket weighted with a pro rata payout of a basket of selected reference assets. The investor might choose one-third of the price upside of an Argentine government bond, one-third of the upside of a Brazilian government bond, and one-third of the upside of a Russian government bond.

This concept can be extended to commodity price performance, first-to-default basket structures, or indexes of any kind. The following term sheet shows an example of a Standard & Poor's (S&P) bear note. The investor receives a payoff at maturity linked to the downside of the S&P 500 index. For every percentage point decline in the S&P, the investor receives one percent over par at maturity. This is a one-for-one payout on the downside of the S&P. If the investor were willing to take some principal risk and risk receiving 98 instead of 100 at maturity, the leverage on the payout could be increased. This type of structure, either a bear structure as shown in the term sheet or a bullish structure, is typical of index-linked notes.

The S&P bear note provides an enhanced return in the event of a sustained weakness in the U.S. equity market while protecting the investors' initial capital outlay. The S&P bear note could also be useful to partially hedge an underlying equity portfolio that the investor may wish to continue to hold for strategic reasons.

S&P BEAR NOTE
Term Sheet

Indicative Terms & Conditions:

Issuer:	AA rated financial institution.
Instrument:	Euro medium-term note.
Size:	Minimum USD 10 million.
Issue Date:	As soon as practical.
Maturity:	One year from issue date.
Issue Price:	100% of size.
Coupon:	Zero.
Redemption:	$100\% \times \{1 + [(\text{S\&P 500}_{Trade} - \text{S\&P 500}_{Maturity})/ \text{S\&P 500}_{Trade}]\}$

expressed as a percent of par.

Minimum redemption 100% of par, where:

$\text{S\&P 500}_{Trade}$ = S&P 500 index at trade date as determined by calculation agent.

	$\text{S\&P } 500_{\text{Maturity}}$ = S&P 500 index closing level two days prior to maturity date as determined by the calculation agent.
Listing:	None.
Arranger:	Investment bank.
Calculation Agent:	Arranger.
Note Seller:	Investment bank.
Suitability:	The bonds will be sold to an investor with such knowledge and experience in financial and business matters to be capable of evaluating the merits and risks of the prospective investment.
Updates:	Calculation agent will provide updated pricing and payoff profile information for this note, upon request.

CHAPTER 7

Synthetic Collateralized Loan Obligations

Balance sheet management requires many tools. While single-name credit derivatives are gaining in popularity, they are an inefficient tool for laying off credit risk for a balance sheet of loans. In many ways, total rate of return swaps (TRORS) and credit default swaps are condiments to be used in conjunction with a broader strategy. We'll talk more about bank best practices and credit management strategies later in this book. Key to the strategy of banks keen to lay off credit risk are synthetic collateralized loan obligations (CLOs).

This book isn't meant to be a guide to securitization. The following discussion gives a brief refresher on some of the key features of securitization, but I won't delve into great detail about the difference between term securitizations and conduits. Later, when I introduce some of the structures, I may leave out features that are not germane to the focus of the discussion, which will center around the imbedded credit derivatives and structural risks. For practitioners interested in more detail, I list some of my favorite resources in the bibliography.

GENERAL COMMENTS ON SECURITIZATION

Most of the following comments apply to U.S. law and tax and accounting treatment, but the issues raised apply to virtually any securitization. Securitizations must address issues of bankruptcy, accounting issues, tax issues, and credit enhancement. In order for investors to have the highest priority claim against the assets in a securitization, they must have protection from bankruptcy of the original owner of the assets (the "seller") or any creditor lien including a government lien involving taxes. If a bank is the seller of the assets, then protection from bankruptcy of the original owner is not an issue. This protection is usually accomplished via a "true sale at law" of the assets to a special purpose entity (SPE). The SPE is a specially created corporation or trust that is "bankruptcy remote" from the original seller of the assets.

Accountants will want to ensure that the financing gets off–balance sheet treatment. Usually this means that the SPE must be legally independent of the seller. For instance, the SPE cannot be a wholly owned subsidiary of the seller, or the assets of the SPE would have to be consolidated on the seller's balance sheet under U.S. general accepted accounting procedures (GAAP).

Sellers want to avoid creating a taxable event by the sale of assets. For tax purposes, the seller wants to characterize this transaction as a financing. Tax laws are independent of bankruptcy treatment and accounting treatment. The securitization is usually structured as seller debt for tax purposes but as a sale for bankruptcy purposes.

Credit enhancement is another key feature of securitizations. Often several strategies for credit enhancement are employed in a single securitization. One method is to purchase a credit wrap purchased from a guarantor. This can be in the form of a surety bond guaranteeing principal and interest, although sometimes just principal is guaranteed. In this instance, the highest rating possible will be that of the credit wrap provider. The amount of credit enhancement depends on the deal structure and is usually expressed as a multiple of the expected loss level. For instance, to get an AAA rating, a general rule is that the credit enhancement must equal five times the expected loss level. The amount of enhancement required declines for lower rating requirements.

Overcollateralization is another form of credit enhancement. This may mean that more assets are placed in the SPE than are required to meet the deal's cash flow needs in a static environment. It may also mean that exogenous collateral, such as U.S. Treasury bills (T-bills) or bank certificates of deposit (CDs), is introduced to provide additional cash flow certainty.

Another credit enhancement method is using tranching to create more than one class of debt within a given structure. The holders of the lower or subordinated classes get a higher return along with higher risk. The subordinated debt holders agree to absorb losses before the senior debt holders. Several tranches may exist in one deal, and the payments due to each tranche holder are defined in the prospectus according to the tranche payment priority. Obviously, the more certain the payment, the higher the credit rating and the lower the return.

Two other methods are cousins and are often confused. The first is use of a reserve fund. The issuer will deposit cash or excess spread in a trust account, and these funds can be used to meet principal and interest payments as needed. The second method also involves excess spread and collateral interest remaining after payment of investor coupons, and fees can be used to offset nonperforming assets.

"Cash flow" transactions focus on the sufficiency of cash flow generated by the collateral pool to meet the interest and principal obligations arising from the notes issued by the CLO. The rating of the notes depends on this cash flow sufficiency. The notes issued in the Secured Loan Trust structure discussed later in this chapter get their ratings based on an estimate of sufficiency of cash flow to be roughly equivalent to those generated by an investment-grade-rated note. If the cash flow deal is properly structured, investors only experience a loss if there are defaults in the collateral pool. Cash flow CLO transactions have a two-to-four-year revolving period. Principal is reinvested, and there is no amortization during this "lock-out" period. The coupon is paid out of interest on the underlying collateral, and fees are also paid from this cash flow stream. During the lock-out period, the excess spread in the deal usually generates cash flows to build cash reserves. Cash flow deals usually restrict trading. The lock-out period is followed by an amortization period in which both principal and interest are repaid usually according to a predetermined amortization schedule. These CLOs may amortize early if one of several unwind triggers is breached. In that case, investors will receive sequential payments of principal and interest. Their payment priority will depend on the tranche in which they invested.

"Market value" CLOs generally do not restrict trading and derive income both from trading and from interest on invested assets. The portfolio of assets is actively managed, and market as well as credit considerations are important to the asset manager. Investors who require a mark-to-market on their investments might prefer these structures. The ratio of the market value of assets to the face value of liabilities is the focus of a market value CLO. The "haircut" (required overcollateralization) of the assets protects investors from the price volatility, or volatility of the market value of the assets. These deals have built-in triggers so that the minimum haircut level must always be maintained or else the assets must be sold to pay down liabilities or the assets must be sold and exchanged for very highly liquid instruments. Market value deals are rarely used in synthetic securitizations because the trigger usually kicks in at the worst possible time. In the trigger scenario, the assets are likely to be at their most illiquid. Nonetheless, we may see more of these deals in a deteriorating economic environment when defaults increase. When the collateral pool includes defaulted bonds or loans, the market value approach may be more appealing because these assets do not generate predictable cash flow streams.

UNWIND TRIGGERS

There are several types of possible unwind triggers that can cause the early termination of a fixed-level structure or that can cause early amortization of an amortizing structure. These triggers will vary by structure and include insolvency of the issuer if applicable, breaching a boundary condition for collateral maintenance, or reaching a certain level of defaults on the underlying reference obligors or assets among others.

Triggers are usually labeled as dynamic or static. The following is a description of a *dynamic trigger*: When a structure is linked to the issuer, if the mark-to-market of the swap reaches a prespecified percent of the market price of the asset, the issuer as swap counterparty may have the right to trigger an unwind. This prespecified trigger, known as the "gap margin," is usually set to 85 percent of the market price of the asset for liquid investment-grade assets, as this is the usual worst-case overnight move in underlying assets. This trigger will be set based on several factors: credit quality of the underlying assets, maturity of the transaction, size of the transaction, price volatility of the assets and derivatives transaction, and available endogenous and exogenous factors related to the quality of the underlying asset and swap. As an added fail-safe feature, this dynamic trigger can be scaled to decline as the public credit rating of the underlying assets declines.

A key factor in determining unwind triggers is the degree of liquidity of the underlying assets. The deal structurer usually conservatively sets unwind triggers to liquidate the underlying assets to cover the expected potential market-risk exposure on an imbedded swap. The potential market-risk exposure is the sum of the mark-to-market exposure on the swap plus the potential move of the underlying asset price and the swap mark-to-market between notice of liquidation and closeout.

Interest-rate swaps imbedded in credit-linked structures are problematic. When they are employed at all, the issues that swaps pose depend on the seniority of the swap counterparty in the event of an unwind. Sometimes credit wraps are applied either to the swap or to the underlying assets themselves. Credit wraps enhance the overall rating of a structure.

A *static trigger* usually comes into play when a certain boundary condition is met. A predetermined level of defaults of the underlying assets, regardless of price, is an unwind trigger. In the event of default of the underlying asset, the Security Trustee liquidates the underlying assets by soliciting dealer bids. In the case of loans, there must be some preagreed pricing mechanism. If there is an interest-rate swap involved, a deal poll will usually provide the mark-to-market on the derivatives transaction. The Security Trustee pays the swap counterparty the positive mark-to-market on the swap (if any) and remits any remaining value to the investors.

Another static trigger takes into account hypothetical worst-case assumptions about absolute price levels as a percentage of par value of the assets. An unwind trigger will be set for the asset prices reaching the estimated recovery value of the underlying assets in the event of default. Additional triggers may be set on a case-by-case basis.

SYNTHETIC CLOs

Investors have become familiar with the concept of tranching risks through products that have been in the market for years: collateralized mortgage obligations (CMOs), collateralized debt obligations (CDOs), and other tranched asset-backed securities. Synthetic CLOs create tranched exposure to a portfolio of reference credits. The difference between a synthetic CLO and another CLO is simply that we employ credit derivatives in the structure of the synthetic CLO. In fact, it is possible to create a synthetic CLO using only credit derivatives.

The terminology applied to synthetic CLOs is often confusing, and the only defense for this problem is to have a clear understanding of the structural features rather than to rely on somewhat arbitrary labels to guide understanding. The benefits of synthetic CLOs vary depending on the structure. In general, they are used to synthetically take assets off the balance sheet, in whole or in part; to reduce the required regulatory capital held against assets; to create a new source or sources of funding; to increase return on equity (ROE); and to increase return on assets (ROA). The effectiveness of various types of synthetic CLOs at accomplishing these goals is arguable. As we shall see later, reduction in asset risk is mixed, reduction in required regulatory capital varies by structure, and internal calculations of ROE or return on economic capital and ROA vary by financial institution.

Synthetic CLOs are sometimes called "balance sheet CLOs" to indicate that the issuer retains risk in the form of a first-loss piece. This first-loss piece is also called the equity piece and provides credit enhancement to the other tranches in the deal. If there is a default, the equity piece will absorb losses first, up to the cap amount indicated for this tranche. The JP Morgan structure discussed in a later section is a balance sheet CLO.

Arbitrage CLOs are created to sell the equity piece to outside investors who want the benefits of high yields and leverage at the cost of high risk. The investor requirements are an important deal driver for these structures. The "securitized loan trust" transaction discussed later is an arbitrage CLO.

One type of synthetic CLO works best for highly rated banks, and it is usually termed a hybrid structure. Credit risk is first imbedded in unrated or rated medium-term notes, and the medium-term notes are then securitized. There are several types of hybrid structures, but the two common major types illustrate the key concepts. First, if the medium-term notes were each linked to a specific balance sheet asset and if the entire credit risk of the asset were imbedded in the medium-term note, the structure would have all the elements of both a balance sheet CLO and an arbitrage CLO. In the event of default of the reference obligation, either the reference obligation would be delivered to the investor in lieu of par at maturity, or the investor would receive an early payout on the medium-term note equal only to the recovery value of the reference obligation. This is the case with some dedicated structures issued by SPEs. Basically this structure is a pro rata basket credit-linked note, which has been dubbed a securitization. The second major type of hybrid synthetic CLO is a balance sheet CLO. Credit-linked notes are linked to the credit risk of a reference obligor but may not specify the exact reference obligation, although the seniority in bankruptcy will be specified. This is usually specified as a senior unsecured debt obligation that would have a recovery value of 51 percent, the average recovery value according to Moody's. This structure may or may not cover all of the risk of the original owner of the asset. If the amount recovered is greater than 51 percent, this is a windfall for the original owner. If the amount recovered is less than 51 percent, the original owner may have residual unhedged risk to the reference obligor's senior unsecured debt. The credit-linked notes are then packaged in an SPE. The resulting pool of credit risks is then tranched and sold to investors. The junior notes are equivalent to the equity, and the original owner of the credit risks retains the junior notes. Because the original credit-linked notes used to create the pool of risks have the credit rating of the original seller of the credit risk, this structure works only for highly rated banks. To get the tightest offering spread possible for the senior tranche sold to public investors, an explicit credit rating is required.

Synthetic CLOs can be linked or delinked transactions. If the bank selling the assets is issuing medium-term notes in its own name with imbedded credit risk of another senior secured reference obligor, the CLO is said to be *linked*. This means that the medium-term-note rating is linked to the bank selling the assets, since the medium-term note can have a rating no higher than the credit rating of the bank selling the assets. If the selling bank's credit rating is not a factor in the structure of the synthetic CLO, the transaction is said to be *delinked*. This is the case for assets that have the status of "true sale under law."

The quality of the portfolio of reference credits is usually strictly controlled with an optimization program, which constrains credit quality, credit enhancement based on historical default levels, maturity, portfolio diversification, asset-to-liability maturity gap, and liquidity eligibility, among other potential criteria. The program uses many data inputs and takes into account recovery rates based on the debt position in the capital structure and collateral type. It is impossible to list all of the possible model inputs and protective covenants. In fact, these may change depending on the collateral and deal structure. Future sections in this chapter will give the reader a better idea of the more common types of synthetic CLOs, and these descriptions should provide some intuition of the types of criteria required for individual synthetic CLOs.

The key to bringing a synthetic CLO to market is understanding how to structure and to sell the synthetic CLO. The structurer must understand the investors' needs, including regulatory, tax, and accounting issues. What investors have in common is that they value diversification as a good. As we mentioned before, the CLO should be structured so that the underlying reference obligations represent a well-diversified portfolio of credits. What constitutes a well-diversified portfolio of credits? One way to determine this is to calculate a Moody's diversity score. For instance, one could map each reference obligor to the appropriate industry classification. Standard & Poor's (S&P) has 39 industry classifications originally developed for collateralized bond obligations (CBOs), but the diversity score concept was first introduced by Moody's. Moody's has classifications for 32 distinct industries. Let's use Moody's for the following example. The mapping may require judgment calls, but one can get advice from Moody's while doing this. Once the reference obligors have been mapped, the structurer can use Table 7.1.

Usually for up to 20 firms in the same industry, the Moody's diversity score is 5.00, but this may be different depending on the names and the overall structure. For instance, if you have three reference obligors that fall into the industry classification "oil and gas," the diversity score is 2.00. Once you have done this for all of your reference obligors and industry classifications, you sum the diversity scores to get the total diversity score for the portfolio. If you have only 32 reference obligors in a given portfolio, the best diversity score you could achieve is 32. This means that you have only one reference obligor in each industry classification. In terms of industry concentration, this is the most diversified portfolio, comprised of 32 reference obligations. Once the diversity score for a given deal is decided, this level must be maintained or bettered throughout the life of the deal, and the diversity score is stated in the deal prospectus.

TABLE 7.1   Diversity Score of Firms in Same Industry

Number of Firms in Same Industry	Diversity Score
1	1.00
2	1.50
3	2.00
4	2.33
5	2.67
6	3.00
7	3.25
8	3.50
9	3.75
10	4.00
>10	Individually determined

Source: Moody's.

The diversity score isn't the entire story, however. The concentration by individual reference obligor is important. The concentration by country and sometimes by region in a country is also important. Synthetic CLOs will have limits on the maximum percentage in any given reference obligor, as well as on the maximum percentage in any given industry classification. If we had only 32 reference obligors, the most diversified portfolio would invest only 1/32 in each name, or 3.125 percent in each reference obligor. Of course, this is a simplified view, because synthetic CLOs generally have many more reference obligations. For multinational deals, there may be limits for country risk concentration and for maturity for any given country. The key is to diversify and to limit concentration risk. For this purpose, an optimization program can be employed to help establish the reference portfolio. As with other models, the optimization program is a helpful guide, not a substitute for some manual labor and management judgment.

RATING CRITERIA

Moody's and S&P designed minimum rating-level criteria for the CBO market that can be adapted to the CLO market. Each rating agency is slightly different. I'll once again focus on Moody's criteria. Moody's provides a table of rating factors to assign to each rating category. The principal amount of the loan is then multiplied by the rating factor for its assigned rating. The sum of these values is the cumulative rating. This cumulative rating must remain at a prespecified minimum level. Table 7.2 gives an example of how this would work for a portfolio comprised of equal amounts of four loans that have their internal credit categories already mapped to Moody's ratings. The weighted average sum of the rating factors is 282.5. On the Moody's

TABLE 7.2 Summary of Asset Rating Factors

Obligor	Amount ($M)	Moody's Rating	Rating Factor
Loan 1	25	Aa3	40
Loan 2	25	A2	120
Loan 3	25	Baa3	610
Loan 4	25	Baa2	360

look-up table, a Baa1 rating has a rating factor of 260, and a Baa2 rating has a rating factor of 360. Therefore, we would assign a rating of Baa2 to this portfolio.

Of course, as we saw before, other considerations such as collateral could affect the portfolio rating. In an actual synthetic CLO, other considerations such as cash flow priority will affect tranche ratings.

In the preceding discussion, I avoided the issue of credit mapping. One of the key challenges for banks and other institutions hoping to securitize loans in the form of a synthetic CLO is mapping internal credit ratings for loans to Moody's and S&P credit ratings. Sometimes banks find that they are not internally consistent in the way they classify loans. This is an especially poignant problem when large banks merge. The merged bank may find they have dueling credit standards and incompatible loan systems. First, the merged bank must overcome these challenges and vet the new loan portfolio. Second, the merged bank must tackle the internal systems issues to be able to organize what is now a massive loan portfolio. The bank must set standards on economic capital to be reserved against the loan portfolio. This should lead to a consistent method for calculating the ROA and the ROE for the loan portfolio. When the bank is finally ready to securitize these assets with a synthetic CLO, it must map its internal credit ratings to the rating agency credit ratings. Now the bank is ready to evaluate the menu of structures available to determine the optimal benefits to reduction of regulatory and economic capital that affect returns. The various structures pose trade-offs in the available benefits, and newly merged banks typically spend more time wrangling with internal politburos than in the actual structuring of the first synthetic CLO.

BLACK BOX STRUCTURES

Many structures in the market present investors with a "black box." This refers to the fact that the collateral in the black box is not disclosed. Figure 7.1 shows one example of this type of structure in which a trust receives the total rate of return (TROR) of a pool of undisclosed assets. The investors receive the total rate of return on the pool of securities less a "funding cost," or fee paid to a bank arranger. The total rate of return to the investor is further enhanced because the investor receives an added premium for assuming the credit default risk in the event of the default of a defined refer-

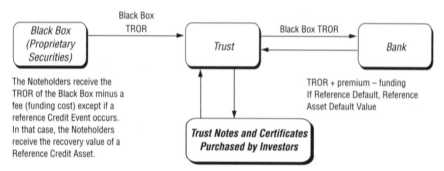

FIGURE 7.1   Credit-Linked Note: Linked to Total Return Swap and a Credit Default Swap

ence credit. The diversified securities in the black box may receive a rating, and the reference asset rating is as high as or higher than the black box.

SECURED LOAN TRUSTS: SYNTHETIC CLOs AND TRORS

Collateralized bond obligations and collateralized loan obligations have been used in the mortgage market for more than 10 years. Just as in the "black box" structure, credit derivatives are used to create slight differences to well-known structures. Insurance companies in particular have become very interested in these structures, particularly for CLOs backed by noninvestment-grade collateral. Whereas securitized loan trusts are created that result in AA rated floaters, the more interesting side of the transaction is the residual piece, also known as the equity piece. Figure 7.2 shows this side of the transaction.

Three major challenges in bringing a successful CLO deal backed by noninvestment-grade collateral to market revolve around the following three issues:

1. Finding appropriate collateral, whether highly leveraged transactions (HLTs), TRORS on HLTs, marginal investment-grade collateral, or a small component of acceptable high-yield bonds.
2. Finding the fund manager.
3. Finding the equity piece buyer compatible with the fund manager choice.

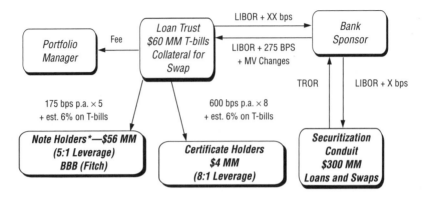

*Note Holders and Certificate Holders have pari passu cash flow priority. Profit and loss is magnified by leverage.

FIGURE 7.2   Secured Loan Trust

The first two pieces, for the note holder and the certificate holder, are traditionally thought of as equity pieces. The equity piece is potentially the most rewarding and the most risky part of the deal.

For CLOs with insurance company investors, the equity piece is tranched into two categories: a note and a certificate. The note is often investment-grade rated and held by an insurance company. Reclassified as a note, these cash flows now receive favorable balance sheet treatment for insurance companies. The certificate is now technically the equity piece. It is pari passu with the note, however. There are structures in which the certificate is subordinated, but it need not be, as in the example shown in Figure 7.2.

The only difference in cash flows is that the certificate has 8:1 leverage whereas the note has 5:1 leverage. The leverage will depend on the collateral and the structure. Rating agencies have strict criteria on how the collateral must be diversified for the note piece to achieve an investment-grade rating.

Diversification is key because it is related to correlation. As we saw earlier with first-to-default basket structures, concentration risk increases with increasing correlation. This is to say that the credit exposure due to event risk increases with increasing correlation. Furthermore, the point of the CLO is to diversify credit risk. Therefore, minimizing correlation among assets is key.

Both the note holders and the certificate buyers put up cash. This is used to purchase T-bills or other highly rated assets, which serve as collateral enhancement for the trust. If loans in the trust default, and if there is insufficient cash flow, the note holders and certificate holders suffer first. The note holder investment-grade rating is not on the entire cash flow amount of the base case scenario. In the case of the example shown in Figure 7.2, that would imply that the note holders receive an investment-grade rating on a note that has a coupon of around 14.75 percent $[(5 \times 1.75\%) + 6\%]$. The investment-grade rating may actually be on return of initial cash investment plus a nominal return. The note is technically investment-grade rated, but only for a low coupon. The potential excess above this low coupon would not receive an investment-grade rating due to the lower probability of receipt of a high, above-market return for a BBB asset.

In this way securitization conduits can obtain additional collateral to enhance a portfolio of assets and create salable equity or residual cash flows.

EQUITY PIECE BUYERS

The buyers of the certificate, or nominal equity piece, have typically been high-yield investors reaching for yield. In the example shown in Figure 7.2, the equity investor has the opportunity to earn interest on the posted Treasury collateral and a net of 600 basis points (bps) per annum (p.a.) with 8 times leverage. If we assume 6 percent for the Treasury collateral, plus 6 percent × 8 for the equity piece, the hedge fund has the opportunity to earn 54 percent. But this comes with a great deal of risk because any losses on the reference obligations will hit the equity holder pari passu with the note holders, but with the impact of greater leverage. A rating is irrelevant to the certificate investors, but the quality and the diversification of the reference obligors are of keen interest to them due to the great risk involved. Certificate holders often demand full disclosure of the composition of the underlying portfolio and perform their own stress tests to satisfy themselves that the potential net reward is worth the risk.

Hedge funds will often ask to receive the equity cash flows in the form of a TRORS, if this is possible. The hedge fund assumes the market risk and the credit risk of the equity piece, but this is a synthetic purchase in the form of a TRORS and has the added advantage of providing additional leverage to the hedge fund as well as a potential tax advantage in some venues.

In the U.S. there are distinct tax advantages to doing a TRORS on an equity piece, as opposed to purchasing the equity piece outright. Netting of interest income and expense can be difficult, and using a swap gets around a possible disallowance for Federal tax purposes. Swaps maintain the character of the income. All swap income is ordinary income. For an outright purchase, equity income can fall into the interest income and capital loss categories. Furthermore, for Federal income taxes, 3 percent of itemized deductions may be disallowed for highly leveraged assets. For state tax purposes, especially in New York where many investors are located, the investor may lose additional deductions.

CASH FLOW OVERVIEW

Earlier we mentioned that the note holders and the certificate holders could receive highly leveraged returns. What is the source of these cash flows? In the example shown in Figure 7.2, $300 million of reference obligations are paying an average coupon of the London interbank offering rate (LIBOR) plus 275 basis points. The loan trust receives these cash flows, and pays LIBOR + XX bps to the bank sponsor. The net cash flow available to pay the note holders and the certificate holders is then 275 basis points per annum on $300 million minus the following: fees to the portfolio manager; XX, representing compensation to the bank sponsor in the form of the funding cost of the loan trust; and any retained spread to enhance the collateral of the loan trust.

Because we stated the returns in the static case environment for the note holders and the certificate holders, we can back out the remaining cash flows. We can ignore the interest-rate return on the collateral because that cash flow stream is not involved in netting out the cash flow stream derived from the reference obligations. For the note holders, the net cash flows in the static case are $56,000,000 \times 5 \times 0.0175$, or $4,900,000. For the certificate holders, the net cash flows in the static case are $4,000,000 \times 8 \times 0.06$, or $1,920,000. The sum is $6,820,000 and represents approximately 227 bps per annum on $300,000,000. The underlying assets throw off 275 bps per annum. The bank sponsor, the portfolio manager, and the loan trust have more than 47 bps per annum to divide among themselves. On a deal $300,000,000 in size, this represents more than $1,410,000 per annum. There are obvious economies of scale in doing these deals, and that is why these deals are usually done with several hundred million dollars in underlying assets.

How much does the bank sponsor require? This figure is negotiable, but it is compared with opportunity costs for the bank sponsor. The bank sponsor is essentially receiving the cash flows of a synthetic floating rate note (FRN). The implied rating of the floating rate note is usually approximately A or at worst BBB. The bank sponsor evaluates the degree of protection provided by the Treasury collateral, the diversification of the portfolio of HLTs, and the structural considerations of the secured loan trust (SLT).

Notice that I started from the point of view of the investor rather than from the point of view of the bank sponsor when I calculated the economics. In practice, this is usually the other way around—the bank sponsor chooses the collateral to create a structure appealing to investors while ensuring that payments to the bank sponsor represent adequate compensation.

RISKS TO THE BANK SPONSOR

Let's take a look at the other risks in this transaction. The TRORS imbedded in this transaction is usually booked in the trading book of the bank sponsor. The bank sponsor engages in a "matched position" TRORS. The TRORS is a "back-to-back" transaction, and the bank sponsor's counterparties for both sides of the TRORS are SPEs. The transaction structure is key to how the bank sponsor views the risk of the TRORS.

The bank sponsor sells HLTs to the securitization conduit, or SPE. Alternatively, the HLTs may be owned by another entity. The securitization conduit pays the TROR of the HLTs to the bank sponsor, and the bank sponsor pays a funding cost. The bank sponsor then pays the TROR to the loan trust, which is a collateral enhanced SPE, thus hedging its position. The bank sponsor receives a "funding cost" from the loan trust. The bank sponsor is laying off the TROR risk with the loan trust, so the diversification of the loans in the securitization conduit and the degree of collateral enhancement are important structural considerations to the bank sponsor.

THE BANK SPONSOR AND COUNTERPARTY RISK

There are two counterparty risk scenarios from the point of view of the bank sponsor: (1) appreciation of the HLTs, and (2) depreciation of the HLTs. The scenarios are depicted in Figure 7.3. If the assets appreciate in value, the bank sponsor has risk to the securitization conduit. This risk can be miti-

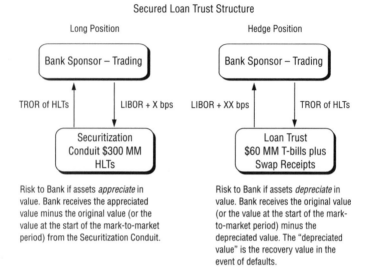

Secured Loan Trust Structure

FIGURE 7.3 TRORS—Bank Sponsor's Risk Perspective

gated by frequently marking the TRORS to market and settling value. U.S. regulatory capital guidelines provide a way to assess this risk. The first step is to mark-to-market on assets used as the underlying reference obligations in the TRORS. The second step is to look up the add-on factor for the reference asset specific risk. Unless one has modeled this risk in a way acceptable to U.S. regulators, one must use the former method for calculating regulatory capital. This method should be checked by venue, as regulations vary. For economic capital purposes, the bank sponsor evaluates the credit exposure to the securitization conduit, using a method similar to that outlined in the credit exposure section in Chapter 2.

The bank sponsor has risk to the loan trust, which as we mentioned before is an overcollateralized SPE. The bank sponsor in effect purchases market risk and credit default protection on its long position from the loan trust. If assets *depreciate* in value, the bank sponsor must receive a payment from the overcollateralized SPE. This should be mitigated by frequent mark-to-market and structural protection. For regulatory capital purposes, evaluating the counterparty risk captures this risk assessment. As we saw before, looking at the risk weight of the counterparty currently captures counterparty risk. In this case, the risk weight can be reduced initially by the amount of overcollateralization, but only because the collateral consists of T-bills, a cash equivalent. Under U.S. market risk guidelines, there is a provision for calculating the regulatory capital requirements. Adding the mark-to-market to the counterparty risk factor captures counterparty risk. The counterparty risk factor is available in a Federal "look-up" table. The economic capital required for the "long" position (receiving the TROR from the securitization conduit) is reduced by the amount of capital relief from the "short" position (paying the TROR to the loan trust).

STRUCTURAL CONSIDERATIONS

If the bank sponsor participates in these transactions, the TRORS payment stream to the bank sponsor from the loan trust must be evaluated in the context of the CLO structure. The key consideration is the ability of the overcollateralized SPE to provide protection in the event of deterioration in the value of the HLTs.

The risk is analogous to a convertible bond. The TRORS sometimes behaves like debt. When there is a rapid deterioration in the value of the HLTs, the TRORS behaves like equity. The main risk to the bank sponsor is a big discontinuous drop in the value of the HLTs.

Without examining the key structural elements related to the TRORS, it is impossible to assess counterparty risk. Key items to consider are shown in the following list, which is not intended to be all-inclusive because new structures raise new issues:

- What is the nature of the early wind-down trigger in the event of deterioration in value of the HLTs?
- What is the nature of the HLT collateral—credit quality, diversification?
- How much protection is provided by the degree of overcollateralization of the loan trust? What do the stress tests show?
- What is the priority of the bank sponsor in the event of an unwind?
- What is the nature of the collateral pledge in favor of the swap (in favor of the bank sponsor)?

Before attempting to view economic capital considerations, these key issues must be addressed.

Some bank sponsors view collateralization as a way for a counterparty to move up in credit class, in the internal implied rating system. Credit exposure, however, is unaffected for the purposes of managing internal credit lines. In the case of the SLT, there is no margin call on collateral. The equity investors and the certificate investors do not post additional collateral. The investors can lose no more than their initial investment. The structure must be evaluated in the context of the initial collateral and potential future risks.

SYNTHETIC SECURITIZATIONS FOR HIGHLY RATED BANKS

On September 10, 1997, SBC Warburg (now UBS) launched a watershed deal in the credit derivatives securitization market. At an original initial offering size of U.S. $1.5 billion, it was the largest credit derivative transaction to date. The deal proved so popular that SBC upsized the deal to $1.75 billion at its launch. Motivated by the need to free up regulatory capital, return on capital considerations, dynamic credit risk management, and client confidentiality, SBC launched a credit-linked vehicle transaction, CLiVe.

Glacier Finance is the name of the special purpose vehicle (SPV) domiciled in the Cayman Islands that issues the senior/subordinated notes that are a part of the CLiVe. The senior notes are rated AA+/Aa1, and the amount of subordination is 8.25 percent. Unlike the CLOs issued previous to this deal, the SBC senior notes are bullet tranches with bullet maturities of five years and seven years. The five-year tranche was priced at LIBOR + 16 bps, and the seven-year tranche was priced at LIBOR + 19 bps.

An especially high degree of importance of client confidentiality is peculiar to Swiss banks because Swiss banking laws are very stringent and call for a 15-year prison penalty for violation of client confidentiality. To preserve this confidentiality, SBC imbeds the client credit risk in credit-linked notes (CLNs)—medium-term notes (MTNs) issued by Swiss Bank's New York branch. SBC chose the New York branch because funding is an expense item for tax purposes in New York. The credit risks arise from investment and commercial banking business: loans, derivatives, securities, and project loans. The MTNs are rated Aa1/AA+, the same as Swiss Bank's rating. The CLNs, the Swiss Bank MTNs, are used as collateral for the Glacier Finance SPV. The CLNs with the imbedded client risks are used in the place of loans. The maturity of the underlying credit risks and of the CLN collateral does not need to match the maturity of the notes issued by the SPV. The CLNs are callable by SBC on any interest-payment date, and SBC can therefore re-volve credits imbedded in the CLNs into and out of the SPV. As CLNs in the SPV mature, the SPV can use the cash to purchase other CLNs.

The MTNs collectively imbed the credit risk of a diversified pool of investment-grade borrowers. These credit exposures are referenced through a trust (see Figure 7.4). These credit risks are then tranched into a five-tranche structure. The mezzanine notes and the junior notes issued by the SBC Glacier Finance Ltd. SPV would merit lower credit ratings than the Aa1/AA+ rated senior notes. Therefore, this structure works best for highly rated banks.

The relationship managers and the line credit officers of the bank do not manage the credit exposures and do not know whether their client's credit is imbedded in CLNs used as collateral for the SPV. Only a few key credit officers have this information. In this way, client confidentiality is preserved because the assets in the SPV are Swiss Bank–issued medium-term notes, the CLNs.

SBC worked for months with Moody's and S&P to meet the diversity score tests for Moody's and the industry and issuer concentration tests for S&P. SBC also mapped their internal bank rating system to the ratings of Moody's and S&P. This allows SBC to continually revolve collateral in the SPV. SBC can call its CLNs and substitute others. This vehicle allows SBC's trading department to manage credit exposures. The rating agencies do not see the individual obligors. This is a blind pool, or a black box.

SBC defines the credit events for the MTNs it issues. The underlying reference credits are never revealed. The underlying credit risk is black box

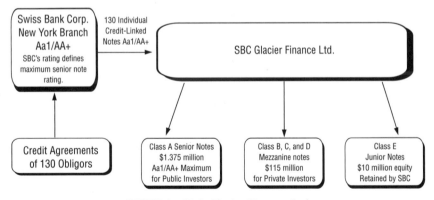

FIGURE 7.4 SBC Glacier Finance Ltd.

structure. The investors have recourse to the CLN, not to the underlying credit risks. If there is no credit event, SBC pays par at the maturity of the CLN. If there is a credit event, SBC calls the CLN and redeems the CLN at the recovery value. The recovery value is determined by the senior unsecured debt obligation of the underlying reference credit. The SPV would receive a payment after 18 days of the determined recovery value. If there is no reference security, the payout is preset at 51 percent. As we saw in our discussion in Chapter 4 on pricing credit default swaps, 51 percent is the average recovery value for senior unsecured obligations according to the Moody's standard.

This structure sold well globally to banks, insurance companies, funds, and money managers. Although the investors bought a black box, the key to investor comfort was the stringent requirements for diversification that SBC had to meet to achieve its target ratings. Unlike first-to-default baskets, senior/subordinated SPVs must meet specific tests to maintain their ratings. For example, there is a concentration limit of 2 percent per obligor, although the individual obligors are not revealed. Diversification tests must also be met to minimize correlation. SBC achieved its goal of regulatory capital relief because the regulators look at the resulting credit protection as cash collateralized exposure.

The credit derivatives imbedded in the MTNs transfer the economic risk but not the legal ownership of the underlying reference assets. There is no sale of assets. In fact, there doesn't need to be an actual reference asset. The credit exposure can be any notional exposure wherever it occurs. The first loss is covered up to 49 percent if there is no defined reference asset because the assumed recovery rate is 51 percent. The structure provides regulatory capital relief and internal economic capital relief, but there is no accounting benefit under GAAP.

BISTROs

JP Morgan's signature product is the Broad Index Secured Trust Offering (BISTRO). Irreverent practitioners claim that the acronym's true meaning is BIS Total Rip-Off because the regulatory capital relief on this structure wasn't as great as originally anticipated. This isn't entirely fair because limited regulatory capital relief is usually a feature of any structure in which the seller bank retains an equity piece. This synthetic securitization is a balance sheet CLO. The overall credit quality of assets referenced in a BISTRO is usually very high—single A and higher. Furthermore, these structures usually have very well diversified reference credits.

JP Morgan brought a five-year maturity private placement structure to market in December 1997, which appeared very similar to a reinsurance structure. JP Morgan referenced $10 billion of a variety of investment-grade exposures while issuing a deal of only $700 million in size.

JP Morgan created an SPV, which took in $700 million in proceeds and invested in U.S. Treasuries. The SPV then sold credit default protection to JP Morgan in the form of a $10 billion notional credit default swap, earning fee income in the process. The credit default swap referenced approximately 300 reference credits, each with a notional size of approximately $35 million and with an average credit rating of A3.

JP Morgan took the first loss piece, which comprised approximately 3 percent of the deal. Approximately 70 percent was an AA rated tranche priced at around LIBOR + 30 bps. The remaining tranche was rated BB. Investors in the SPV's tranches received cash flows derived from the U.S. Treasuries plus the fees from the credit default swap with JP Morgan.

By June 2000, JP Morgan had closed 20 BISTRO transactions. The underlying exposures of the deals totaled more than $90 billion. By the time JP Morgan finished with its own balance sheet, it had developed a marketable technology. JP Morgan now structures BISTROs for other banks for millions of dollars in fees for each deal closed. It seems that the only thing inhibiting faster growth in the number of deals done is education in the banking community. The cost of funding BISTROs versus traditional CLOs is lower. Because legal ownership of the underlying assets is not transferred, the deals seem simpler legally. BISTROs also seem structurally simpler than traditional CLOs yet solve many of the economic and regulatory problems facing banks.

BISTROs employ credit default swaps using Morgan Guarantee Trust (MGT) as the credit protection purchaser, which pays a fee to the investors in exchange for the investors making a contingent payment to MGT under the conditions outlined for the investor-purchased tranche of the structure. These structures may also employ credit-linked notes in a fashion similar to the Glacier deal to transfer the risks of the portfolio of reference entities. The notes can be issued by either an SPE or by a bank. As with the Glacier deal, the exposures can derive from any number of sources, including loans, bonds, structured securities, or derivative transaction counterparties.

BISTROs allow synthetic securitization of the risks of both funded and unfunded commitments.

The bank seller of the credit risks usually retains the first loss piece, or the equity piece. This first loss piece is also referred to as the "junior piece." It is sometimes misleading to say junior piece because many long-time structurers refer to subordinated tranches, which are lower-rated nonequity tranches, as junior pieces. When professionals discuss junior pieces, it is a good idea to ask for clarification to be absolutely sure which tranche is being referenced. Investors usually do not invest in the first loss (equity) piece.

The credit events are based on International Swaps and Derivatives Association, Inc. (ISDA) credit swap definitions. JP Morgan usually calculates the loss by soliciting bids from the market on senior unsecured obligations or even for specific bank credit facilities. As we shall see in Chapter 9's section on basis risk, we can no longer confidently refer to the documentation used in BISTROs as the industry standard. Practitioners are questioning ISDA credit swap definitions for credit events, especially where "restructuring" is used as a credit-event trigger. The market is now sensitive to the fact that different senior unsecured obligations may have very different price levels after the breach of a credit-event trigger. This may lead to careful scrutiny of documentation used in the creation of synthetic CLOs.

Investors may still take comfort in the overall high-credit quality of the underlying exposures, albeit the pool is usually on the order of 10 times the principal amount of the notes. Traditional CLOs are on the order of one-to-one, although this is a generalization. Overcollateralization may change that ratio. The key is the investor's loss exposure and the amount of credit enhancement. The rating is based on the former.

The motive of the bank credit-risk seller is regulatory and GAAP, if possible, capital relief. Notice that the original bank seller of the credit risks usually retains the equity piece. This means that the bank seller keeps the underlying credit risks on the balance sheet up to the threshold of the equity piece. This threshold provides credit enhancement for the buyers of the more senior tiers of the CLO.

The retention of this risk may be problematic for banks. The original sellers of the risks haven't really rid themselves of all of the credit exposures. Rather than make generalizations about the treatment of equity pieces, one should check the regulations appropriate for the venue. This may be as much as 100 percent capital to a lesser amount, depending on the venue and on the structure. If one requires further capital relief, it may be possible to securitize all or a portion of the first loss piece using technology for principal protected notes as discussed later in this chapter.

THE SUPER SENIOR TRANCHE

The good news is that balance sheet CLOs are creating investment opportunities in the form of the super senior tranches. The marketplace rewards investors who take the time to examine these structures by currently paying them above-market spreads for these AAA rated tranches. An added bonus for U.S. investors is that the Federal Reserve deems these tranches to have a 20 percent risk weighting, provided the deal has been structured properly. Other venues may follow suit with this favorable treatment. Investment in these high-quality, above-market-coupon, 20 percent Bank of International Settlements (BIS) risk-weighted assets is often a particularly good deal when compared to underwriting a single-name loan with a lower rating and a 100 percent BIS risk weighting. Banks issuing balance sheet CLOs should strongly considering retaining the super senior tranche of their own deals and accumulating the super senior tranches of foreign banks that cannot yet benefit from this favorable regulatory capital treatment.

SECURITIZING FIRST LOSS RISK WITH PRINCIPAL PROTECTED NOTES

Virtually anything can be securitized. Even the first loss pieces of CLOs can be securitized. Hedge fund purchasers of the certificates in SLT structures sometimes seek to perform just this type of securitization. The first loss equity piece is combined with either a Treasury zero-coupon bond or a corporate zero-coupon bond. The zero-coupon bond provides enhanced protection to the potential return of the original principal investment. Figure 7.5 shows an example of a principal protected structure.

I'll simplify the economics of this transaction to illustrate the basic concept (see Figure 7.5). The investor pays par for the note. The proceeds are used to buy a zero-coupon bond trading at a discount to par. Suppose the investor pays $10 million for a five-year maturity note. The investment bank takes out $250,000 in fees for structuring the note. If the five-year U.S. Treasury (UST) zero rate is 6 percent, the note will trade at a price of about

Note: Fees are usually deducted from the note proceeds.

FIGURE 7.5   Securitizing First Loss Risk with Principal Protected Notes

74.4. The remaining $2,310,000 can be used to invest in a pro rata portion of a basket of first loss pieces or even in a single equity tranche. At the end of the five years, the zero will accrete to par, and the investor will receive that amount at maturity with the credit assurance of the Treasury. Typically a Treasury zero or a zero-coupon investment-grade-rated corporate bond is used for these structures.

The coupon on this security is another matter. Suppose the investor purchased the certificate for the SLT structure we mentioned earlier. The static case coupon was 54 percent, so the static case coupon on this note would be 23.1 percent of that (remember the fees), or 12.4 percent. This seems great! The investor has principal protection and a very high static case coupon. But what is the certainty that the investor will realize this coupon? That depends on the defaults in the original SLT structure. In other words, the investor should not be indifferent to the type of equity piece and the quality of the underlying SLT structure.

The expected loss to the equity tranche-based interest component of a principal-protected structure will be significantly greater than the expected loss to the principal component of the transaction. The effect of the greater expected loss on the expected loss to a transaction as a whole depends, in turn, on the relative current values of the interest and the principal components. Thus the longer the life of the transaction and the higher the promised interest rate, the greater the effect that the credit risk associated with the interest component of the transaction will have on the expected loss.

To determine the expected loss to the principal-protected investor, the current values of the principal and the interest components of the certificates and the expected loss to each are combined. The expected loss to the entire instrument is the sum of the expected loss to the principal piece and the expected loss to the interest piece, each weighted by its respective present value.

The rating of a principal-protected note depends on how the "promise" of the note is structured. The rating is usually dependent on one of three scenarios:

1. The rating is based on potential return of principal only.
2. The rating is based on return of principal plus a "minimum" coupon. Or
3. The rating is based on return of principal plus all cash flow from the collateral.

Usually Moody's is the rating agency of choice for principal-protected notes. In each case the rating is based on the expected loss to the investor from the benchmark of the promise. It is very important to refer to the benchmark on which Moody's is basing its rating.

Note that if the principal-protected note is rated AAA, the rating is almost certainly based on return of principal only. The cash flows thrown off by the SLT certificate investment, which contributes the coupon cash flows, would not merit an investment-grade rating. The combined principal and "minimum" coupon-based rating might be investment grade. This would depend on the stated level of the minimum coupon and on the certainty of the cash flows. The third scenario is even more problematic. This rating will depend on the ratio of the principal to the more uncertain coupon cash flow stream and on the overall probability of receipt of the combined cash flows.

CREDIT ARBITRAGE FUNDS

Very few banks have managed to set up a successful credit arbitrage fund. This is ironic, given the fact that credit arbitrage is one of the key businesses of banking. As mentioned earlier, Citibank was very successful with the credit arbitrage funds set up in its subsidiary. This was mainly due to the organization and the expertise of the people Citibank had working for it. Former staff from Citibank have now started their own successful funds or joined other banks to form funds, leaving trained personnel behind. The critical mass of people, talent, effort, and long lead time is usually the sticking point for banks. An additional stumbling block is that many bank boards have difficulty understanding what is basically a very simple structure. The following discussion is a simple outline of the credit arbitrage fund structure that describes the basic features without giving away any trade secrets.

The usual structure is to establish an independent Cayman Island incorporated SPE with limited liability. The SPE engages in the activities of an investment company within proscribed parameters. A separately established "Investment Manager" conducts the investment activities of the SPE, which is in essence a credit arbitrage fund.

The purpose of the SPE is to invest in bonds, notes, debentures, certificates of deposit, and debt securities of all kinds. Sometimes investment in credit derivatives is also possible. The SPE may enter into options, futures, and other types of hedging transactions. The SPE has the ability to raise funds and to carry on other incidental activities to support its investment portfolio.

Often the SPE will be a qualifying special purpose entity (QSPE) for U.S. accounting (FASB 125) purposes; that is, it will be an off–balance sheet, bankruptcy-remote entity. The SPE may have a wholly owned subsidiary, with a name along the lines of SPE Finance, Inc. (where SPE is the name given to the original Cayman SPE). This is usually a company incorporated under the laws of the state of Delaware for the sole purpose of issuing and selling debt securities as a nominee for the SPE. The Cayman SPE guarantees debt issued by SPE Finance, Inc.

The SPE typically funds itself with a Euro medium-term note (EMTN) program and a U.S. Euro commercial paper program. SPE Finance, Inc., will also usually have a U.S. commercial paper (CP) program and a U.S. medium-term-note program. The Cayman SPE guarantees the obligations of SPE Finance, Inc., under the U.S. commercial paper program and the U.S. medium-term note program. The SPE may borrow and raise money in any currency and grant security over its assets to secure borrowings.

Program credit enhancement is provided by capital raised in the market. The SPE's capital will consist of "A" shares and "B" shares and capital notes denominated in a variety of currencies. The rights of the holders of the capital notes are subordinated to the rights of all other creditors, including holders of notes, on a winding up of the SPE. The economic rights of the A and the B shares are of equal rank. The returns are paid out to capital investors every six months. The returns are floating in character, and investors earn LIBOR plus a spread. The ratio of issued and paid-up capital to investments under management is on the order of one to ten ($2 billion for $20 billion under management).

Liquidity is usually obtained from liquidity facilities provided by Prime-1 (P-1) rated banks and liquid investment assets. Notes issued by these SPEs have ratings of P-1/Aaa, and CP issued by these SPEs have ratings of P-1. Any downgrade of any program rating triggers an unwind of the entire program.

The ultimate size of the asset portfolio is usually specified, and $20 billion is typical. Investments are strictly controlled with an optimization program, which constrains credit quality, maturity, portfolio diversification, asset-to-liability maturity gap, and liquidity eligibility. The SPE purchases a portfolio of high-grade assets, generally with an average AA credit quality. Average credit composition for the fund is approximately as follows: AAA/Aaa: 30 percent; AA/Aa: 40 percent; A/A: 20 percent; and BBB/Baa: 10 percent. The SPE is allowed to lever AA rated investments, usually up to eight times, but must use less leverage for lower-rated securities and may use more leverage for AAA assets. The SPE cannot invest in assets with a rating lower than a specified rating, usually BBB, with limited exceptions. The SPE may hold BB-/Ba3 assets if original holdings are downgraded up to a 10 percent portfolio concentration; typically no assets with a lower rating may be held in the portfolio under any circumstances.

The vehicle funds itself to the extent possible by match funding CP and MTNs with purchased assets. It is desirable to have access to the derivatives pricing models and derivatives expertise to check value of the custom-tailored swaps (matching roll dates and so forth) required for this fund.

Distribution of the capital shares and notes has traditionally been done through a bank's capital market's sales force if the fund managers don't already have relationships with buyers. Typical buyers are capital preservation funds and high-net-worth individuals. Marketing pieces can be developed by the fund builders, and marketing sales calls are generally done as a joint fund/capital markets effort.

Capital markets contacts with the investment banking firms that will distribute the fund's CP and MTNs are very valuable to establish the necessary swap credit lines and distribution attention required to maintain low funding costs for the fund.

The return on investment for share and capital note holders has an excellent track record. Management corporations contract with the A and the B share and capital note holder to earn a percent of the excess return above LIBOR plus some minimum number of basis points on the A and B shares and capital notes. Investors have earned 50 percent of the excess return above LIBOR + 50 bps on the A and B shares and capital notes. Typical experience is that after a period of two to four years, the returns level off at a maximum of LIBOR + 400 bps.

Investors in the A and B shares and capital notes of the SPE have no recourse to the sponsoring bank, only to the assets in the SPE. Investors in the MTNs and CP issued by the SPE also have no recourse to the sponsoring bank. Often the sponsoring bank will invest in the form of liquidity and in the shares and capital notes of the SPE, but this is not a fast rule. This is usually viewed as a strong positive signal to other potential investors, however.

The investment experience in these funds has been excellent, due to the nature of the risk and how it is managed. Investors in the CP and MTN issuance of the SPE receive assets of the highest rating backed by a pool of well-managed and credit-enhanced collateral. The fund makes no maturity, interest-rate, or currency bets and invests in high-grade assets.

Investors in the A and B shares and capital notes are subordinated to other creditors. They receive above-market returns on a stream of cash flows for the degree of risk assumed. The unwind triggers, the restrictions on the investment criteria of the fund, and the credit arbitrage nature of the fund combine to create a very low probability of default for the investors. Investors in similar funds have never experienced default, have received full return of principal, and have enjoyed high coupons relative to the degree of credit risk assumed on their investment.

Set up properly, these funds are good transactions for both the fund managers and the investors. While this seems a natural fit for most banks, the critical mass of credit talent for the investments, derivatives talent for the funding, structuring talent, and marketing talent is difficult to find.

CHAPTER 8

Selected Documentation, Regulatory, Booking, and Legal Issues

For even the most simple credit default transaction, three different jurisdictions can be involved: (1) the jurisdiction of the default protection seller, (2) the jurisdiction of the default protection buyer, and (3) the jurisdiction of the reference credit. Within each jurisdiction, different regulatory bodies may have a say in treatment of the transaction: bank regulatory authorities, insurance company regulatory bodies (for insurance company investors), the International Swaps and Derivatives Association, Inc. (ISDA), ministries of finance, tax authorities, the Bank for International Settlements (BIS), and securities firm regulatory authorities, just to name a few.

This book does not attempt to cover all of the issues involved with these transactions. It is the responsibility of the participants in these transactions to determine the documentation, regulatory, booking, and legal issues involved. In this chapter, I highlight certain issues as an attempt to illustrate helpful issues to bear in mind while investigating the various considerations involved in these transactions.

As of yet, there is no international standard for the documentation of these transactions. The ISDA, the Federal Reserve Board (the Fed) in the United States, the Office of Comptroller of the Currency in the United States, and the Bank of England have opened discussions in an attempt to formulate some standards.

The Bank of England circulated a discussion paper in November 1996 to identify regulatory capital and exposure management issues and followed with an amendment in summer 1997. The following pivotal papers are available by calling or writing the Bank of England: "Developing a Supervisory Approach to Credit Derivatives," November 1996, Bank of England; and "Credit Derivatives: Amended Interim Capital Adequacy Treatment," June 5, 1997, Bank of England.

The Federal Reserve comments and papers on this subject are available by calling the Federal Reserve in New York or by simply printing the reports from their Web site on the Internet: <www.bog.frb.fed.US\boarddocs\SRLETTERS>.

In Germany, the Bundesaufsichtsamt fuer das Kreditwesen has not yet developed definitive guidelines, and French banking authorities are currently investigating the regulatory implications of credit derivatives.

The Bank for International Settlements in Basle recently proposed new regulatory treatment of credit risks (Basle two). The proposal is expected to be adopted sometime between late 2001 and late 2003. If that occurs, the risk-weight treatment of credit risks will change. This will result in fewer credit default swap (CDS) transactions with banks for highly rated investment-grade product, but it will create other opportunities.

A few major U.S. banks have adopted a draft of an ISDA confirm provided by ISDA on December 15, 1997. This confirm refers to the ISDA master agreement. Most transactions happen only between counterparties that have an ISDA master in place. Most of the standard definitions referred to in confirms come directly from the ISDA master.

This need not be the case, however, as we are dealing with many different counterparties and many jurisdictions. Some Japanese institutions documented credit default protection as loan participations on the bank book. As this market matures, we can expect to see a greater push to standard documentation, however.

There is no substitute for good legal advice for credit derivatives documentation. There is no substitute for checking with local regulatory authorities for proper capital treatment of transactions. And there is no substitute for professional accounting and tax advice to determine the booking treatment of credit derivatives transactions.

HIDDEN COSTS IN DEFAULT LANGUAGE

Among the issues discussed earlier is the "bid/ask" of documentation. Buyers of credit default protection will attempt to put as many trigger events as possible into the credit default protection language. The ISDA master documentation allows for a variety of trigger events and provides many standard definitions. ISDA has attempted to standardize credit derivative confirmation language by issuing draft confirmations such as the International Swap Dealers Association's "Confirmation of OTC Credit Swap Transaction Single Reference Entity Non-Sovereign," December 15, 1997, ISDA. Despite ISDA's attempts, the market resists standardization, but these documents are good references for dealers, and the standard definitions are useful for final documentation.

Do not be misled if you are told the documentation will be "standard." A close read of a document will reveal many idiosyncrasies. Users of credit derivatives have thrown in other triggers, including events leading to lack of convertibility of the currency, war, confiscation of nonlocal bank assets, and hostilities as well as broadly defined government actions.

The following language sample is typical of what a large U.S. international commercial bank will introduce as a credit event definition when it is the default protection buyer. This is adopted from the standard ISDA language from the "OTC Credit Swap Transaction Single Reference Entity Nonsovereign" draft of December 15, 1997. This is made generic for a sovereign obligation but includes triggers normally reserved for corporate debt. Just insert the particular sovereign in place of the bracket phrase [relevant government entity].

Credit Event

Each of the following shall constitute a credit event and shall apply to this transaction:

bankruptcy;

credit event upon merger;

cross acceleration;

cross default;

currency convertibility;

downgrade;

failure to pay;

governmental action, including war, hostilities, and confiscation;

market disruption;

repudiation;

restructuring.

When determining the existence of occurence of any credit event, the determination shall be made without regard to (a) any lack or alleged lack of authority or capacity of the reference entity to enter into any obligation, (b) any actual or alleged unenforceability, illegality, or invalidity with respect to any obligation, (c) the failure of the reference entity to make any payment as a result of compliance with any applicable law, order, regulation, decree, or notice, however described, or the promulgation of, or any change in, the interpretation by any court, tribunal, regulatory authority, or similar administrative or judicial body with competent or apparent jurisdiction of any applicable law, order, regulation, decree, or notice, however described, or (d) the imposition of or any change in any exchange controls, capital restrictions, or any other similar restrictions imposed by any monetary authority.

Credit Event Definitions

Bankruptcy means the reference entity or any government entity: (1) is dissolved (other than pursuant to a consolidation, amalgamation, or merger); (2) becomes insolvent or is unable to pay its debts or fails or admits in writing its inability generally to pay its debts as they become due; (3) makes a general assignment, arrangement, or composition with or for the benefit of its creditors; (4) institutes or has instituted against it a proceeding seeking a judgment of insolvency or bankruptcy or any other relief under any bankruptcy or insolvency law or other similar law affecting creditors' rights, or a petition is presented for its winding-up or liquidation, and, in the case of any such proceeding or petition instituted or presented against it, such proceeding or petition (a) results in a judgment of insolvency or bankruptcy or the entry of an order for relief or the making of an order for its winding-up or liquidation, or (b) is not dismissed, discharged, stayed, or restrained in each case within 30 days of the institution or presentation thereof; (5) has a resolution, order, or decree passed for its winding-up, official management, or liquidation (other than pursuant to a consolidation, amalgamation, or merger); (6) seeks or becomes subject to the appointment of an administrator, provisional liquidator, conservator, receiver, trustee, custodian, or other similar official for it or for all or substantially all of its assets; (7) has a secured party take possession of all or substantially all of its assets or has a distress, execution, attachment, sequestration, or other legal process levied, enforced, or sued on or against all or substantially all of its assets and such secured party maintains possession, or any such process is not dismissed, discharged, stayed, or restrained, in each case within 30 days thereafter; (8) causes or is subject to any event with respect to it, which, under the applicable laws of any jurisdiction, has an analogous effect to any of the events specified in clauses (1) to (7) (inclusive); or (9) takes any action in furtherance of, or indicating its consent to, approval of, or acquiescence in, any of the foregoing acts.

Credit Event upon Merger means the reference entity consolidates or amalgamates with, or merges with or into, or transfers all or substantially all of its assets to another entity and the creditworthiness of the resulting, surviving, or transferee entity is materially weaker than that of the reference entity immediately prior to such action.

Cross Acceleration means the occurrence of a default, event of default, or other similar condition or event (however described), other than the failure to make any required payment, in respect of the reference entity or any government entity under one or more obligations or government obligations in an aggregate amount of not less than the default requirement that has resulted in any such obligations or government obligations becoming due and payable before they would otherwise have been due and payable, unless the reference entity or government entity shall have made all payments on the date that such obligations or government obligations became due and payable.

Cross Default means the occurrence of a default, event of default, or other similar condition or event (however described), other than a failure to make any required payment, in respect of the reference entity or any government entity under one or more obligations or government obligations in an aggregate amount of not less than the default requirement that has resulted in any such obligations or government obligations becoming capable at such time of being declared due and payable before they would otherwise have been due and payable.

Currency Convertibility means any governmental or regulatory authority, agency, or instrumentality of the [relevant government entity], after the date hereof, (1) imposes exchange control policies or material convertibility restrictions on the [relevant domestic currency], (2) otherwise seeks to regulate the exchange rate of the [relevant domestic currency] into or for any other foreign currency including, without limitation JPY, DEM, or USD, or (3) imposes any law, rule, regulation, or policy, or official interpretation of any of the same having an effect substantially similar to the foregoing.

Downgrade means the credit rating reaches or is lower than the specified rating or the downgrade obligation is no longer rated by any rating agency.

Failure to Pay means, after giving effect to any applicable notice requirement or grace period, the failure of the reference entity or government entity to make, when due, any payment equal to or exceeding the default requirement under any obligation or government obligation.

Governmental Action means (1) any governmental or regulatory authority, agency, or instrumentality, or any court or tribunal (a) asserts that the performance by the reference entity or any government entity of any covenant or obligation under any reference obligation or government obligation is unlawful or unenforceable against the reference entity or any government entity, or (b) declares a moratorium on the payment or performance of all or any portion of any reference obligation or government obligation, or (c) declares a general moratorium on banking activities in the [relevant government entity], or (d) asserts that the purchase or sale of any reference obligation or government obligation or the exercise of any right of a holder under any reference obligation or government obligation is unlawful or unenforceable in relation to the covenants and obligations of the reference entity or any government entity, or (e) purports to divest title to or beneficial or economic interest in any reference obligation or government obligation from any holder or group or class of holders of any reference obligation or government obligation; or (2) the occurrence of any war, insurrection, revolution, armed conflict, or outbreak or escalation of hostilities that substantially impairs the functioning of the government of, or banking activities in, the [relevant government entity].

Market Disruption means (1) trading generally shall have been suspended or materially limited in London, Tokyo, or [relevant government entity]; or (2) there shall have occurred any war, insurrection, revolution, or armed conflict, or outbreak or escalation of hostilities or any change in financial markets or any calamity or crisis that, in either case, is material and adverse to the reference entity or any government entity or the markets for the reference obligation or any government obligation.

Repudiation means the reference entity or any government entity disaffirms, disclaims, repudiates, or rejects, in whole or in part, or challenges that validity of, any obligation or government obligation.

Restructuring means a waiver, deferral, restructuring, rescheduling, standstill, obligation exchange, or other adjustment occurs with respect to any obligation or any government obligation, and the effect of such is that the terms of such obligation or government obligation are, overall, materially less favorable from a credit or risk perspective to any holder of such obligation or government obligation.

General Definitions

[Relevant Domestic Currency] means the lawful currency, from time to time, of the [relevant government entity].

Government Entity means the [relevant government entity], or any political subdivision or agency of the [relevant government entity], or any person controlled or supervised by and acting as an instrumentality of the government of the [relevant government entity].

Government Obligation means with respect to a government entity, any obligation (whether present or future, contingent or otherwise, as principal or surety or otherwise) for the payment or repayment of money (in any currency whatsoever).

Reference Entity means the issuer of the credit obligation.

Reference Obligation means with respect to the reference entity, [any obligation (whether present or future, contingent or otherwise, as principal or surety or otherwise) for the payment or repayment of money] [any obligation (whether present or future, contingent or otherwise, as principal or surety or otherwise) in respect of borrowed money] [the following obligations:] [the reference obligation(s)].

This contract throws in just about every definition. Notice that a credit default protection seller who agrees to the foregoing conditions accepts triggers that do not reflect lack of payment on the reference obligation or other financial obligations of the relevant sovereign. Lack of convertibility of the currency may not mean that the debt of the sovereign is in default. It could be a worrisome event to holders of the sovereign debt obligations, however. The same might be said for outbreak of hostilities. By these definitions, the Gulf War would have been a credit-event default trigger for U.S. government debt.

All language is negotiable, however. The default protection seller does not have to accept this language. Indeed, most of the default protection language examined in Chapter 4 was much less stringent than the foregoing language. See also the section on geared default options in Chapter 4 to review a sample of other pitfalls in term sheet and confirmation language.

We also saw earlier that credit default language often includes protection for market risk for the default protection buyer. This is usually in the form of a clause in which the default protection seller agrees to pay hedge termination costs for the default protection buyer. Strictly speaking, this is not sovereign risk at all. The hedge might be a cross-currency swap or a spot forward currency transaction. No one has forced the buyer to connect such a transaction with the reference obligation. The buyer will often ask the default protection seller for indemnification for these costs, however. The default protection seller can and should demand additional premium for this convenience.

GUARANTEES, INSURANCE, AND CREDIT DERIVATIVES

The Federal Reserve views credit default protection as a guarantee for purposes of the banking book. This means that credit default protection sold from the banking book does not have to be marked to market.

It is generally best not to use the word *guarantee* in a credit default swap contract. The legal versus the regulatory interpretation can be subtle, but important. In England, for instance, a special body of rules applies to contracts of guarantees, but not all of these rules will necessarily apply to credit default protection.

If credit derivatives were to be classed as insurance contracts, this could create problems in certain jurisdictions. In England, for instance, this could mean that the seller of a contract is creating a criminal offense if the seller is conducting unauthorized insurance business. The contract may be unenforceable and the buyer of the protection may have the right to recover any fees paid.

The problem is that credit default protection and convertibility protection look a lot like insurance. These contracts have many of the elements of an insurance contract. Indeed, the export finance companies refer to this protection as insurance, and private insurers write insurance contracts for this protection. Banks have long been in the legal business of providing credit guarantees, however, in the form of letters of credit (LOCs).

There are key differences between credit derivatives and insurance contracts, however. Often, even if a counterparty has not suffered a loss, a payment must be made. In the case of credit spread options, for instance, or in the case of a credit default option in which the protection buyer does not hold the reference asset, a payment is not necessarily related to an actual loss.

Law firms such as Allen & Overy in the United Kingdom have opined that credit default swaps are not insurance for purposes of U.K. law. Credit default contracts should be reviewed by legal counsel to avoid potential problems.

BOOKING ISSUES

As we saw with the first-to-default options, booking issues can be very important in the way a credit derivatives trader recognizes profitability. Further, there is no clear guidance on how credit derivatives must be booked. Several Japanese and Swiss banks sell credit default protection and do not mark these positions to market. This transaction is viewed as "bank business," as a guarantee that does not have to be marked to market. The credit default premium is taken into income as a fee, just as a fee for an LOC or an unfunded loan would be taken into income.

This treatment does not work for other banks that want to reduce "loan" exposure. Often credit default protection is traded out of a separate credit derivatives trading book. This position must be marked to market. In this case, a buyer of credit default protection, who sells protection simultaneously, wants to net off his position. Both positions must be marked to market.

Certain bank sellers of convertibility protection are also booking this protection as a country guarantee. This position is not marked to market. Other bank sellers trade this protection out of their credit derivatives trading book and must mark this position to market. As we saw in the section on convertibility pricing, marking convertibility protection to market is very difficult. Marking convertibility protection to "model" is nearly impossible.

There is an advantage for banks and other institutions that are not required to mark their positions to market. There is a significant savings in administration and a significant savings in model booking. There is also a significant savings in time required to satisfy other bank managers that marking techniques provide reasonable, reproducible, and defensible results.

REGULATORY CAPITAL

Regulatory capital treatment is in a state of flux. There is no clear guidance in any country, and the meager existing guidance varies by country. This is a key issue because it affects banks and some of the government-sponsored export finance companies that have investment and trading portfolios. Regulatory capital is the capital that banks must reserve against assets or against transactions. The Bank for International Settlements in Basel sets general guidelines. Currently, the minimum amount of capital that banks must reserve against assets is 8 percent. This minimum applies to transactions or assets that have a 100 percent BIS risk weighting. Banks will often inquire as to the BIS risk weighting of a transaction. This is the number to which they are referring, the 100 percent risk weight.

Even though 100 percent is the maximum, Organization for Economic Cooperation and Development (OECD) bank risk has only a 20 percent risk weight. OECD sovereign obligations, even OECD sovereign obligations rated lower than certain bank obligations, have a zero percent risk weight. Non-OECD sovereign obligations have a 100 percent risk weight. Therefore, the sovereign obligations of Mexico, an OECD member, have a zero percent BIS risk weight; and the sovereign obligations of Brazil, a non-OECD member, have a 100 percent BIS risk weight.

The reason this is important to banks, in particular, is that the risk weight affects the rate of return-on-capital (ROC) calculation. This is not return on economic capital; rather it is the return on regulatory capital. The following example shows the rate of return for a bank that holds a 100 percent risk-weighted asset. This is compared with the cash flows in which the bank holding the asset hedges the risk with a lower-credit-quality bank that has a higher funding cost. The hedging bank can choose the lower of the risk weighting of the bank counterparty *or* the asset on which it purchases credit default protection.

Let us reconsider our earlier example of the AAA institution holding a BBB asset and a single-A institution holding a BBB asset. If we compare an outright purchase by both banks, with the AAA bank purchasing the asset and simultaneously purchasing credit default protection from the single-A bank, the economic capital treatment for the two alternatives would be as shown in Figures 8.1 and 8.2.

Often presentations and market literature will show examples similar to that shown in the example in Figures 8.1 and 8.2 and include income for the invested regulatory capital. The assumption is that regulatory capital is invested in riskless market instruments such as U.S. Treasury bills (T-bills). This suggests a higher return on regulatory capital than the numbers shown in the example. I think this approach overstates return on capital because it does not take into account cost of capital. If I assume my cost of capital is roughly the same as the return from investing in T-bills, the cost of regulatory capital and return on investment of regulatory capital nets to zero.

Using the off–balance sheet credit derivative to hedge the position of the AAA bank improves the position of the AAA bank dramatically. Not only does the AAA bank create a synthetic AA asset with a synthetic coupon of LIBOR plus 10 basis points (bps), it also reduces the regulatory capital requirement. Despite a lower net spread after hedging, the return on capital increases from 6.88 percent to 21.88 percent, a multiple of 3.18.

Notice that I assume that the single-A rated bank books this credit de-

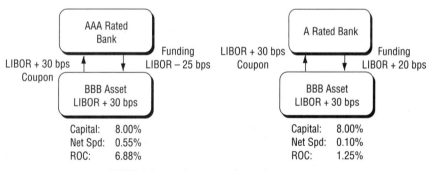

FIGURE 8.1 Cash Ownership of BBB Asset

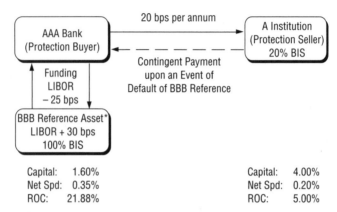

FIGURE 8.2 Regulatory Capital Effect of Credit Default Swap to Offset BBB Asset

rivative as an unfunded letter of credit (LOC) to achieve a 4 percent BIS capital treatment versus an 8 percent capital reserve for the outright purchase. Nonetheless, the return for the bank with a funding cost of LIBOR + 20 bps is very low. This illustrates why banks with high funding costs are generally reaching for yield. While the return of the single-A bank is still low, the difference between owning the asset outright and taking in premium is 1.25 percent versus 5.00 percent. This is a 400 percent improvement in the return on capital. Regulatory capital applies to the banking industry, but because banks make up the majority of the credit derivatives transactions, regulations that affect banks indirectly affect the entire market.

From the point of view of capital, the difficulty banks face in using credit derivatives is that there is no clear guidance on how credit derivatives should be treated for regulatory capital. As we saw in the section on first-to-default basket options in Chapter 4, the current suggested regulatory capital treatment can seem punitive. The Bank of England currently suggests that the buyer and the seller consider capital and exposure using the worst-case scenario. *Both* the buyer and the seller can't experience the worst-case scenario at the same time, however. Further, both can experience an intermediate scenario from the worst case for either of them, even in the event of default of one of the credits in the basket (which may never happen).

The current dogma on regulatory treatment gives market professionals an uneasy feeling. I often hear complaints: The regulations seem incomplete, the regulations seem arbitrary, the regulations seem unsatisfying. This is often true of new products, which are not easily pigeon-holed into existing categories.

As we saw earlier, for total rate of return swaps (TRORS), an investor bank that hedges a long position by paying the total rate of return to a counterparty versus receiving a floating rate payment can choose the lower of the risk weight of the counterparty *or* the reference long position. In this case, the counterparty, the receiver of the total rate of return, is a protection seller. For example, if the investor bank's reference asset is 100 percent BIS risk weighted and the counterparty is an OECD bank, the risk-based capital required for the investor bank hedging a long position is reduced from 8 percent of the principal amount to 1.6 percent of the principal amount. This is because OECD banks enjoy a 20 percent risk weighting no matter what their credit rating. Some state-sponsored finance companies, such as Finnish Export Credit and Swedish Export Credit, are also 20 percent BIS risk weighted. As we saw in the earlier examples in this section, a reduction in the required regulatory capital from 100 percent to 20 percent has an enormous impact on return on equity.

To make life even more interesting, there are anomalies in regulatory treatment in different banking jurisdictions. The Bank for International Settlements in Basel sets the guidelines for regulatory capital treatment, but these guidelines are subject to interpretation by ministries of finance and central banks in various countries. It is not uncommon to have different regulatory capital in Germany, England, and the United States for various transactions. For a time special purpose vehicles (SPVs) collateralized with Italian government debt were interpreted by most German banks to have a 100 percent BIS risk weight, whereas the Bank of England allowed a 20 percent BIS risk weight. In the future, in the credit derivatives market, I expect to see similar anomalies, which may motivate certain types of cross-border transactions.

U.S. and European banks generally view bank debt as 20 percent BIS risk weighted and bank holding company debt as 100 percent BIS risk weighted, but that is not true everywhere. In Japan, bank holding company debt is treated as having a 20 percent BIS risk weight. From a regulatory capital view, it is more advantageous for a Japanese bank to purchase a credit-linked note from a bank holding company issuer than for a European bank to do so.

Many Japanese banks offer and document their sales of credit default protection on corporates as standby credit facilities. As an undrawn facility, it attracts only a 50 percent BIS risk weight.

In general, many OECD banks interested in reducing regulatory capital requirements are eager to buy credit protection on Brazil or Argentina while simultaneously selling credit protection on Mexico. The reason is that Brazil and Argentina, non-OECD countries, attract a 100 percent BIS risk weighting, whereas Mexico, an OECD country, attracts zero percent BIS risk capital. In general, OECD banks will be interested in reducing regulatory capital by doing business with other OECD banks. Citibank, for example, transacts credit derivatives business only with other OECD banks.

German banks attract the reference-asset BIS risk weight for writing credit default protection. This is generally true globally. What is unique, however, is that some German banks get a zero percent BIS capital treatment for writing credit spread options. In other words, there is a tremendous capital advantage to selling credit protection in the form of a credit spread option rather than as a credit default swap.

Just as some German banks put zero percent capital behind credit spread options, other European banks have received internal bank approval to put zero percent capital behind investment-grade referenced credit default options on the theory that they have an extremely low probability of exercise. The logic behind this treatment is that a credit default swap or a credit default option is the same as a very deep out-of-the-money option. *The option is worthless in normal trading conditions.* The credit default option creates an exposure only in the event of a default event. For the case of an investment-grade asset, the low probability of default makes the option nearly worthless. This argument is not as good, however, for noninvestment-grade product or for first-to-default baskets of investment-grade product where the cumulative probability of default can be quite high.

The U.S. Federal Reserve opinion on this topic is clear. If a U.S. bank buys credit default protection from another bank, the buyer of the credit default protection may choose the lower of the risk weight of the reference asset *or* the risk weight of the bank protection seller. For example, if a U.S. bank purchases credit default protection on a United Mexican States bond with a zero percent risk weight from an OECD country bank with a 20 percent risk weight, the U.S. bank can choose to use a zero percent risk weight for the transaction. In the case where the total return swap creates an unhedged long position, this bank must use the risk weighting of the reference credit issuer. The Federal Reserves treatment is outlined in its opinion letter SR 9617 dated August 12, 1996. This document is available on the Internet at <www.bog.frb.fed.US\boarddocs\SRLETTERS>.

Although most regulators agree that the U.S. Federal Reserve guidelines make sense, the regulations for a given jurisdiction may be different; and until there is official clarification, many banks will use the most conservative approach.

Hedge funds, which are 100 percent risk weighted, often receive the total return in a swap. Hedge funds typically put 10 percent collateral up front and use TRORS as a synthetic financing to enjoy the leverage provided by many bank counterparties. Most jurisdictions allow for a reduction in required risk capital equal to the amount of cash or cash-equivalent collateral posted in a swap. A hedge fund that posts 10 percent cash collateral would therefore have a 90 percent risk weight.

Notice that the risk capital treatments discussed here apply to the case in which the reference asset credit default protection or the reference asset for the TRORS matches the asset being hedged. This is not always the case, however. If the reference asset and the asset being hedged are obligations of the same legal entity and have the same level of seniority in bankruptcy and same maturity, the Federal Reserve considers the asset 100 percent hedged. In the case where the reference asset differs from the hedged asset, the transactions must be linked internally for documentation purposes. Further, the regulatory capital treatment is unclear. If a bank can demonstrate a high correlation between the credit derivative reference asset and the asset being hedged, the bank may treat the asset as hedged. But what degree of correlation and what evidence are suitable for regulatory purposes? There is no clear guidance on this issue, and it is a good idea to get a separate opinion memo from the relevant regulatory body so that the hedge treatment is not disallowed at a later date.

Regulatory treatment also varies depending on whether a credit default swap is held on the banking book or on the trading book. The Bank of England is now leaning toward holding credit default swaps on the trading book. Instruments held in the banking book get 8 percent of the notional value held against them. Instruments held in the trading book usually attract between 0.25 percent and 1.6 percent of the notional value as capital held against assets.

The Federal Reserve's guidelines state that if a credit derivative is held in the trading book, the capital requirements will be the same as for other derivatives in the trading book. Banks can use internal models to determine regulatory capital requirements and to add on capital to account for counterparty risk. The trick is to classify credit derivatives as eligible for booking in the trading book. Consider a credit default swap that uses a letter of credit as a reference asset. If a bank receives a premium for providing credit default protection on the LOC and agrees to take delivery of the LOC if it is funded, can this credit default swap be booked in the trading book? After all, if a default event occurs, it appears an LOC would be a banking book asset. The same logic seems to apply for a credit default swap on a loan. Wouldn't the credit default swap booking depend on the type of reference asset? The regulatory agencies are still grappling with definitions of credit derivatives and haven't yet dealt with all of the implications of the various types of credit derivatives and reference assets.

These ambiguities make the credit derivatives market ripe for trades based on regulatory capital treatment arbitrage. In principle, there is nothing wrong with this. This is regulatory capital *avoidance*, not regulatory capital *evasion*. This is the same concept as exploiting cross-border or home jurisdiction tax rules for tax avoidance, which is legal, as opposed to tax evasion, which is illegal. As more banks become clear on how to exploit these differences, the market will see an upsurge in regulatory capital-based transactions.

I am usually in favor of improving balance sheet performance on a regulatory capital basis, but there is an important caveat. Notice that regulatory capital treatment has very little to do with the credit quality of the counterparty. The sovereign debt of Mexico, rated Ba2, has a zero percent risk weight, as does the debt of the United States, which is rated Aaa. The debt of General Re, rated Aaa, gets a 100 percent risk weight. This doesn't make much sense, but those are the rules. Whenever regulatory rules depart from pure economics, there are ways to use them to one's advantage. One can manipulate the balance sheet to show improved performance according to the rules. This is a double-edged sword, however. When transactions are done to optimize performance according to arbitrary regulations, noneconomic transactions may occur. Transactions that cosmetically improve performance in this fashion may actually put an institution at greater credit risk. This is not always true, but the temptation exists. In my experience, whenever the temptation exists, someone succumbs.

These differences in regulatory capital will bias banks to behave differently toward the credit derivatives market. Keeping track of these regulatory differences will also give an edge to banks that take the time to understand which transactions have the most value to their counterparties.

BOOKING IN NONBANK ENTITIES

Because U.S. banks cannot book high-yield securities on the bank balance sheet, many banks have set up special purpose vehicles or commercial paper (CP) conduits in which to purchase assets. These vehicles can also receive the total rate of return on a TRORS without attracting adverse BIS capital treatment. The primary motivation for most banks in setting up these conduits is to avoid high capital treatment charges. Another motive is to book cash assets or to receive the total return on certain assets that normally cannot be booked on the bank balance sheet. In the United States, this helps banks avoid complications of the Glass-Steagall Act—a U.S. federal law that prohibits banks from underwriting or trading corporate bonds (among other restrictions).

The challenge that many banks face is that many banks do not want these vehicles as counterparties. Unless there is an explicit guarantee by a bank for these vehicles, the credit worthiness of the vehicle is usually a negative question mark.

SELECTED CROSS-BORDER ISSUES

Selling securities cross border poses special problems. Tax and legal issues can arise, which are not easy to foresee in advance. The markets can pose myriad questions: Does a credit-linked note linked to default of a country that normally withholds tax to the investor create a withholding tax on the credit-linked note's interest income? Can European transactions be subjected to value-added tax? Does the local-language newspaper in the Philippines qualify as a financial news source? Will global firms have the resources to track local-language financial publications or, for that matter, local English-language publications in each of the venues in which it deals?

If prospectuses and indenture agreements for hard-currency sovereign debt are not carefully read, other problems may occur. Some sovereign reference bonds may not pay off in hard currency in the event of default. What happens if a credit default contract is poorly crafted? What if the reference asset does not necessarily pay off in a hard currency, but the credit default swap contract references only USD prices—how is the currency exchange rate and currency convertibility handled?

If there is a change of government in the country of a bank guarantor, will these contracts continue to be legal and enforceable? Would you consider buying credit default protection from an Iraqi bank or, for that matter, from an Iranian bank?

These questions and others like them are still under active discussion. There is no substitute for the services of a good international law firm and tax firm to protect the interests of both parties in a contract.

CHAPTER 9

Future of the Global Market

The credit derivatives market is growing rapidly and will continue this trend for the foreseeable future. Banks will cause the most explosive growth in the credit derivatives market as credit derivatives change the way in which banks do business. Once banks adopt models for the trading book that allow them to treat these products like other traded derivatives, credit derivatives will be compelling. This is a key development in the credit derivatives market in the United States. Once this is widely adopted, the rest of the global banking community will eventually follow suit.

The driving force for this revolution in banking is the fact that the Bank for International Settlements (BIS) risk weighting of the trading counterparty will become irrelevant. The magnitude of the credit exposure as expressed by trading models will determine regulatory capital requirements. All banks will have an incentive to figure out ways to move assets from the bank book to the credit derivatives trading book. Trades, which did not make sense from a past regulatory capital perspective, will make sense in the future whether the bank is buying or selling credit protection. The regulatory capital charge in the trading book is a fraction of the charge in the bank book, and exposure netting makes trading book management viable.

Banks will buy credit default protection from nonbank institutional investors with no concern about the BIS risk weight of the protection seller. Banks will be able to sell credit exposures and buy credit protection for a few basis points (bps), and the transaction will make sense from both a regulatory capital point of view and an economic point of view.

The early stages of the credit derivatives market have seen confusion from bank and insurance regulatory, tax, accounting, and market professionals. As this regulatory confusion disappears, market professionals will learn how to trade within and to exploit established guidelines. Regulations are a bit like inflation. Inflation itself is neither good nor bad for trading a market. If the market has a common consensus about inflation, one can trade the market accordingly. It is uncertainty that brings the market to a grinding halt. As confusion about cross-border and domestic regulations is resolved, additional participants will enter the market and existing participants will trade more boldly.

The banking community especially will benefit from regulatory clarity. As banks learn how to use intermediaries for regulatory arbitrage and as banks become more adept at using their balance sheets for financing counterparty positions, trading volume will increase. Banks will gradually become more willing to actively trade credit risks. Banks are globally hiring and educating existing staff on this new product line, and the number of new major global bank entrants in the market increases monthly.

Banks are in the business of taking credit risk. They are natural providers of protection. As a result, they can become natural sellers of credit risk as their lines become full to capacity, while their appetite to do profitable business with a counterparty continues. Banks are just beginning to exploit the potential advantages of trading lines with each other. The U.S. market, with its broad number of regional banks, the strong presence of cash-rich banks eager for U.S. credits, its single currency, and its relatively long history of credit data, is poised to become the largest interbank-credit-line trading market in the world.

As we have seen, these products are very documentation intensive. It takes time to build new departments. It takes time to build an infrastructure of people, paperwork, and management support. Nonetheless, in a relatively brief time, the trading volume in interbank credit derivatives has mushroomed, and it will continue to do so at an exponential rate.

The European Monetary Union (EMU) will have a dramatic effect on trading of credit derivatives. As banks move to a standard currency, the ease of laying off credit risk among European banks will be much easier. The variable of credit exposure due to currency exposure will be eliminated. The European banking community is sitting on huge portfolios of local credit risk and is in need of diversification as well as of increased lines to local customers.

Global banks in particular will become more active in structured products. Products such as the collateralized loan obligation are newcomers to the market, yet have imbedded credit derivative components. The Swiss Bank Corporation deal discussed in Chapter 7 in the section on collateralized loan obligations was collateralized with credit-linked notes. It is the largest global loan underwriting to date. It is also the largest credit derivative transaction ever. The initial size was USD 1.5 billion. The deal was quickly upsized to USD 1.75 billion.

SBC is not alone in its willingness to securitize low-yielding loan portfolios. By monetizing loans, which have a low return on capital, SBC frees up funds to invest in more lucrative transactions. At the same time, SBC is freeing up credit lines and reducing overall exposure on its books. Even if SBC does this transaction at break-even levels, it will end up better off than it was prior to the transaction. Many other global banks, including Chase, Bank of America, Union Bank of Switzerland, and others, have large loan portfolios and are eager to monetize these positions.

Project finance creates an ongoing need to lay off global credit risk. Enron plans to create a fund populated with project finance loans. If possible, it plans to use credit derivatives to mitigate some of the sovereign credit and currency convertibility risks, while earning a high spread. Many banks are currently planning to create funds that will offer high returns in exchange for the risk of project finance loans in emerging market countries. These funds will have higher returns, but the risk will not be hedged. The value of the funds is the diversification of the credit risks and the fact that most institutional and private investors have no other access to these specific risks and these high returns. Most of the risks are in emerging-market countries.

The nonstandardization of documentation, evolving economies, and evolving legal and regulatory environments in these countries will create a continued strong demand for credit products and continued confusion in pricing and documentation issues for the near future. The Latin American market, considered by many to no longer qualify as an emerging market, is already showing signs of increased standardization. Eastern Europe, Korea, Thailand, China, Vietnam, and the Philippines will continue to provide high margin opportunities and higher risk in documentation.

BASIS RISK: DELIVERY OPTIONS AND CREDIT EVENTS

Several earlier sections of this book discussed basis risk. Sloppy documentation can create its own kind of basis risk. Another kind of basis risk has to do with acceptable delivery and with what constitutes a credit event in the first place. Although we already saw several examples of areas of concern for interpretation of a credit event, one particular type is worth revisiting.

In the fourth quarter of 2000, the credit derivatives dealer community was up in arms about credit default protection on Conseco. Banks that owned and underwrote Conseco loans included restructuring as a credit-event trigger. This was fairly standard in credit derivatives documentation. Delivery in the event of a credit event could be either a bond or a loan. This also was fairly standard in credit derivatives documentation. This is precisely why we spent so much time on the potential documentation risk of credit derivatives earlier in this book. The documentation in this transaction led to significant risk to the credit default protection providers.

A restructuring of Conseco loans by the banking community triggered a credit event, and the banking community delivered long-dated deeply discounted bonds to the credit default protection providers. The long-dated bonds were susceptible to both market risk and credit risk. Furthermore, as we discussed earlier, long-dated bonds often trade at drastically reduced prices to short-dated bonds under workout situations. The price disparity between long-dated bonds and loans is even more pronounced in these situations. The credit default protection providers had to pay the difference between par and the market price of the discounted bonds. Meanwhile, the loans, which motivated the protection purchase in the first place, were valued at a much higher price. The dealer community felt burned two ways. They felt the banking community was closer to the Conseco situation, given that they had underwritten the loans. They also felt that the banks had some control over the restructuring. Finally, by delivering the deeply discounted bonds, the banks were not acting in good faith.

There is nothing wrong with imbedding a delivery option into credit default documentation, but one should get paid for the imbedded option. That didn't appear to be the case in this instance.

The credit default protection providers were surprised. I was surprised, too. I was surprised that the protection providers seemed to be unaware that they had exposed themselves to this risk. Delivery matters. If I give my counterparty the option of delivering a menu of possible choices with potentially different market values, I have just written a delivery option. This delivery option has an economic value. I don't want to give away that option for free. I'm not indifferent between delivery of a bond or a loan. Often, I'm not indifferent to which in a possible menu of bonds I'm being delivered, as we saw in the section on geared default options.

The reaction was swift, and this incident sensitized the entire dealer community. Credit default contracts are now being written excluding restructuring as a credit event. Banks hedging loans cannot use those credit default options, however. When banks buy credit default protection against their loan portfolios, they require that restructuring be specified in the credit default protection contract. The banks in the Conseco transaction that took the short-term opportunity nearly closed the door for themselves for future credit hedging transactions.

This kind of upset is good for a new market. Eventually cooler heads will prevail, and solutions and compromises to this problem will be negotiated. As of this writing, there is no standard solution. But already sound proposals are being presented to the International Swaps and Derivatives Association (ISDA).

In an attempt to eliminate "gaming" from the settlement procedure, practitioners proposed language to ISDA to tighten up the definition of restructuring as a credit event. They are proposing the deletion of some of the more troublesome points in the ISDA language on restructuring and the addition of provisions to describe the limitations to what can be delivered. In the case of a credit-event triggered by a restructured loan, some practitioners are proposing either delivery of the restructured loans or cash settlement somehow tied to the perceived market value of the restructured loans. This will be difficult because the market value of restructured loans is very difficult to ascertain. One proposal calls for five quotes on loan prices. The high and the low prices would be discarded, and the price used would be the average of the remaining three loan prices. It may be difficult at times to get five banks to offer quotes. Another proposal would allow delivery of a floating rate note (FRN) with a maturity shorter than or equal to the final maturity of the credit derivatives contract. This is an attempt to limit market risk while capturing the credit risk. The difficulty here is that floating rate notes with the required maturity may not be available in the market.

Even delivery of the loan presents challenges. It takes time to arrange for all the required consents to a loan assignment. There is variability in the lag time between settlement of distressed loans and the trade date for a distressed loan. The Loan Syndications and Trading Association (LSTA) and

ISDA have formed a joint working group to advise ISDA's credit derivative documentation group on issues that arise in connection with the physical delivery of a loan as settlement for a credit derivatives transaction.

I speculate there may be broader implications. Synthetic collateralized loan obligations (CLOs) that have this imbedded risk in the credit default documentation may have to be reexamined. This may be of particular concern to investors in the mezzanine pieces of synthetic CLOs. One might argue that since banks usually retain the equity, they would play games with the recovery values, but the above incident raises some concerns.

It seems clear that the market trend is to create clearer documentation. Lawyers can help in this process, but they cannot determine the business risks that one is willing to underwrite. There is no substitute for a good lawyer. Equally there is no substitute for business units to clearly define the risks they are willing to take for a given price and the risks they are not willing to take for a given price. In the end every risk has its price, but before one can price the risk, one has to define the risk.

BANK BEST PRACTICES

So, you want to be a contender? You realize that your bank's major risk is credit risk. What does it take to catapult your bank into the top tier of credit mangers? What sort of infrastructure do you need to build? Although the final execution will vary, based on a bank's regulatory, accounting, and tax constraints, the most successful credit management operations seem to exhibit a common pattern. It may be helpful to take a look at what others have found to be a reasonable approach.

The first step is to find people at the top of the bank who have their lights switched on. This is critical. The global banking community is stuffed with complacent, inert, self-indulgent managers whose most obvious talent is providing support for the other members of their internal politburo. Hard work is a distant bad memory to these people. You will have trouble getting this type of person to actually read a well-written proposal, much less take the time to understand it. Banks are not pure meritocracies. Political connections often matter more than the merits of your program.

Sometimes the program sponsor is only one powerful person at the executive-committee level or on the board of directors. This person must have the ear of the chief executive officer (CEO) and influence within the bank. If the CEO is the only sponsor, a bank may not be able to get this program off the ground, because CEOs—even the competent ones—tend to have short attention spans.

You'll also need a critical mass of key professionals committed to changing your bank's old paradigm for managing credit risk. The following sections will help you draw conclusions about the number and qualifications of the people required. The global banking community is experiencing a widening expertise gulf that got worse in 2000. Talented credit professionals frustrated with the lack of expertise and support at their legacy institutions have been migrating to banks promising them support for their initiatives. The smarter banks are getting smarter.

Enterprise-Wide Credit Risk Transfer Pricing

To successfully manage credit risk on an enterprise-wide basis, you'll require new tools, several new credit products, and a unified strategic approach. Your goal is to create a credit risk transfer-pricing unit for the bank. Your driver for rationalization of pricing is value at risk for credit. This requires the coordination of multiple areas within the bank: the loan portfolio/investment book, treasury, accounting, legal, tax, compliance, risk management, credit officers, quantitative research, systems, trading, structuring, and the executive committee.

The overlay for the credit risk transfer pricing is the investment portfolio or the loan portfolio. Most banks do not do a rigorous analysis for pricing credit risk for loans. They usually do an even worse job of pricing the imbedded options often written into loan agreements. Once a bank gets the knack of pricing credit risk, questions regarding the rationale behind loan syndication and loan inventory come next. Prepare to make people uncomfortable. Buy a dog—you will need a friend.

Most banks do not mark their loan portfolios to market. It is not a requirement for banks. The theory was that loans would be held to maturity, and banks would take all of the credit risk. Regulators and banks understand the folly of that thinking. There comes a point when the risk doesn't justify the reward and you want to get out of what has evolved into a bad deal. This scenario is obvious to almost everyone. What is less obvious is when a deal is new or appears fine. Banks are less willing to put these deals under the microscope and to second-guess existing pricing.

JP Morgan marks its loan portfolio to market and attempts to put a price on credit risk everywhere in the bank, no matter where it occurs. Other banks in the United States grudgingly recognize that JP Morgan is doing the right thing. It is also the inconvenient thing. By setting a high standard and sticking to it, JP Morgan will force other banks to live up to this standard. Several of the top U.S. banks are a couple of years behind JP Morgan and won't be able to meet this standard in the year 2001 or even 2002.

It isn't clear whether JP Morgan rigorously prices imbedded options in loan documentation, however. For instance, I cited an earlier example of a two-year loan that can extend an additional year after one year has passed. The loan with an original maturity of two years becomes a three-year loan. Usually there is some handwaving and a number of basis points is assigned as the value, but banks rarely use option models to price this option. There are obvious market and credit price issues with this sort of structure. The trend will be to rigorously price these risks using some form of consistent analytical framework.

As we saw earlier, measuring credit exposure both on a departmental and an enterprise-wide basis is crucial to the ultimate objective. Your bank will require global credit monitoring and global credit limits of various sorts. The price of credit risk doesn't matter if you can't measure the risk in the first place. Often a merger of large banks will set the merged institution back at least two years. Perhaps the most underestimated cost of a merger is the time, people, effort, software, and hardware it will take to successfully integrate information-reporting systems for a merged bank. Most banks aren't very good at it on a stand-alone basis. Once two large banks merge, they've completely lost the plot for some period of time.

In the last section of Chapter 2 on TRORS, we discussed the general approach for pricing credit exposure. You may wish to use much more complicated models to determine your credit exposures. While using complicated models may force you to make up data, it may give your management the comfort that you are using a consistent and defensible approach. There is merit in that, and models combined with common sense and experience can help you organize your entire pricing approach.

Once you've sorted out your credit exposures, you'll need a credit value-at-risk (VAR) model. The challenge with all of the models is not the model itself but rather the *data*. Correlations, recovery values, default rates, and credit migration rates are based on often-limited data, especially for credits outside the United States. As mentioned before, the KMV model, which has the best available first-world database, does a good job of measuring expected default frequencies (EDFs). Even if you use KMV's data and models and supplement the data with additional data purchases, you will probably need to supplement with another portfolio tool. You will want another credit model, such as CreditMetrics or CreditRisk+. For example, CreditMetrics software is easier to use than KMV, the report generation engine is highly developed, and the results track very closely to the KMV model. This model also allows the use of KMV EDFs as an input and allows time horizons as short as one quarter (as opposed to six months for KMV). Some users report they are happier with CreditRisk+ because they've reported problems with CreditMetrics data and with the mark-to-market. The actual pricing of credit risk is typically strongly dependent on market intelligence as well as on these rather simple credit models.

If you've gotten this far, you'll want to price the credit risk. The key work on fair-value models evolved because of demand on the trading side, not the credit portfolio side, of financial institutions. You'll need to manage the credit risks and market risks in traditional lending products in a manner similar to the way you manage exposures in a market-making activity. This requires the use of a fair-value model, even though banks don't reflect changes in the fair value of loans and lending commitment products in earnings reports or on the balance sheet. The effects of market conditions and events are more readily evident with a fair-value model, and this leads to better decision making and diversification.

While I made the claim that the trading books price their risks, it isn't strictly true. For instance, most banks do not calculate a credit valuation adjustment for interest-rate swaps and other types of interest-rate derivatives. The theory was that the credit risk in the swap market was the average credit risk of the major interest-rate swap market makers. This market hallucination usually puts the implied credit risk at a strong single A or a weak AA risk. Therefore, dealers never rigorously priced the credit risk to their interest-rate swap counterparties. When banks do business with lower-rated corporations, they usually deal with the question of credit risk with a generalized program of limiting transaction maturity, periodic mark-to-market, mutual midmarket puts, collateral, or a combination of all of the former. Very highly rated banks and sovereigns will often request collateral from lower-rated banks. This may give credit managers comfort, but it isn't the same as actually pricing the risk of the credit exposure. Sometimes a bank will act as an intermediary for another bank and charge a small fee. If a bank doesn't have a credit line, it will purchase protection in the event that this swap counterparty defaults and the protection buyer is owed money on the swap. The protection provider "stands in the middle," or acts as intermediary, in the swap transaction. These generally—but not always—involve rather small fees, and these small fees are not rigorously priced, and sometimes aren't even marked to market as required. There is inconsistency even in the trading area of banks and financial institutions. To correct for this, institutions like JP Morgan are attempting to make a valuation adjustment for this credit risk. This valuation adjustment is simply the estimate of credit loss using the derivatives portfolio exposure profile and market prices for credit risk based on spreads for credit derivatives, asset swaps, and bonds.

All of these models have their challenges and are cumbersome to use. There is no substitute for common sense, quantitative skill, and good judgment in evaluating inputs and results. There is also no substitute for observing market credit spreads. You will need market prices in various markets, including credit derivatives, asset swaps, and bonds. This means you need to set up a credit trading operation for these products. To improve return on equity (ROE), you will eventually want to move credit risks off the investment book and into the trading or flow book.

Trading, Structuring, and Securitizing Credit Risk

Banks must use securitizations with imbedded credit derivatives and along with name-specific credit default swaps to reduce credit risk in their credit investment portfolios. Credit derivatives are the key tool of the credit transformation strategy. Banks need the ability to contemplate structures where every tranche is a derivative, so they need credit-derivatives expertise in both their investment and trading areas. These products enable a bank to reduce credit risk and total capital used for credit activities.

Banks need multiple tools that include a variety of hedging choices in addition to diversification of the credit portfolio. Hedging rather than diversification is sometimes the better answer to mitigate credit risk. This may sound like a surprising statement. Diversification is often used to justify higher exposure to new credit risks, but diversification is not a guarantee against loss, only against losing everything at once.

Banks can begin employing some of these strategies even before they measure the fair value of the entire credit portfolio. In general, the credit management books can be broken into four groups, with the investment book as the driving force. A general schematic might look as follows:

	Investment Book	
Structuring	Flow Book	Exotics Book
Synthetic CLOs	Single CDs	Super Senior Risk
Synthetic CDOs	TRORS	Baskets
Conduits	Asset Swaps	Basis Risk
Credit-Linked Notes	Balance Sheet Trades	Correlation Risk
Securitization	Credit Spreads	Convertibility Risk

Although you may not participate in all of these products, the successful banks participate in structuring, flow products, and exotic products in various forms. Distribution efforts are usually organized to support this effort so as to get synergy and cross-product selling.

The credit trading area often becomes a centralized source of market intelligence. *The spread is where the spread is because that's where the market says it is.* There is no substitute for market intelligence, and most banks are very weak in this area. Banks should set up a credit trading area and should transact credit derivatives, asset swaps, and tranches of structured deals for profit, not just to lay off their own credit risk. This desk should also keep data of credit spreads in the bond markets.

Many credit trading desks still do not mark to model. Often banks provide flexibility for deal approvals via an issuer risk matrix available to all trading books. This avoids the problem of seeking internal approvals (inaction by committee) for each deal and satisfies the need to transact swiftly and to position credits. Capital allocation is rationalized.

Desks are often authorized to trade as long as they are within limits for investment-grade deals. Authority to book noninvestment-grade deals may require a separate area with special approvals, if it is done at all. Alternatively, some banks coordinate with emerging-markets trading desks to share their lines and to make some profit accommodation for the joint nature of the business.

An increasing number of credit trading desks are able to price tranches of credit risk using a model such as Savvy Soft. These desks have the authority to position the super senior risk of CLOs, including taking the super senior piece of their own bank's deals. They sometimes take on basis risk and hedge out the subordinated portion. The formerly mentioned super senior tranches are especially attractive to U.S. banks because the Federal Reserve (the Fed) grants these risks a 20 percent BIS risk weight.

Credit trading desks are both buyers and sellers of credit risk. They may be authorized to buy credit risk either in basket form or on a single-name basis. In the spring of 2000, a five-name BBB basket with a three-year maturity would trade at a price (where the bank buys the credit risk) of approximately 155 bps per annum. The price gradually widened throughout the year.

These desks usually also execute total rate of return swaps (TRORS) with the top tier of commercial and investment banks. The collateral varies, but all deals are 20 percent BIS risk weighted. Banks earned LIBOR (London interbank offering rate) + 26 bps to LIBOR + 40 bps with this group of counterparties over a six-month-to-one-year time horizon for deals booked in 2000. These deals are best documented like a TRORS, not a credit derivative.

The preceding list is not exhaustive; it is only meant to highlight the concept of active credit products trading.

The portfolio area, the structuring desk, and the credit trading areas are symbiotic. The portfolio group needs to hedge credit risks and components of portfolio structures. The trading desk needs the credit lines of the bank. That requires the blessing and sponsorship of the portfolio area.

The bank strategy is to improve return on assets (ROA) and ROE on both economic and regulatory bases. Once a bank prices and mitigates credit risk, each incremental deal comes under the spotlight of opportunity cost. That is the blessing and the bane of credit risk pricing. If you free up a line, what is the return on capital of the alternative deal? The next best deal may be a loan, or it may even be a credit derivative.

INTERNET TRADING

Internet trading blossomed after the first credit trade was closed over the Internet by CreditTrade in September 1999. Paul Ellis, CEO of CreditTrade, which was founded in 1999, said that revenues in 2000 achieved several times the level of expectations at the beginning of the year. In September 2000 alone, CreditTrade transacted over 150 trades with notional value of nearly $2.5 billion. CreditTrade has an estimated 40 percent share of interdealer trades from both brokerage and Internet sources.

Internet trading in credit derivatives is still in the very early stages. The market is trying to come to grips with a transition between voice-brokered deals and Internet delivery. CreditTrade and Prebon Yamane formed a joint venture to promote a hybrid delivery system. Most of their transactions are executed by the brokers, but the Internet may have provided a means of generating interest, and a small percentage estimated as less than 25 percent of their transactions are executed on the Internet.

At first it was difficult to distinguish whether the Internet provided any advantage over Bloomberg as a screen quote device. It appears that the Internet does have advantages and that there is growing acceptance, albeit only a small number of trades are actually executed online. The Internet's main advantages appear to be ease of posting documents, ease of creating a central posting place for traders from various firms, and the potential to communicate on line.

Rupert Walsh of CreditTrade feels that it has only been in the past year that the credit derivatives market has become reasonably well commoditized. ISDA short-form confirms for credit derivatives helped greatly in this effort. But some traders actively arbitrage documentation. As long as some practitioners do not pay attention to these subtleties, this activity is unlikely to stop. The credit derivatives market is a new market and seems to suffer periodic stress tests. One such stress test was the Russian crisis. Protection buyers, who thought they bought credit default protection for Russian domestic obligations, found to their dismay that their confirms only referenced Russian Eurobonds. Mr. Walsh feels that the Conseco restructuring is another stress test. The trend is to tighter documentation and greater awareness of the need to properly vet documentation.

In general, the Internet itself poses some risk issues. The main issues are the same whether the purpose is credit derivatives trading or other business-to-business (B2B) commerce. The key risks are as follows:

- Operational Risk: System or hardware failures; computer sabotage; viruses; inadequate network or system capacity.
- Legal Risk: Lack of cross recognition of legality; repudiation; lack of uniformity.
- Sovereignty: Venue for dispute jurisdiction; privacy; taxation.
- Fraud Risk: Impersonation and identity theft; Web-page tampering; unauthorized trading.
- Credit Risk: Verification of credit lines; settlement.

For successful global trading, one must be able to span geopolitical boundaries and to comply with legal and operational requirements. If traders want to communicate online, they must have confidence that no outside party can eavesdrop on their trade. Traders must be able to authenticate the identity of both their individual sender and their counterparty online. Traders must also have confidence that no one can tamper with the information they are sending online. These requirements are basically the same as for telephone trading, where traders must "know the counterparty."

Digital certificates are usually acceptable to prove Internet identity, and digital signatures are usually acceptable to provide integrity. For credit derivatives Web sites, a password and a user ID are usually all that is used. This may be part of the reason why very few trades are executed online.

Other new Web sites include Creditex and CFOweb. As of December 2000, very few trades have been done online on these Web sites. CFOweb seems to be a more generalized Web site for a variety of financial markets needs. Creditex specializes in credit derivatives and has aspirations to become a credit derivatives trading warehouse. They don't use voice brokers, and it remains to be seen whether this is a mistake. Voice brokers are believed to provide an important source of liquidity by actively working the phones to find a price. There is some evidence that people new to the market are the heaviest users of credit derivatives trading sites. One of the reasons they seem to gravitate to the Internet is because they don't have the relationships in the market and are looking for information and service.

Very good credit derivatives Web sites are available through the major players in the market, with the JP Morgan Web site, morgancredit, being the best in my personal view. Salomon, Morgan Stanley, and Goldman also have good Web sites. Web sites are constantly evolving.

AN INEVITABLE SHAKE-UP

As in any new market, the unscrupulous or the ill-informed may pick off new entrants. Already, structures that have no economic value are being touted in the market. Credit default protection from banks "guaranteeing" their own senior debt will lead to dissatisfied customers.

Banks who put senior guarantees on their own subordinated debt are adding marginal value, although in the event of a bank default, it is problematic as to how much value that will be. Furthermore, a bank that offers a senior guarantee on its own subordinated debt changes the capital structure of the bank. The senior versus subordinated debt ratio is effectively changed, and hidden transactions like this may lead to revaluation of overall debt ratings.

The National Association of Insurance Companies (NAIC) in the United States is looking into credit derivatives. Insurance companies receiving the total rate of return in a TRORS with a bank counterparty consider the credit rating of the bank and not the reference asset. The NAIC is concerned about the actual credit impact for insurance companies and is keen to see that no abuse takes place.

Leveraged credit-linked notes and first-to-default basket structures are offered to clients who have virtually no ability to analyze the economics of the transaction. One can only wonder at the degree of disclosure involved in the marketing efforts of these transactions. Interestingly, the more aggressive leveraged structures are not offered to savvy investors.

Collateralized loan obligations have had their share of problems in the United States. Insurance companies often contribute part of the collateral. Nonetheless, several CLOs are rumored to be underfunded. In 1997, several banks had deals rumored to be short of necessary collateral. Banks that fail to meet funding deadlines may be on the hook for cash flow payments if they cannot find the loan collateral to populate their deals. Banks eager for the high-fee income available for structuring the CLO may have gotten ahead of themselves.

As we saw before, Korean banks are eager to sell credit protection on other Korean banks—and even on themselves. Correlation between the protection seller and the reference asset is rarely accounted for in any rigorous quantitative fashion. If there is ever a problem with transactions of this ilk, dissatisfied credit protection buyers may seek reparations from the firms that arranged these transactions.

These types of challenges are not unique to the credit derivatives market. These types of challenges are not even unique to the derivatives market. These challenges are endemic to every new financial market. The potential for negative publicity and minor shake-ups in this market abound. It won't be surprising to read articles about "seven-day scandals"—abuses of client trust and abuses of credit derivative applications in the future. Some market participants will get their education the hard way. It is an inevitable part of the product life cycle.

TREND TO A COMMODITY MARKET

As in the early days of any new product, opportunities to earn higher margins abound. As with any product cycle, the relentless movement toward a commodity-like market will occur in the credit derivatives market. Total return swaps on well-traded credits already exhibit these characteristics. Over the next couple of years, TRORS on well-traded U.S. credits will become "cookie-cutter," with fairly standardized prices.

Other areas of the credit derivatives market will be more immune to the threat of commoditization. This is because the barrier to entry in the form of models needed—for first-to-default basket options, for instance—or the economic barrier for obtaining the necessary information to estimate default probabilities and recovery rates is too high. Nonetheless, we have seen margins in other complex derivatives, such as Bermuda options, decline rapidly over time as more and more market participants learned how to trade these products and manage the risk.

Emerging markets offer an opportunity for higher returns because the depth and the breadth of those markets are less and the volatility of the markets is higher than that of established U.S. and European markets. This may be the area of greatest reward for professionals who establish active trading units. There will be an element of risk that cannot be hedged in some of these markets, however, as suitable hedge instruments do not always exist. A firm with the ability to manage risk and to exploit timely market information and good marketing distribution has the greatest chance of reward. Even this market will see compressed margins over time as more firms develop the knack for managing books of emerging-market credit derivatives and compete more aggressively for customer business.

The near future holds the greatest rewards for participants in complex credit derivatives. As the market becomes more established and as seasoned professionals are lured from profitable operations to new firms, the margins will gradually decline.

selected bibliography

Altman, E. "Financial Ratios, Discriminant Analysis and the Prediction of Corporate Bankruptcy." *Journal of Finance*, 1974, 589–609.

Bank of England, "Credit Derivatives: Amended Interim Capital Adequacy Treatment." Bank of England, June 5, 1997.

———. "Developing a Supervisory Approach to Credit Derivatives." Bank of England, November 1996.

Banks, Erik. *Complex Derivatives*. Chicago: Probus Publishing Company, 1994.

Banks, Jim. "Comfy with Credit." *Futures & Options World*, July 1996, 30–33.

Brand, Leo, Joseph Rabbia, and Reza Bahar. *Ratings Performance 1996 Stability and Transition*. Standard & Poors, February 1997.

Brealey, Richard, and Stewart Meyers. *Principles of Corporate Finance*. New York: McGraw-Hill, 1981.

Carty, Lea, and Dana Lieberman. "Defaulted Bank Loan Recoveries." New York: Moody's Investors Service Global Credit Research, 1996.

Carty, Lea, Dana Lieberman, and Jerome S. Fons. "Corporate Bond Defaults and Default Rates 1970–1994." New York: Moody's Investors Service Global Credit Research, 1995.

Ciruentes, Arturo, Jeremy Gluck, and Eileen Murphy. *Mind the Gap: Moody's Ratings of "Low-Coupon" Structured Investments*. New York: Moody's Investors Service Global Credit Research, February 28, 1997.

Efrat, Isaac, Jeremy Gluck, and David Powar. "Moody's Refines Its Approach to Rating Structured Notes." Moody's Investors Service, July 3, 1997.

Fabozzi, Frank J. *Handbook of Structured Financial Products*. Frank J. Fabozzi Associates, 1998.

Federal Reserve. For download of all Federal Reserve papers on the subject of credit derivatives: <http://www.bog.frb.fed.US\boarddocs\SRLETTERS>

Ghose, Ronit, ed. *Credit Derivatives: Key Issues*. London: BBA Enterprises, 1997.

Gluck, Jeremy. *Tripping Tigers: The Impact of Asian Events on the CBO Market*. New York: Moody's Investors Service Global Credit Research, January 30, 1998.

Hessol, Gail I., Francis Parisi, Mark Puccia, and Joanne W. Rose. "Credit Comments." Standard & Poor's Structured Finance, November 1995.

International Swap Dealers Association. "Capital Requirements for Credit Derivatives." ISDA, August 12, 1996.

———. "Confirmation of OTC Credit Swap Transaction Single Reference Entity Non-Sovereign." ISDA, December 15, 1997.

———. "Memorandum to Primary and Risk Management." ISDA, February 12, 1997.

Ketcha, Nicholas J., Jr. *Supervisory Guidance for Credit Derivatives*. Federal Deposit Insurance Corporation, Division of Supervision, August 15, 1996.

Lee, Peter. "Masters of Credit or Hype?" *Euromoney*, July 1997, 44–49.

Leong, Kenneth. "Estimates, Guesstimates and Rules of Thumb." *Risk*, February 1, 1991.

Nelken, Israel, ed. *Option Embedded Bonds*. New York: Times Mirror, 1997.

Office of the Comptroller of the Currency. "Credit Derivatives." OCC *Bulletin*, OCC 96–43, August 12, 1997.

Parsley, Mark. "Credit Derivatives Get Cracking." *Euromoney*, March 1996, 28–34.

Rai, Shaun, and Hal Holappa. "Credit Derivatives: The New Wave in Risk Management." *The Journal of Lending & Credit Risk Management*, May 1997, 26–33.

Roever, Alexander W. *Securitization 101: Understanding and Demystifying Asset Backed Transactions*. Bank One, January 1, 1999.

Rosen, Dan. *Effectively Measuring and Integrating Market Risk & Credit*. New York: Algorithmics, 1997.

Spinner, Karen. "Building the Credit Derivatives Infrastructure." *Derivatives Strategy*, June 1997, 35–51.

Westlake, Melvyn. "The Credit Crucible." *Emerging Market Investor*, February 1997, 10–14.

Winkler, Robert L., and William L. Hays. *Statistics Probability, Inference, and Decision.* New York: Holt, Rinehart, and Winston, 1975.
Interesting Web Sites (these are .com addresses):
    bakred.de—Bundesbank Regulations and Guidance.
    barra—Risk management sales and research link.
    bloomberg—Online version of the system we know and love.
    CFOWeb—Financial markets trading.
    Credittrade—Internet trading site for credit derivatives.
    Creditex—Internet trading site in early stages.
    Derivatives—Financial derivatives and risk management news.
    Enroncredits—Enron Corporation's credit trading web site.
    frbservices.org—U.S. Federal Reserve Regulations and Guidance.
    GARP—Web site for Global Association of Risk Professionals.
    Gloriamundi.org—Web site for VaR resources and risk professionals.
    csfb.com/creditrisk/—Web site for CreditRisk+.
    kamakuraco—Hawaii-based software for risk management.
    loanpricing—Loan Pricing Corp.'s Web site.
    Margrabe—Unique risk management and financial engineering boutique.
    Moodys.com—Moody's Investor Services homepage.
    Risk.ifci.ch/—Introduction to risk management.
    RiskMetrics—Risk management tools.
    Savvysoft—Cutting-edge financial engineering software developers.
    Wilmott—Quantitative finance consulting and software.

index

Algorithmics, 18
All-or-nothing payment structure, 75, 109
Altman Z score, 12
American option, 74
Argentina, 208–211
  BIS risk weight for, 29
  convertability risk protection term sheet, 208–211
Asian market crisis of 1997, 190–191, 220
Askin, David J., 45, 46
Askin Capital Management, 45
Asset swap swap. *See* Asset swap switch
Asset swap switch, 75, 142–145 (Figure 4.1)
Assets, diversification of, 8
  See also Reference assets; Synthetic assets
Asymmetry, 102
Auction pricing method. *See under* Market value
Austria, 196–198

Balance sheet management, 149–155
  exposure management, example of, 62 (Figure 2.13)
  and relative value, 59–62
  with TRORS, 41–44

Bank of America, 139
  Risk Management Analysis Group, 140
Bank Arranger, 83
Bank of Boston, 216
Bank of England:
  on regulatory capital treatment, 30, 181, 183, 266, 276
  on worst-case-scenario approach to basket protection, 181, 183, 276
Bank for International Settlements (BIS), 28
  on regulatory capital treatment, 266
  See also Risk weight, BIS
Bankruptcy, 268
Banks:
  balance sheet comparison, 32 (Table 2.2), 34 (Table 2.3)
  best practices of, 288–294
  highly rated, 254–256
  managers of, and exposure management, 153–155
  minimum capital requirements for, 28–30
  motivations of, 28–34
  and need to both buy and sell risk, 154–155
  sponsors of, and risk, 251–253

Basil, Philip, 76–77
Basis risk, 99–103, 165–171
  and delivery options/credit events,
    285–288
  sources of, 103–106
  and substitution, 106–108
Basket credit default swap, 172–173
    (Figure 4.7)
  pricing, 175–181
  termination, 174 (Figure 4.8)
  term sheet, 172–173
Basket structures:
  applications suitable for, 174
  first-to-default, 171–172
  and index-linked notes, 233–234
  vs. pro rata default structures, 186
  regulations on, 181–183
Best's credit rating scale, 9 (Table 1.1)
Binary payment. *See* Termination
    payments
BIS. *See* Bank for International
    Settlements (BIS)
BIS risk weight, 28–29, 274
  future irrelevance of, 283
  importance of, 31–32, 38
  sample TROR on, 31 (Figure 2.2)
  and super senior tranches, 259
BISTRO. *See* Broad Index Secured Trust
    Offering (BISTRO)
Black box structures, 200–201, 246–247
Bonds
  Brady, 191–192
    Brazilian, 196–198
  determining market value of, 43–44
  vs. loans (*see* Loans, vs. bonds)
  nonpar, 111–113
  zero-coupon, 191, 259–260
Brazil, 78–82, 88–89, 91, 114–119
  and Brady bonds, 196–197
  and convertibility protection, 216
  credit default swap, indicative term
    sheet, 78–82, 114–119
  credit protection quotes, 138
  default language, 88–91
Brazilian Eurobond, 138
British Bankers Association (BBA), 5

Broad Index Secured Trust Offering
    (BISTRO), 256–259

Callable step-up structure, 155–159
Capital asset pricing model, 7, 8
Cash flows:
  country, 221
  for equity piece, 250–251
Cash flow transaction, 239
Cayman Island incorporated SPE, 262
CBO. *See* Collateralized bond obligation
    (CBO)
CFOweb, 296
Chan, Dr. Hei Wei, 214
Citibank, 261–262
CLO. *See* Collateralized loan obligation
    (CLO)
CMO. *See* Collateralized mortgage
    obligation (CMO)
CMT. *See* Constant maturity treasury
    (CMT)
Coca-Cola Femsa, 100 (Figure 3.5)
Collateralized bond obligation (CBO), 6
  vs. first-to-default basket structure,
    171–172
Collateralized loan obligation (CLO), 6
  arbitrage, 242
  balance-sheet type, 242
  vs. BISTRO, 257
  equity piece (*see* Equity piece)
  vs. first-to-default basket structure,
    171–172
  hybrid, 242–243
  market-value type, 239–240
  and noninvestment-grade collateral,
    247–248
  structures, 253–254
  synthetic, 241–246
    linked vs. delinked, 243
    rating criteria for, 245–246
Collateralized mortgage obligation
    (CMO), 44–45
Commercial paper (CP) market, 42, 43
Commodity market, trend toward, 298
Commodity money, 202, 203
Concentration risk, 245, 248

Conduits:
  to avoid high capital treatment
    charges, 280
  securitization, 251
  for transfer of risk, 42–44
Confirmation, 54
Conseco, 286–287
Constant maturity treasury (CMT), 61
Convertibility. *See* Currency
    convertibility.
Convertibility event, definition, 207
Correlation:
  asset, 8, 85–87, 99–100
  and concentration risk, 248
  between emerging markets, 190
Counterparty, 5
  importance of, 103, 140
Counterparty risk, 33, 251–254
Covariance, 8
Crean, Louise Rowsell, 76–77
Credit. *See* Credit money
Credit arbitrage funds, 261–264
Credit default event, 96–99
Credit default protection:
  applications suitable for, 74
  buyer of, 5
  key inputs for model, 127
  pricing, 127, 128
  seller of, 5, 82–88
  seller/buyer motivations, 136
  as TRORS, 31, 34 (Figure 2.3)
Credit default risk premium, 213
Credit default swap/option, 73, 74
    (Figure 3.1)
  basic/traditional, 77–82
  Emerging Markets Investor definition
    of, 108
  and hedge costs, 120–121
  market issues, 88
  plain vanilla, 77–82
  premium, 73–74, 75 (*see also* Credit
    default swap/option termination
    payments)
  pricing, 122–133, 138
  regulatory jurisdictions for
    transactions, 265, 277

  sample term sheets, 78–82, 91–95,
    97–98, 110–111, 112, 114–119
  structures, 75
  vs. TRORS, 73, 74–75
Credit default swap/option termination
    payments, 108
  common calculation method, 110
  defining, 108–121
  digital cash structure, 108–110
    binary, 75, 109
    fixed cash payment, 109
    par minus market (recovery) value,
      75, 110
  initial price minus market value, 110–
    113
  and market value, 119–121
  and nonpar bonds, 111–113
  normalized price method, 113–119
  and senior unsecured bonds, 132–133
  and senior unsecured debt, 121
Credit derivatives, 8
  applications unsuitable for, 82–83
  booking issues, 273
  classification of as insurance contract,
    272–273
  market history, 7–12
  market size, 5–6
  National Association of Insurance
    Companies (NAIC) on, 297
  regulatory capital guidelines for (*see*
    Regulatory capital treatment)
  reasons for entering into, 5, 84, 126
  tranched asset swap (*see* Tranched
    asset swaps, vs. total rate of
    return swaps [TRORS])
Credit event:
  on basket of loans, 175
  definitions, 267–271
  example, 229–232
  materiality test for, 106
  upon merger, 269
  redefining credit default event as, 96–
    99
  term sheet definition, 206
Credit event exchange swap, 153–154
Creditex, 296

Credit exchange agreement, 145
Credit exposure:
    calculating, 66, 70, 180–181
    changing the maturity of, 35–36
    and conditional probability of
        default, 62–71
    due to event risk, 180–181
    for U.S. dollar interest-rate swaps,
        151 (Table 4.1)
        and black box structure, 247
          (Figure 7.1)
        linked to credit event, 229–232
        linked to default, 226–228
        major structures of, 224–225
Credit-linked note (CLN), 161–164,
    223–235, 254–256
Credit-linked vehicle (CLiVe)
    transaction, 254
CreditManager software, 12–15, 17
    typical report, 14 (Figures 1.2, 1.3)
Credit mapping, 246
CreditMetrics methodology, 12, 15, 291
    and asset correlation, 86
CreditMetrics Monitor, 63
Credit money, 202, 203
Credit plays, 298–201
Credit quality, and funding cost
    arbitrage, 136–137
Credit rating systems, 9 (Table 1.1)
Credit risk:
    key parameters of, 13
    measurement techniques, 12–18
    models of (*see* Statistical models)
    sovereign, example of, 161–164, 165–
        168
    trading, structuring, and securitizing,
        292–294
    transfer pricing, 289–292
Credit risk measurement Altman Z
    score, 12
    CreditMetrics, 12, 15
    KMV Corporation credit risk model,
        17, 18
    regret model, 18
CreditRisk+, 291
Credit risk switch, 145 (Figure 4.2)

Credit spread forward/swap, 147
Credit spread migration, 70–71
Credit spread option, 147–148, 192
CreditTrade, 294–295
Credit trading desks, 293–294
Credit wrap, 238
Credits, investment-grade, 178–179
Cross-acceleration, 269
Cross-border issues, 220–221, 281
Cross-default, 269
Currency, 201–221, 271. *See also*
        Currency risk; Money, types of
Currency convertibility, 201–208, 270
    and default language, 271–272
    and default risk, 221
    option premium, 213
    protection, 206–208, 211–212, 216
        pricing, 212–220
    sample term sheet, 208–211
    See also Convertibility event
Currency convertibility risk, 208–211
Currency risk:
    key to evaluating, 205
    solutions to, 206–212
Currency transferability, 201–208

Dealer poll. *See under* Market value
Debt:
    inside vs. outside, 102, 132
    public vs. nonpublic, 138
    recovery rates for, 131, 132
    senior unsecured, recovery rate for,
        121
    sovereign, 281–282
        rated in local vs. foreign currency,
          198–201
        uses of, 202–203
    subordinated, vs. loans, 59–62
Default:
    expected default frequency (EDF), 65
    individual vs. basket rates, 177–178,
        179–180
    pro rata structure, 186–187
    recovery rates, 129–130, 130–132
    risk of (*see* Default probability;
        Default risk)

Default event:
 defining, 88–91
 example of, 101
 with respect to credit agreements, 76
Default probability:
 assessing, 176–181
 characteristics of, 128–129
 common formula for, 123–124
 conditional
  calculating, 64–66
  and credit exposure, 62–71
 currency convertibility, 221
 joint, 38–41, 63
Default protection:
 buyer motive in callable step-up,
  155–157
 sovereign, 195 (Table 5.2)
Default risk, 133
Delivery:
 and basis risk, 165–167
 of loan settlement, 286, 287–288
Demilitarized zone of investment, 8
Digital cash payment structure, 108–
 109
Digital cash structure, 75. *See also*
  under Credit default swap/option
  termination payments
Disclosure, 103
Diversification:
 vs. hedging, 292
 and synthetic CLOs, 243–244
Diversity score, 244
Documentation, 285, 288
Downgrade, 270
Duff & Phelps (D&P) credit rating
 scale, 9 (Table 1.1)
Dresdner Bank, 201
Dresdner Kleinwort Benson, 228–229
Dun & Bradstreet (D&B) credit rating
 scale, 9 (Table 1.1)
Duration, 104–105
 MacCaulay, 104
 modified, 104–105

Economic development corporations
 (EDCs), 126–127
Ellis, Paul, 294

Emerging markets, 189–221, 285
 and Brady bonds, 191–192
 countries classified as, 190
 currency issues, 201–221
 definition, 190
 Eurobond prices, 193–194 (Table 5.1)
 and sovereign risk, 189–221
 and tax arbitrage, 196–198
Equity piece, 247, 248
 and BISTRO, 258–259
 buyers, 249–250
 cash flows for, 250–251
Eurobonds:
 Brazilian, 138
 prices for selected emerging markets,
  193–194 (Table 5.1)
 Russian, 139–140
European Monetary Union (EMU), 284
Euro swaps, 58–59
Event. *See* Convertibility event; Credit
  default event; Credit event;
  Default event; Event risk
Event risk, 70, 203–206. *See also*
  Default probability, conditional
Expected default frequency (EDF), 65
Expected-loss-to-issuer formula, 132
Export credit agencies, 212
Exposure:
 credit (*see* Credit exposure)
 vs. risk, 13, 14 (Figure 1.3)
Exposure management, 153–155
 and balance sheet swaps, 149–155
 and bank managers, 153–155

Failure to pay, 270
Federal National Mortgage Association
 (FNMA), 29
Federal Reserve. *See* U.S. Federal
 Reserve Board (the Fed)
Fiat money, 202, 203
Financial management, key to all, 7
Financing, TRORS, 24. *See also* Total
 rate of return swaps (TRORS)
Financing cost, 20
First-loss risk, 259–261
Fitch credit rating scale, 9 (Table 1.1)
Floaters, 16–17

Floating rate note (FRN), 59
Floating rate payment, 20
Foreign exchange (FX) spot rate, 211
Forward:
　credit spread, 147
　vs. future, 76–77
Funding cost arbitrage, 38–41, 133–140
　and credit default swap/option, 122–123
　of the investor, 20
　TRORS, 24
Futures, 76–77

Gap margin, 240
Geared default options, 160–165
Glass Steagal Act, 281
Gordian Knot Limited, 10, 11
Governmental action, 270
Government entity, 271
Government obligation, 271
Greece, 225, 226–228, 251–253
Guarantees, 272

Hanil Bank, 83, 84
Hedge costs, 56, 120–121
　calculating, 167–168
Hedge funds:
　and equity cash flows, 249
　and HLTs, 46
　vs. investment-grade loans, 57
　and leverage, 26–27, 55–59
　limited disclosure by, 56–57
　and loan TRORS, 44–47
　and regulatory capital treatment, 279
Hedging:
　vs. diversification, 292
　and mark-to-market, 30–31
　recognizing, 30–31
Highly leveraged transactions (HLTs), 46
　and counterparty risk, 251–253
　See also under Total rate of return
　　swaps (TRORS)
High-yield bonds, 175

Index-linked notes, 233–235
Indonesia, 190, 220
Insurance contracts, 272–273

Interest-rate swaps. *See* Swaps, interest-rate
International Swap Dealers Association
　(ISDA):
　on credit-derivatives confirmation
　　language, 266, 267
　on credit event vs. restructuring, 287
Internet risk, 295
Internet trading, 294–296
Investment, book, 292–293
Investor credit rating:
　and repurchase rate, 45
　and TRORS, 38
Iran, overthrow of shah of, 203–204

Japan, 9
　Ministry of International Trade and
　　Industry (MITI), 212
　and Tesobono trade, 217–220
Jewish community, and formation of
　banking practices, 202
Joint probability of default, 63–66
　benefit equqation, 64–65
JP Morgan, 12, 72, 228–229, 289–290
　morgancredit Web site, 296
　See also Broad Index Secured Trust
　　Offering (BISTRO);
　　CreditManager software
Junior piece, 258
Junk bonds. *See* High-yield bonds

Kealhofer, Stephen, 17, 85. *See also*
　KMV Corporation
KMV Corporation, 17, 85, 128, 129–130, 290–291
Knock-in default swap/option, 75, 184
　and materiality clauses, 104
Knock-in structures, 184
Knock-out structure, 148
Korea, 85–87
　Hyundai, 86
Korea, South. *See* South Korea
Korea Exchange Bank, 86
Kurtosis, 15

Language, 63
　bond market, 142–143

Language *(continued)*
    convertibility protection, 206–208
    credit default/event, 102–103, 267–272
        and issuer's credit rating, 101–102
    credit derivatives market, 77
    currency convertibility protection, 214–215
    default, 228, 272
        fallibility of, 96
        hidden costs in, 267–272
        nonsovereign/corporate, vs. sovereign, 91–96
        sovereign, variations in, 101–103
        and trigger events, 267
    materiality *(see* Materiality)
    swap, 75
    total return swap, 21, 22–24
Latin America, 75
    debt restructuring of 1980s, 191
    as emerging markets, 190, 285
    See also Argentina; Brazil; Mexico
Leverage, 25–27
    and hedge funds, 26–27
    and net returns to counterparties, 26 (Table 2.1)
    See also Total rate of return swaps (TRORS); *see also under* Hedge funds
LIBOR. *See* London interbank offering rate (LIBOR)
Loans:
    vs. bonds, 47–48
        average prices one month after default, 132
        documentation, 102
        and senior secured debt, 130–131
    and credit risk transfer pricing, 289–290
    delivery of settlement, 286, 287–288
    investment-grade, 57
    price robustness of, 131
    vs. subordinated debt, 59-62
    See also under Maturities, mismatched
Loan Syndications and Trading Association (LSTA), 287–288

Loan TRORS. *See* Total rate of return swaps (TRORS), loan
London interbank offering rate (LIBOR), 10, 20
Long-term credit ratings. *See* Credit rating systems
Loss in the event of default (LIED), 185–186

Market-contingent risk, 141–142
Market disruption, 270–271
Market risk, 33
    and credit default language, 272
    and maturity mismatches, 36
Markets, emerging. *See* Emerging markets
Market value:
    auction pricing method, 121
    dealer poll, 121
    and termination payments, 119–121
Marking-to-market:
    increasing frequency of period, 64
    issues of, 273–274
Materiality, 104
    clauses, 104
        price adjustment feature of, 105
    issues of, 106
Materiality test, 106
Maturities:
    limited market for larger, more lengthy, 139
    mismatched, 35–36
        loans and synthetic CLOs, 71–72
        vs. tranched asset swaps, 36
    "rolling down the yield curve," 148
McQuown, John, 17, 85. *See also* KMV Corporation
Medium-term note. *See* Notes, medium-term (MTN)
Mexico, 96–99, 110–111, 112, 161–164, 165–168, 229–232
    BIS risk weight for, 29
    and tequila effect, 217–218
    and Tesobono trade, 217–219
Money, types of, 202
Moody's Investor Service:
    and CLOs/CBOs, 6, 245–246

credit rating scale, 9 (Table 1.1)
cumulative default rates, 130 (Table 3.3)
marginal default rates, 129 (Tables 3.1, 3.2)
portfolio diversity score, 244
and principal-protected notes, 261
recovery rates, 131 (Table 3.5)
Morgan Guarantee Trust (MGT), 257–258
Mortgage swap agreement (MSA), first ever, 20
Multilateral Investment Guarantee Agency (MIGA), 212

Nonbank entities, booking in, 281
Normalized price method. *See under* Credit default swap/option termination payments, digital cash structure
Notes:
    bear, 234–235
    boosted coupon, 225, 226–228
    vs. certificates, 248–249
    credit-linked (*see* Credit-linked notes)
    credit-sensitive, 233
    index-linked, 233–235
    limited recourse (*see* Credit-linked notes [CLNs])
    medium-term (MTN), 254–256
    motivation to buy, 223–224
    principal protected, 225, 259–261, reduced coupon, 226
Notional amount, 6, 150

Off–balance sheet transactions:
    HLTs, 46–47
    TRORS, 20
Office of the Comptroller of the Currency (OCC), 30
Options, 16
    American, 74
    barrier, 75 (*see also* Knock-in swap/ option)
    call, on a spread, 146–147
    credit event trigger swaps (*see* Knock-in default swap/option)

credit exposure, 151–152
credit spread, put vs. call, 148
currency convertibility, marking-to-market of, 218–220
geared default, 160–165
knock-in credit default basket, 184
mortgage/Treasury spread, 146
put
    and tranched asset swap, 36–37
    out-of-the-money, 76, 184
    reduced loss credit default, 184–186
    See also Credit default swap/option; Knock-in default swap/option
Organization for Economic Cooperation and Development (OECD), 29, 33–34, 274, 277
Overcollateralization, 238
Overseas Private Investment Corporation (OPIC), 212

Par minus market (recovery) value. *See under* Credit default swap/option termination payments
Pooled structure, 186
Portfolio concept, 7
    diversification, 17–18
    diversity score, 244
Price adjustment, 104, 105
Price risk, 66–71
    and maturity mismatches, 35–36
Price robustness, 131
Pricing, "rule-of-thumb," 186
Principal protected structure, 260–261. *See also* Notes, principal protected

Qualifying special purpose entity (QSPE), 262

Rating agencies, 8–9. *See also individual rating agencies*
Recovery rates. *See* Default, recovery rates
Reference assets:
    correlation of, with risk, 99–100
    HLT, 46–47
    intrinsic values of, 29–30

Reference assets *(continued)*
  loan, sample term sheet, 48–54
  maturity of, 35–36
  price of, and interest rates, 36
  suitable for TRORS, 20
Reference entity, 271
Reference obligation, 271
Regret. *See under* Statistical models
Regulatory capital treatment, 28–34,
      274–281
  arbitrage, 280
  and basket structure, 181–183
  confusion concerning, 283–284
  for credit derivatives booked on bank
      book vs. on trading book, 30–33
  and currency convertibility protection,
      213
  effects of skewedness of, 31–32
  fluctuations in guidelines for, 30–31
  key issues with respect to credit
      derivatives, 30
  OCC guidelines for, 30
Repo rate. *See* Repurchase rate
Repudiation, 271
Repurchase agreements, 24, 44–45
Repurchase rate, 24, 45
Reserve fund, 239
Restructuring, 271, 287
Return on capital, 274–275
Risk, 33, 141–142
  components of under new market-risk
      proposal, 33
  vs. exposure size, 13, 14 (Figure 1.3)
  "fire-hydrant" or "lifting a leg," 59
  and repurchase rate, 45
  transferring via conduit, 42–44
  See also Basis risk; Concentration
      risk; Counterparty risk; Credit
      default risk premium; Credit
      risk; Currency convertibility risk;
      Currency risk; Default
      probability; Default risk; Event
      risk; Internet risk; Market risk;
      Market-contingent risk; Price
      risk; Sovereign risk; Specific risk;
      Tax-law-interpretation risk;
      Unique risk

Risk exposure model, 34 (Figure 2.3)
Risk management, 8
Risk protection, fallacy of guaranteed,
      7–8, 11, 45–46
  hazards of, 272
  and hedge funds, 57
  See also Statistical models, vs. market
      observation
Risk-vs.-reward concept, 7
Risk weight:
  assumptions, 29
  and return on capital, 274–275
  See also BIS risk weight
RJR Nabisco, Inc., 91–95
Russian civil war, 204–205
Russian debt, 138–139

Salomon Brothers, 20, 143
Savings and loan disaster (U.S.), 125
SBC Glacier Finance Ltd., 254–256
SBC Warburg, 254–256, 285
Secured loan trust structure, 239, 242,
      247–249
Securitization, 292
  applications suitable for, 259
  and credit enhancement, 235
  for highly rated banks, 254–256
  key features of, 237–240
Semantics. *See* Language
Seniority of obligation, 130–131 (Table
      3.5)
Sigma Finance Corporation, 10–11
Skewness, 15
Sloane, Sandy, 57–58
South Korea, and 1997 war crisis, 87n.
Sovereign risk, 206
Special purpose corporations (SPCs), 200
Special purpose entities (SPEs), 238
  and credit arbitrage funds, 262–264
Special purpose vehicle (SPV), 217
Specific risk, 33
Spreads:
  credit, conventional uses of, 146–148
  knock-in, 148
  market reliance on, 125
  net, and BIS risk weight, 31
  See also Credit spread migration

Standard & Poor's (S&P):
 bear note, 234–235
 credit rating scale, 9 (Table 1.1)
 jointly supported ratings, 40 (Table
  2.4)
 and sovereign debt ratings, 198
Statistical models, 127
 challenges to, 290–291
 for default risk/probability, 64–66,
  128
 key to, 15
 vs. market observation, 124–125
 and market risk, 67–71
 and new regulatory capital treatment,
  33
 for pricing credit swap spreads, 124–
  125
 Regret, 18
 usefulness of, 15
 See also Askin, David J.; Credit risk,
  measurement techniques
Stripped yield, 191
Structures. *See* Basket structures; Black
  box structures; Callable step-up
  structure; *subentries under*
  Credit default swap/option
  termination payments
Substitution, 106–108
Swap mark-to-market, 169–170
Swaps, 75
 basket credit default, 171–181
 credit default, regulatory capital effect
  of, 276 (Figure 8.2)
 credit event exchange, example of,
  153 (Figure 4.4), 154 (Figures
  4.5, 4.6)
 credit event trigger. *See* Knock-in
  default swap/option
 interset-rate, 150–152
 See also Asset swap switch; Mortgage
  swap agreement; Switch; Total
  rate of return swaps (TRORS);
  Tranched asset swap
Swap switch, asset. *See* Asset swap
  switch
"Swap"/"switch" confusion, 75, 142–
  143

Swiss bank confidentiality, 254
Switch, 75, 142
 credit risk, 145 (Figure 4.2)
Synthetic assets, 35
Synthetic CLO. *See* Collateralized loan
  obligation (CLO), synthetic;
  Maturities, mismatched, loans
  and synthetic CLOs
Synthetic credit facility (SCF), 160
Synthetic floating rate note (FRN), 59
Synthetic lending facility (SLF), 46, 159–
  160

Tax-law-interpretation risk, 196
Terminations payments, 108–121
 digital cash payment, 108–109
  binary payments, 109
  fixed cash payments, 109
 initial price minus the market value,
  110–113
 and market value, 119–121
 normalized price method, 113–119
 par minus market value, 110
Terminology. *See* Language
Term sheets:
 vs. confirmations, 54
 legal status of, 228
 See also Materiality; Substitution
Tesobono trade, 217–218 (Figure 5.2),
  219 (Figure 5.3), 220
Thailand, 190, 220
 baht crisis, 87, 220
Total rate of return (TROR), 19
 and black box structures, 246–247
 bond swap, 22–24
 payer, 20, 25, 27, 37–38
 receiver, 20–21 24–27
Total rate of return swaps (TRORS),
  19–72
 for balance sheet management, 41–44
 and bank sponsors, 251–253
 basic transaction, illustrated, 21
  (Figure 2.1)
 vs. credit default swap, 73, 74–75
 and credit exposure, 62–71
 and equity piece, 249–250
 funding arbitrage, 38–41

Total rate of return swaps *(continued)*
  and hedge funds, 55–59
  HLTs, 56 (Table 2.5)
  joint probability of default, 38–41
  and leverage, 25–27
  loan, 44–54, 55 (Figure 2.9)
  market price determination for, 121
  mismatched maturities, 35–36
  payments, 20
  possible reference assets, 20
  primary use of, 24, 25
  and regulatory capital treatment, 277
    (*see also* Regulatory capital
    treatment)
  relative performance, 44
  vs. repurchase agreements, 24
  sample term sheet, 48–54
  terminated due to default, 21
  vs. tranched asset swap, 36–38
  transaction flows, 39 (Figure 2.6)
  transaction standards, lack of, 24
Tranched asset swap, 36–37
  and maturity mismatches, 37 (Figure
    2.4)
  vs. total rate of return swaps
    (TRORS), 36–38
Tranched asset swap return, 37
Tranches:
  and credit enhancement, 238–239
  interest-only, 44–45
  super senior, 259
  and synthetic CLOs, 241–245
Trigger event, definition, 206
Triggers, 240–241, 267

TROR. *See* Total rate of return
TRORS. *See* Total rate of return swaps
    (TRORS)

Union Bank of Switzerland, 6
Unique risk, 18
Unknowable unknowns, 123–124
U.S. Federal Reserve Board (the Fed):
  on basket first-to-default swaps, 182–
    183
  on credit default protection, 272,
    278–280
  on regulatory capital treatment, 30,
    32–33, 266 (*see also* Regulatory
    capital treatment)

Value, components of, 142
Value-at-risk (VaR), 66, 67
  due to credit, 14 (Figure 1.2)
Value-at-risk (VaR) model:
  and callable step-up structure, 159
  credit, 290
Variance, 68
Vasicek, Oldrich, 17, 85. *See also* KMV
    Corporation
Verbal ("gentlemen's") agreements, 47,
    103, 120
Volatility:
  calculating, 66–68
  as measure of total market risk, 68–71

Web sites, 296

Zero-one payment structure, 75, 109